CHANGING OUR SCHOOLS

CHANGING EDUCATION

Series Editors:
Professor Andy Hargreaves, Ontario Institute for Studies in Education
Professor Ivor Goodson, University of Western Ontario

This authoritative series addresses the key issues raised by the unprecedented levels of educational change now facing schools and societies throughout the world.

The different directions of change can seem conflicting and are often contested. Decentralized systems of school self-management are accompanied by centralized systems of curriculum and assessment control. Moves to develop more authentic assessments are paralleled by the tightened imposition of standardized tests. Curriculum integration is being advocated in some places, more specialization and subject departmentalization in others.

These complex and contradictory cross-currents pose real challenges to theoretical and practical interpretation in many fields of education and constitute an important and intriguing agenda for educational change. *Changing Education* brings together leading international scholars who address these vital issues with authority and accessibility in areas where they are noted specialists. The series will commission books from all parts of the world in an attempt to cover the global and interlinked nature of current changes.

Published titles

David Corson: *Changing Education for Diversity*
Gill Helsby: *Changing Teachers' Work*
Colin Lankshear: *Changing Literacies*
Kenneth Leithwood: *Changing Leadership for Changing Times*
Shirley Steinberg and Joe Kincheloe: *Changing Multiculturalism*
Louise Stoll and Dean Fink: *Changing our Schools*

CHANGING OUR SCHOOLS

Linking school effectiveness
and school improvement

LOUISE STOLL AND
DEAN FINK

OPEN UNIVERSITY PRESS
Buckingham · Philadelphia

Open University Press
Celtic Court
22 Ballmoor
Buckingham
MK18 1XW

email: enquiries@openup.co.uk
world wide web: http://www.openup.co.uk

and

325 Chestnut Street
Philadelphia, PA 19106, USA

First Published 1995
Reprinted 1996, 1997, 1999

A catalogue record of this book is available from the British Library

ISBN   0 335 19290 4 (pb)   0 335 19291 2 (hb)

Library of Congress Cataloging-in-Publication Data
Stoll, Louise, 1956–
     Changing our schools : linking school effectiveness and school improvement
Louise Stoll and Dean Fink.
       p.   cm. — (Changing education)
     Includes bibliographical references and index.
     ISBN   0-335-19291-2 (hardbound)   ISBN   0-336-19290-4 (pbk.)
     1. School improvement programs. 2. Effective teaching. 3. Educational
   change. I. Fink, Dean, 1936–   . II. Title. III. Series.
LB2822.8.S86   1996
379.1'54——dc20   95-42288
                                                                                          CIP

Typeset by Type Study, Scarborough
Printed in Great Britain by St Edmundsbury Press, Bury St Edmunds, Suffolk

To Vivienne, Henry and Ramona

CONTENTS

SERIES EDITORS' PREFACE

Around the world, schools and the societies of which they are part, are confronting the most profound changes, the like of which have not been seen since the last great global movement of economic and educational restructuring more than a century ago. The fundamental forms of public education that were designed for an age of heavy manufacturing and mechanical industry are under challenge and fading fast as we move into a world of high technology, flexible workforces, more diverse school populations, downsized administrations and declining resources.

What is to follow is uncertain and unclear. The different directions of change can seem conflicting and are often contested. Decentralized systems of school self-management are accompanied by centralized systems of curriculum and assessment control. Moves to develop more authentic assessments are paralleled by the tightened imposition of standardized tests. Curriculum integration is being advocated in some places, more specialization and subject departmentalization in others.

These complex and contradictory cross-currents pose real challenges to theoretical and practical interpretation in many fields of education, and constitute an important and intriguing agenda for educational change, and for this series which is intended to meet a deep-seated need among researchers and practitioners. International, social and technological changes require a profound and rapid response from the educational community. By establishing and interpreting the nature and scope of educational change, *Changing our schools* will make a signification contribution to meeting this challenge.

We are delighted that Louise Stoll and Dean Fink are opening this series with their thoughtful, panoramic yet practical account of school change. Stoll and Fink are uniquely placed to analyse and communicate just what is involved in the difficult enterprise of *Changing our schools*. Louise Stoll brings to the text her former experience as a school district researcher on both sides of the Atlantic, and her current experience as a prominent researcher and writer in the field of school improvement and educational change. Dean Fink draws on years of experience as an effective and innovative school district administrator who has committed himself to and (like most good innovators) has also been candidly self-critical about a number of complex educational change initiatives for which he has been responsible in his own district and many others.

Together they have written an intellectually provocative yet highly accessible account of school change strategies in the postmodern world. They show how our paradigms of teaching and learning are changing, and why. They describe how strategies of school effectiveness and school improvement take us some way to grappling with these new paradigms, but why they have not gone far enough. These approaches, they show, may have helped us create some good schools – but only according to the standards of 1965!

Stoll and Fink explore not merely what is needed to make schools more technically adequate or effective by well-worn, and increasingly inappropriate standards. They also examine why the basic structures of schooling need to change and how this can be achieved. They address how schools can be *recultured* to build stronger professional cultures of collaboration, trust, risk-taking and shared learning among the teaching force. And instead of joining the politically fashionable chorus of researchers who scapegoat the 'failing schools' of the vulnerable few, they draw attention to the shortcomings of those many 'cruising schools' whose teachers avoid their obligations to improve or examine what they do by hiding in the slipstream of their high academic achievers.

Changing our schools is a clear, well written book. It connects the big picture of social change to concrete examples of what this means in practice. It builds a rare bridge between creative, cutting-edge thinking about change, and practical guidance that can be acted upon in classrooms and schools right now. Far too many books on change, improvement and effectiveness in education either bemuse teachers with excessive jargon and methodological intricacy, or insult them with superficial thinking and step-by-step solutions. *Changing our schools*, however, brings together imagination, research and practical experience in a powerful narrative that will always engage its readers, yet never demand too little of them. Once they have read it, thinking practitioners everywhere will return to this book again and again to guide them and stimulate reflection as they pursue their own struggles for positive change and school success.

Andy Hargreaves and Ivor Goodson

PREFACE AND
ACKNOWLEDGEMENTS

There is a story, apocryphal no doubt, about two people lost in the woods of northern Canada. They staggered from the bush into a small town, tired, hungry and dishevelled; they asked the first local, 'how do you get to Toronto?' The local's laconic answer was, 'Well, I wouldn't start from here'. In some ways, this book is like our story. It is not the one we originally set out to write. We both had spent a number of years heavily involved in an effective schools project with the Halton school district in Ontario, Canada, and had documented the project thoroughly. The 'Halton Story' would have been easy to write and, we thought, a timely contribution to the change literature. Like most things in education in the past few years, events moved much too quickly. School systems throughout the world have come under political attack. Decentralization, market-based reforms and high stakes testing, among other changes, have become accepted practice. A retrospective about a system-led change process, therefore, seemed somewhat out of step with the times. So we shifted our focus to a riskier, but we think more useful approach to change. We attempt throughout to describe a future which we believe is both inevitable and desirable. Our Halton years, our experiences since we left the Halton Board, and developing areas of research have led us in directions which we had scarcely contemplated when we first began our discussions about a book.

We intend this book for anyone seriously interested in changing schools to improve the lives of all pupils. In particular, it is written to assist principals/heads, school development teams, all school partners and education students to conceptualize the issues and to provide them with some concrete suggestions. It is our intention also that the academic community will find it a useful adjunct to the school effectiveness and school improvement literature.

By integrating concepts and constructs from a number of different disciplines, we try to paint as holistic a picture of school change as space will allow.

It has been argued that all knowledge claims are 'intelligible and debatable' only within their context, paradigm, or community: 'Reality is the result of the social processes accepted as normal in a specific context' (Rosenau 1992: 111). Chapter 1 initiates this theme by suggesting that history is about change and continuity and ours is an age of discontinuity. It is within a context of unrest, questioning, diversity, complexity, and changing concepts of time and space that schools must adjust to compelling but contradictory forces. By framing the paradoxes which face schools, we attempt to help the reader to understand the broad context in which schools must operate and why standing still or returning to some mythical past are unacceptable alternatives.

In response to these paradoxes, throughout the world a great deal of effort and money has been expended in the name of educational change. There is little sense, however, in attempting to improve schools unless there is a moral purpose and a very clear idea of what is to be achieved. If you don't know where you are going any destination will do. This is the second theme of Chapter 1; we return to it throughout the book. Equally, there is little sense in defining purpose and describing outcomes unless there are means to account for the uniqueness of schools and ways for them to make the improvement journey. By linking the *why* of change (moral purpose), the *what* of change (school effectiveness), and the *how* of change (school improvement), we attempt in the remainder of the book to assist all those committed to changing schools by providing both a theoretical critique and practical advice.

Chapter 2 introduces the three waves of educational reform in the 1980s and 1990s – school effectiveness, school improvement, and reform or restructuring – within our context of the 'Halton Story'. This chapter assists the reader to understand the experiences which helped shape our beliefs about school change and particularly our conviction that school effectiveness must be linked to school improvement if authentic change is to occur in schools. Chapter 2 also describes the experiences of a school system and one of its schools as they attempt to make substantive changes based on contemporary research. It provides the backdrop for in-depth looks at school effectiveness, school improvement and school development planning, which are the substance of Chapters 3, 4 and 5 respectively.

In Chapter 3 we review the evolution of school effectiveness studies from the early days – when schools were described as effective if they showed progress in basic skills on standardized tests – to more sophisticated views which try to determine 'value added' by schools over time. It is a paradigm which has evolved from a simple input-output model to a more detailed and thus complicated notion of effectiveness. School effectiveness research has shifted the focus of school change to pupil progress as a result of schooling. It is also based on the very democratic concept that a school must be effective for all its pupils, not just those who achieve or come from advantaged homes. By focusing on best practices of schools, school effectiveness contributes direction for the *what* of change.

Chapter 4 examines the *how* of change, school improvement. By synthesizing major contributions to the process of change, this chapter provides an outline of conditions and strategies which have proven useful in many contexts in helping schools to negotiate the paradoxes of contemporary society. It also examines some of the challenges that beset improvement attempts. The chapter concludes with attempts to link school effectiveness and school improvement to create a meaningful approach to change.

Chapter 5 is a derivative of school improvement because it examines the concept of total school development planning. We look at different models and identify key components of the process. More importantly, we derive from our own experiences and the literature a number of issues, often irrational, which must be attended to before such rational approaches as school development planning will work. We argue that these issues must be addressed if school development planning is not merely to be a time-consuming paper exercise.

Structures such as school development planning only succeed within rich cultures which build collaboration among teachers to promote school improvement. We define culture as others have done, in fairly simple terms, as 'the way we do things around here'. From this definition, in Chapter 6 we describe ways in which cultures evolve. We propose a typology of school cultures and a set of cultural norms which promote development for all pupils. This chapter also suggests practical ways in which schools can build more collaborative and developmental cultures.

Studies of organizational cultures, school effectiveness and school improvement agree on the importance of leadership. There is less agreement on a definition of the role of leaders within the different research traditions. In Chapter 7 we examine the evolution of the leadership literature and suggest that the contradictions of our times require a different conception of educational leadership. Such a leadership model should be flexible, dynamic, inclusive, humane and dedicated to moral purposes. To this end we define, describe and provide examples of invitational leadership. The chapter concludes by applying this style of leadership to the school typologies described in Chapter 6.

Invitational leadership is built on the belief that people are able, responsible and worthwhile. Chapter 8 applies this conviction to the teaching-learning process. This is the *why* of change. Much of the reform which has taken place – and certainly a great deal of the rhetoric – has had limited positive impact on pupils and their teachers. This chapter describes traditional approaches to learning and how they have affected teaching, and discusses an emerging paradigm which will and should change what is taught, how it is taught and how we know that it has been taught. This emerging paradigm, we predict, will require significant changes in the ways we organize and support schools to promote learning for *all* pupils.

Schools are not islands; they need support. Each school has multiple stakeholders. If change is to occur, the goals and activities of these various individuals and groups must be coherent. School systems, parents, school councils, community agencies and groups, businesses and universities (among others) can be effective and powerful partners in assisting schools and their pupils. All too often, however, schools have adopted a seige mentality which isolates or antagonizes potential sources of support. Chapter 9, therefore, analyses the roles of various partners and provides examples and suggestions as to how schools and their partners, by using 'positive politics', can build productive connections.

A learning organization is both an organization that learns and one that attends to the learning of all its people. Since the substance of the book up to this point focuses on organizational learning, Chapter 10 deals with the professional learning of teachers, leaders and some of the schools' partners. It describes principles of adult learning as well as guidelines for 'interactive professionalism'. We provide a number of examples of effective staff development programmes.

Doubt is the beginning of wisdom, and good information through enlightened assessment is crucial to ensuring that professional learning is focused on things that matter to pupils. Unfortunately, poorly conceived accountability models in many countries have reinforced the distrust of people in schools towards the forces outside its walls. Chapter 11 suggests that schools and school systems need to be more forthcoming and 'evaluate what they value'. We contend that, with some thought and goodwill, accountability and empowerment can be compatible. A related challenge described in this chapter is how to measure change. To this end we have developed a model which suggests that in addition to baseline data, change agents will need to collect data on how well the process is proceeding, data on intermediate outcomes related to teacher and school effectiveness, and finally pupil outcome data based on the goals of the change.

To show the interrelationship of concepts and summarize our approach to change in Chapter 12, we have designed a comprehensive model. The model briefly highlights some of the key concepts articulated throughout the book and attempts to bring some closure to its more pervasive themes. The book concludes by considering the connection between school effectiveness, school improvement and restructuring, and by addressing a concept which is seldom discussed when we talk about change, reform, improvement, development or whatever words people put to the notion of transforming schools to meet the needs of the future. It is a 'soft' and 'fuzzy' concept which in our hyperrationalistic world is thought to be somewhat old-fashioned. It is difficult to measure, yet the survival of our schools and – we do not think it too melodramatic to suggest – the survival of our civilization depends on our capacity for caring: caring enough to ensure success in school and in life for *all* children.

This book is an international collaboration and intended for an international audience. Our choice of words has required considerable compromise. Like most compromises our choices will not make everyone happy but we hope that no one will be too put off. When we refer to a particular context, however, we do use the language of that particular setting. The following list reflects our attempts to be ecumenical in our choices:

Our choice	*Other meanings*
pupils	students
principal	head
assistant principal	deputy head, vice principal
district	school board, Local Education Authority
school councils	governing bodies, school advisory councils
primary schools	elementary schools
secondary	high school
teacher unions	teacher federations
appraisal	teacher evaluation
administrators	Senior Management Team

Acknowledgements

For us to acknowledge all the people to whom we are indebted we would have a book longer than *War and Peace*. To our many colleagues and friends in Halton who have helped us and supported our work, thank you. We would particularly like to acknowledge the dedication, leadership and hard work of the original members of the Effective Schools Task Force: Eleanor Adam, Ron Beckett, Larry Davis, Karen Erskine, Milree Latimer, Ed Miazga, Terry Parry, Moe Pennock, Bert Radford, Larry Zavitz and Joanne Zywine. To Bob Williams, our boss during much of our work, thank you for modelling invitational leadership. We would also add our appreciation to our many colleagues in the International Congress for School Effectiveness and School Improvement for showing us the possibilities for change in schools.

We offer our appreciation to the following scholars and friends who have challenged our thinking and helped to shape it and this book: Lorna Earl, Michael Fullan, Harvey Goldstein, Andy Hargreaves, David Hopkins, Ken Leithwood, John MacBeath, Peter Mortimore, William Purkey, John Novak and David Reynolds. The scholarship and friendship of the late Desmond Nuttall have contributed significantly to our undertaking this project and to our understanding of school effectiveness. We also wish to thank Kate Asbill, Amanda Claremont, Peter Earley, Corrie Giles, Sue Harry, Barbara Mac-Gilchrist, Kate Myers, Pam Sammons, Jane Savage and, especially, Jo Kerr who has helped us pull the text together magnificently and kept us sane! We are most grateful. Our appreciation goes to Eleanor Adam for her contribution to the Frontenac story in Chapter 2. Thanks also, to our series editors, Andy Hargreaves and Ivor Goodson, for encouraging us to write this book; to Shona Mullen, our commissioning editor, Open University Press and John Skelton, managing director at Open University Press, for all your support.

We are particularly grateful to the following friends and colleagues: the Associate Directors and Associates of the International School Effectiveness and Improvement Centre (ISEIC); the Alliance for Invitational Education; schools and districts with whom we have worked, especially Lewisham LEA; and colleagues from the ESRC Seminar Series on School Effectiveness and School Improvement. Thank you. Since there are two authors, each with family and friends, we move to singular acknowledgements.

Louise Stoll: on a personal level, I would never have written this book without the ongoing support of my family: my parents, Vivienne and Henry; my sister and brother and families, Liz, David, Erika, Bernie, Oscar and little Abigail, who always brings a smile to my face. My friends in Britain, Canada and elsewhere mean so much to me and have sustained me through this endeavour. Special thanks to Debbie and Lorna for the long and often expensive phonecalls, and to Mike Moore, for all the joy he has given me. Finally, my thanks go to Steven for his good humour, encouragement and incredible patience.

Dean Fink: to my long-time friend John Walker: your attitude and courage in the midst of adversity are a daily inspiration. To the women in my life: my mother, Marjorie, who taught me the meaning of a caring family; my mother-in-law, Mona, for her ongoing support; my children Danielle and Tracy – for who you are and what you are, thank you. To Ramona my wife and strongest supporter for 33 years, words cannot express my love and appreciation. To our newest member, my grandson Zachary, thanks for keeping me young and tired.

It is not the custom for co-authors to acknowledge and thank each other. Since this is not a 'customary' book on change, we think it appropriate to go against the grain. When we have made presentations together, we have been introduced as 'the odd couple'. We differ in almost every way that two people can differ. In addition to the obvious – age, gender and nationality – we think, write and conceptualize differently. Our challenge was to ensure that these variances were complementary and in this we hope we have succeeded. We are still great friends and appreciate each other's contributions to this effort.

one

GOOD SCHOOLS IF THIS WERE 1965: THE CONTEXT OF CHANGE

During a recent trip one of us took to Kharkov in Ukraine, the tour guide and interpreter Valery pointed to a large factory and commented, 'this factory makes very good watches', then he paused and smiled: 'if this were 1965'. This comment speaks eloquently of the problems of not only Ukraine but of the entire former Soviet Union. They make products that are antiquated and unsaleable in the western world. They are, therefore, unable to earn the capital necessary to upgrade their factories and their workforce. This catch-22 is endemic in these societies and instructive to those of us who care about education. Many of our schools are good schools 'if this were 1965'. They got this way because society tends to predict the future by looking into the rear-view mirror. The historian Gustavson (1955) captures this idea when he states that people

> are afraid of drastic innovations, partly because [they] prefer the familiar, and partly because the vested interests of most people are normally bound up with the existing set up. Added to the weight against change is what might be called an institutional inertia, a proneness to keep the machinery running as in the past unless strong pressure for change materializes.
>
> (p. 72)

Much of human history and particularly institutional history is more about continuity than about change. Most people operate on the premiss that history is linear and what has happened in the past will continue into the future. This kind of thinking makes life seem more predictable, stable and comfortable.

There have been periods in history, however, of profound discontinuity, when events turned in ways which significantly altered every social structure. The Enlightenment of the eighteenth century, for example, ushered in an age in which people turned away from faith as a way of knowing, to science, rationality and a belief in progress. The application of science and the development of new and powerful technologies led to the industrialism of the nineteenth century. For the first time, people left their homes where they had made their livings through farming and cottage industries and made their ways to a new kind of economic organization, the factory. Here they became an adjunct to technology. The factory model required workers to leave their humanity at the door and function as part of the overall mechanistic structure. Workers were expected to be punctual, take orders, and above all never question authority. In time, basic skills such as reading, writing and arithmetic were added to the list of requirements.

Since compliance was a prerequisite to effective functioning, a managerial class evolved and over time bureaucratic structures developed to control people and information. As organizations became larger and more complex, specialization was introduced as a way to promote efficiency. These specialities often became fiefdoms within larger structures. They emphasized their differences through the use of uniquely specialized language and customs. 'Modernity' in the twentieth century has come to mean a society which is stable, stolid, predictable, compartmentalized and bureaucratic.

These social and economic changes prevented the extended family from educating children in traditional ways. State-run schools, therefore, gradually emerged for children of the less privileged. These schools copied the organizational model of the factory where the children's parents worked:

> schools mirrored the national economy, with standard assembly-line curriculum, divided neatly into subjects, taught in predictable units of time, arranged sequentially by grade, and controlled by standardized tests intended to weed out defective units and return for reworking.
>
> (Reich 1992: 226)

Schools and school systems gradually took on the trappings of other modern institutions. They became departmentalized and bureaucratized, but also stable, predictable and comfortable for most children, parents and educators. Recently, much has been made of failing schools, particularly in Britain. The underlying task for the future, however, is not only to deal with the really disastrous schools, but also the comfortable schools that on the surface appear effective or at least satisfactory and enjoy public support, but which are in reality mediocre: 'the good schools – if this were 1965'.

An age of discontinuity

It is becoming increasingly clear that we are in the midst of another age of discontinuity which offers 'indeterminacy rather than determinism, diversity rather than unity, difference rather than synthesis, complexity rather than simplification' (Rosenau 1992: 8). Changing social forces are compelling western societies to move into the emerging information age. Drucker (1993) contends that ' "the means of production" – is no longer capital, nor natural resources, nor labour. It is and will be knowledge . . . Value is now created by "productivity" and "innovation", both applications of knowledge to work' (p. 8).

If one considers the industries which many consider will drive our economies into the new millennium: microelectronics, biotechnology, the new materials industries, civilian aviation, telecommunications, robots plus machine tools and computers plus software – all knowledge industries (Thurlow 1992) – one can see the basis for Drucker's argument. Simply stated, we are living in a postmodern world. Hargreaves (1994a) describes postmodernity as 'a social condition in which economic, political, organizational and even personal life come to be organized around very different principles than those of modernity . . . The post modern world is fast, complex, compressed and uncertain' (p. 8).

Reich (1992) makes the link between postmodernity and education when he says: 'There will be no national products or technologies, no national corporations, no national industries. There will no longer be national economies . . . Each nation's prime assets will be its citizens' skills and insights' (p. 3). He contends that the real challenge for a nation 'is to increase the potential value of what its citizens can add to the global economy, by enhancing their skills and capacities and by improving their means of linking those skills and capacities to the world markets' (p. 8).

Patterns of work and living have to and will change. Knowledge workers, for instance, can work from their homes as workers did before industrialism. Layers of bureaucracy have been eliminated in both the private and public sectors because they are no longer needed to ensure compliance and to control knowledge. The factory metaphor is being replaced by other organizational metaphors such as the 'shamrock' organization suggested by Handy (1991). In this organization, a highly educated élite core of knowledge workers is surrounded by the other leaves of the shamrock, the contractors who come and go as their services are needed and the part-time workers who are also hired on a needs basis. Rather than lifetime employment with an organization, he suggests that we will have to develop a portfolio of skills and competencies to enable us to fit into a flexible and dynamic system. Family structures, parenting patterns and, of course, education will change.

After years of being a minor part of the political and economic agenda in most western countries, the urgency to adjust to the postmodern world has elevated the discussion of education to a position of pre-eminence. It is the economic agenda, driven by powerful forces in our societies, which has provided the popular answer to the philosophical question, 'what are the purposes of education?' If one was to accept the logic of corporate élites, the purpose of education is to prepare pupils to adapt to the technological revolution so that they will be more useful to the international corporate world. Such logic is profoundly anti-democratic and anti-individual. The free market and democracy are not necessarily synonymous. The already unconscionable gap between rich and poor in most western countries has the potential to grow even wider as some adapt to the new age and others are kept from its rewards.

Clearly, an educational purpose seemingly lost in the market rhetoric of educational discourse is the notion of education for democratic citizenry. The necessity of producing an informed citizenry which sees itself with rights and responsibilities within and to a larger community has long been a stated goal of most western societies. Giroux (1989) summarizes this need to refocus education:

> Education reform needs to address the most basic questions of purpose and meaning. What kind of society do we want? How do we educate students for a truly democratic society? What conditions must we provide for both teachers and students for such an education to be meaningful and workable? These questions link schooling to the issues of critical citizenship, democratic community, and social justice.
>
> (p. 729)

This dilemma of educational purpose, between serving the needs of the market-place and the requirements of democratic living, is but one of the many postmodern paradoxes facing schools. In the following section we identify other paradoxes or ironies that define the context in which schools must function.

The paradox of change and continuity

Handy (1994) describes our times as an age of paradox. Social forces which impact our lives have within them trends or patterns which are contradictory, ironic, and thus paradoxical. A. Hargreaves (1995), in his review of paradoxes affecting education, includes 'stronger orientation to the future creates greater nostalgia for the past' (p. 15). This is the paradox of change *and* continuity, and this is the fundamental paradox for schools.

They must attend simultaneously to the forces of change and continuity, and the pressures of postmodernity and modernity. Schools' efforts to move towards an image of education which will prepare pupils for the vagaries of a postmodern age, therefore, must occur within a society and policy structure which looks backwards to some halcyon days in education which never existed. As the American humorist Will Rogers once said, 'Schools ain't what they used to be, and never was'. The changes required in the 'deep structures' of schooling (Cuban 1990) are counterbalanced by powerful forces which emphasize continuity in education.

The discontinuity of our times has made the educational scene quite unstable internationally. Very sane people throughout the world resist ill-conceived, mindless changes to the continuity factors of education which they feel enabled schools to succeed in the modern era. In doing so, however, changes to the 'deep structures' which are overdue and necessary to equip students for the postmodern world are also resisted.

Practitioners today are swamped by innovations. Fortunately for sanity, many new ideas seem to come and go with incredible speed. Teachers and administrators have learned to treat innovations like kidney stones: they may cause considerable pain but, in the last analysis, 'this too shall pass'. In many situations this is the sane and sensible thing to do. Change, instability and resistance in all facets of society, not just education, are compelling realities for contemporary life. While inevitable, changes are not necessarily always positive. Principled people resist change perceived to be harmful to pupils. To resist, however, is to be considered irrational. In education, ill-designed and poorly implemented change projects have made many educators with any kind of memory sceptical of mandated changes and, in some cases, outright hostile. Since these are the people who have to implement educational change and who have been largely left out of policy debates, schools have become fundamentally conservative institutions which have historically resisted change and sought to preserve continuity with their past experiences.

Change in schools is made even less rational by the public nature of schools. Since most people have attended school at one point in their lives, to suggest that schools need to change in substantive ways becomes a critique of one's own education. In what Galbraith (1992) calls this 'age of contentment', people who vote in elections tend to focus on short-term gain: that is, stability and minimal upset and leave the future to take care of itself. Educational reformers throughout the world have failed to convince their publics of the benefits of change (Mirel 1994). The context within which public educators work, therefore, is inherently conservative and in some situations reactionary or at least nostalgic.

One need only look at reform efforts in Britain, Canada, Australia and the United States, among others – with their emphasis on conformity of curriculum, testing for compliance and decentralized decision making – to confirm the distrust politicians and technocrats hold for educators in general, and teachers in particular.

It is instructive to note that as we move into the postmodern information age, the best that well-publicized educational critics can propose are 'back to the basics' and 'free market' approaches to education. The former dooms children to redundancy because the basics have changed. It would appear that 'free market' approaches to education create the same social inequities in schooling that exist in the distribution of wealth in the market-place. It is ironic that the same national, political and business leaders who advocate teamwork, decentralized decision making and flat-lined organizations in business, support structures in education which are centralized, competitive and authoritarian.

Most of us who have spent our working lives in education have always lived with such contradictions: demands for school improvement but reduced costs; greater accountability but more flexibility; more structure, less structure; more discipline, greater caring; work harder, work smarter, and so on. If the contradictions of the past were confusing, the 'change-continuity' paradox we experience today is truly confounding, and society's love/hate attitudes towards teachers even more bewildering.

Contrary to popular mythology, teachers have adapted to the changing clientele in schools. It is teachers who have learned to modify curricula, develop new teaching and assessment strategies and deal with the myriad of social problems society has dumped on schools. Teachers have made these adjustments out of their desire to serve pupils not because of political or bureaucratic mandates. Pupils are not standardized and teaching is not routine. Teachers need knowledge of child development, multiple teaching strategies, a variety of assessment strategies, as well as insight into children's learning styles. Teaching is as much an art as a science. Historically, teachers have been treated like semi-skilled tradespeople. Someone devised a change and then through writing new curriculum guidelines or manuals, using political clout to change textbooks, or by mandating tests for pupils and/or for teachers, expected teachers to improve learning for pupils.

These attempts have failed in the past and will fail in the future because teachers have not been involved in the changes and find little personal meaning in them. The sooner teachers are seen as knowledge workers, professional educators and leaders, the sooner schools will improve. Stenhouse (1984) captured this idea well:

> Good teachers are necessarily autonomous in professional judgement. They do not need to be told what to do. They are not professionally the dependants of researchers, of superintendents, of innovators or supervisors. This does not mean that they do not welcome access to ideas created by other people at other places or in other times. Nor do they reject advice, consultancy or support. But they do know that ideas and people are not of much real use until they are digested to the point where

they are subject to the teacher's own judgement. In short, it is the task of all educationalists outside the classroom to serve the teachers; for only teachers are in position to create good teaching.

(p. 69)

While teachers and schools have changed significantly over time in most western countries, they have done so through slow incrementalism characteristic of most institutional change rather than massive reform movements. In spite of significant change, however, the continuity in education – grouping by age and ability, separate subject disciplines, secondary school departments and isolated classrooms – has remained fundamentally unchanged for decades. Efforts to develop policies to force change have largely ignored the increasing diversity and polarization of society.

The paradox of quality-equity

Policy development usually involves an interplay among three competing priorities: quality, equity and efficiency. New initiatives raise such questions as, does it improve the quality of pupil learning? Does it raise the quality of learning for *all* pupils? Can we afford to make the changes? The reforms proposed in most countries have been made in the name of quality and efficiency. They provide the rhetoric of equity but fail to accommodate the changing nature of society. Indeed many changes tend to be ways for the 'haves' to escape from the 'have nots'. Grant-maintained schools in Britain which have become selective in their intake, American charter schools which choose their clientele, and various choice and voucher initiatives are popular political responses which gain favour with the affluent but ignore the impact of postmodernity on the least empowered elements of society. Reich (1992) states that

> Each nation's primary political task will be to cope with the centrifugal forces of the global economy which tear at the ties binding citizens together – bestowing even greater wealth on the most skilled and insightful, while consigning the less skilled to a declining standard of living.

(p. 3)

The fundamental problem is stated by Britain's National Commission on Education (1993), but is also relevant to many other countries: 'The most serious shortcoming of education in the United Kingdom . . . is its failure to enable not just a minority but a large majority of young people to obtain as much from their education as they are capable of achieving' (p. 2).

The widening gap between the social classes has meant an increasing percentage of children live in poverty. In Britain families with children under

16 years of age compose an increasing percentage of the lowest 20 per cent on the socio-economic ladder. One in four children currently live in poverty, compared to one in five in 1991 (Smith 1995). The number of children on free school meals – a good indicator of economic disadvantage – has increased 40 per cent since 1991. This is heightened by a considerable geographic stability of low income families in certain areas.

Smith correlates the disparity in socio-economic levels with school performance, and indicates that pupils in the highest outperform the lowest disadvantaged areas by two to one on secondary examination results. It is no accident that the first dozen failing schools identified by Britain's new inspectorial arrangement were found largely in areas of urban or small town deprivation (Hofkins 1995).

Data from the United States are equally bleak. Hodgkinson (1991) states that since 1987, a quarter of all preschool children have lived in poverty. Every year 350,000 children are born to mothers who are addicted to cocaine. Fifteen million children are raised by single mothers who live in poverty. At least two million children have no afterschool supervision each day and between 50,000 and 200,000 children have no home to go to on any given night.

In a report to the Ontario government, the Premier's Council on Health, Wellbeing and Social Justice (1994) indicated that in Canada's most affluent and industrial province, the percentage of children living in poverty had risen from 12 per cent in 1987 to over 17 per cent in 1990. The Council chronicled the changing family. Real income growth in Canada has stagnated at 1970s levels, and has declined in young families (under age 35). Among families with a head under 25, the incidence of poverty nearly doubled from 21 to 37 per cent between 1981 and 1991.

In 1961, the traditional 'male as earner' and 'stay at home' wife constituted almost two-thirds of Canadian families. By 1991, this structure accounted for only 12 per cent. By 1996, 80 per cent of Canadian women, who still perform the primary childrearing and housekeeping roles, will be in the workforce. More than 70 per cent of preschool children are in non-parental care arrangements.

The complexity and instability of postmodernity have impacted on families and, through families, to the classroom in challenging ways. The Premier's Council (1994) states that:

> The 'leisure society' promised in the 1960's has become instead a society of exhausted workers for whom time – time for children, time for relaxation, time for community involvement, time for sleep – seems an ever more precious and elusive commodity. Not surprisingly . . . women who work full time outside the home and had young children were most likely to be severely time stressed.
>
> (p. 17)

While all of these socio-economic factors are crucial to an understanding of a school's context, even greater pressure is created by gender, race and cultural issues. On gender issues Shakeshaft (1993a) writes:

> Few schools offer an equitable environment in which all students can grow. Most offer white males more options in an environment that is hospitable to their needs. White females and all members of minority groups, on the other hand, must obtain their education in systems that are at best indifferent and at worst hostile to them.
>
> White women and all people of colour learn that their concerns, their lives, and their cultures are not the stuff of schooling. They discover that school is not a psychologically or physically safe environment for them and that they are valued by neither the system nor the society.
>
> (p. 87)

She goes on to argue that educational goals, organizational structures, curriculum and learning materials are heavily weighted to advance the learning of boys. Traditional gender-specific subjects such as home economics for girls and industrial arts for boys still separate according to sex role stereotypes. Mathematics and science are seen by girls as more difficult and less interesting (Halton Board of Education 1993a).

Males receive more attention than females in class (Sadker and Sadker, 1986; Mortimore *et al.* 1988). 'The average female is ignored – neither reprimanded nor praised – and the high achieving female receives the least attention of all students' (Shakeshaft 1993a: 89). Even more alarming, studies in New York State reveal that many female students are subjected to sexual harassment. Shakeshaft and Cohen (1990) report that of the 300 reported incidents of sexual harassment, 97 per cent involved a male heterosexual teacher and, in 74 per cent of incidents, a female student. While it is difficult to generalize to other contexts, we would suggest that this is a universal issue.

King and Coles's (1992) research reflects girls' negative self-perception. They asked 11-, 13- and 15-year-old Canadian girls and boys to respond positively or negatively to such statements as: 'I like myself'; 'I have confidence in myself'; 'I often wish I were someone else'; 'I would change how I look if I could'. Boys were much more positive about themselves on all items. The last item, on body image, showed girls to be much more critical of themselves (p. 80). In their international comparison which asked girls and boys from ten nations 'Do you ever feel lonely?' more girls than boys in all ten countries responded in the affirmative. In eight of the ten nations, Norway and Sweden excepted, girls by 15 years of age were far less involved in physical activities than boys. In our own work on self concept (Halton Board of Education 1993b), in response to the item 'I like myself', we found twice as many 12- and 13-year-old girls (19 per cent) as compared to boys of the same age (nine per cent) answered negatively.

Context issues related to gender also involve boys. Boys outnumber girls in vocational schools in Ontario by two to one and boys are more likely to be one or two years behind grade level in the United States (Carnegie Council on Adolescent Development 1989). American data suggest that boys are more likely to be the perpetrators and victims of violence (Hodgkinson 1991). In Britain, boys outnumber girls by two to one in schools for pupils with learning difficulties. Boys trail girls on many important school achievement measures. Barber (1994) asks the rhetorical question: 'It is a pitiful performance by boys that now requires a radical rethinking of attitudes to equal opportunities. The question is: have girls had it too good for too long while society has complacently accepted that boys will be boys?' (p. 7).

Another question remains. If girls are doing so well, why are their aspirations and feelings of self so low? (Myers, personal communication). These gender paradoxes sit in most classrooms every day and it is up to the teacher to attend to differing needs.

Pupils who are members of racial or cultural minorities, or recent immigrants, are particularly vulnerable when policies are pursued that fail to account for the unique contexts of schools and classrooms. An American report stated that minority students 'attend the weakest schools, have access to the least adequate health services, and have the fewest clearly visible paths to opportunities in the mainstream' (Carnegie Council on Adolescent Development 1989: 25). Oakes's (1985) study of ability tracking demonstrated that these students are segregated into vocational or non-academic programme tracks, that do little more than purify the mainstream programmes for middle-class and upper-class students. Minority students have a much higher chance of being retained in a grade and have significantly higher school dropout rates (Carnegie Council 1989). Even physical harassment is part of the school context for many minority students (Klein 1995).

While considerable gains have been made in responding to the needs of multicultural pupils (Banks 1993), these gains are threatened by fears that multiculturalism is undermining mainstream culture (Pyke 1994). In the United States, renowned historian Arthur Schlesinger (1991) presents this view, and has been well received, especially among American conservatives. In Canada, popular books which advocate a return to 'traditional' values, practices and curriculum content reflect the increasing uneasiness of many Canadians with the changing racial and cultural compositions of the nation and its schools (Gairdner 1993; Nikiforuk 1993).

Debates in Britain and the United States about the contents of textbooks and the reading lists for English programmes reflect this tension between groups within the community: those who feel schools must respond to their increasing multiculturalism and others who see traditional values and traditions threatened (Garcia 1993). Attempts to address the problems of people who have been marginalized have in many places precipitated a 'modernist' response which has historically enabled the majority culture to win and minorities to lose. This reaction has lead to the reaffirmation in some jurisdictions of ranking, streaming, competition, standardized tests and a focus on basic skills. Anything less to the critics of multicultural programming is evidence of a civilization that has become soft and indulgent and, of course, non-competitive economically. Regardless of this controversy swirling around them, the reality for teachers and schools is that they must enhance the learning of individual pupils with a diversity of backgrounds and needs.

Conclusion

While the contradictions we have described are beyond any school's ability to resolve, educators can, by framing them, at least understand and begin to manage them to benefit pupils. In our own work in both Canada and Britain, we have had the opportunity to observe many schools and educators as they seek to respond to these paradoxical social pressures. Two patterns have emerged: in one, schools and school systems have attempted to fix the parts, a structural change here, a new programme there, usually with limited impact. The other response has been to force change through policy mandates. Once again these reform efforts focus on a few aspects of schooling, oblivious to schools as part of larger systems. In our view these approaches have not and will not work.

As we move into the twenty-first century, we need to rethink our conceptions of how to respond to our rapidly changing contexts. The modern world has been built upon the mechanistic world view of Cartesian-Newtonian logic which guides most of our academic traditions and tends to look at the parts of a system rather than at the whole. Capra (1983) suggests that we must see our society and its schools as interconnected systems rather than as the sum of its parts. Our best chance to change our schools in ways which prepare our pupils for the vagaries of the twenty-first century is to look at schools and their contexts as ecosystems. To this end, we attempt throughout this book to make connections. Not only do we link the school effectiveness research and the school improvement literature, we have tried to develop a comprehensive picture of the change process by relating these research areas to such concepts as culture, leadership, learning theory, partnerships, adult learning and evaluation.

In the next chapter, we outline an example of a school system and a school within that system which attempted to look at change in this holistic way.

Since we were both involved in these efforts, these stories provide the context for much of our understanding of the change processes described in the remainder of the book; we hope they are instructive to others who are charged with facilitating change.

two

THE HALTON EFFECTIVE
SCHOOLS PROJECT:
A STORY OF CHANGE

The following two stories describe the evolution of a school system, the Halton Board of Education and one of its schools, Frontenac Public School. The first narrative provides a case-study of a system which has evolved from a highly centralized organization to a system which now can be described as 'co-managed' (Louis 1990). The second depicts a school which evolved from a '1965' school to one which is providing leadership to other schools in the system.

History as context

The Halton Board of Education, located 30 miles from Toronto Ontario, serves 44,000 students in 66 elementary schools and 17 secondary schools. Organized in 1969 as part of the government of Ontario's reorganization of school boards, the Halton board consolidated ten smaller school districts into one larger and more comprehensive school district.

It was organized as a typical 1970s bureaucracy. Curriculum was initiated at central office and delivered by subject coordinators to the schools. Quality was to be assured through a number of assistant superintendents who had the job of inspecting principals and teachers. Senior administrators not only set policies, they annually conducted a rigorous on-site inspection of each school and its principal to ensure compliance. High expectations were established for principals and those who did not measure up were summarily demoted. Needless to say, an annual visit by the senior administration was an event to survive, not to anticipate as a growth experience! Change was initiated at the Board of Education office, developed into policy by a compliant school board and delivered to the schools by the bureaucracy.

In response to a perceived lack of influence, principals developed associations within the system to represent their interests. Over time, the elementary and secondary principal associations became so powerful that the system could be administered with significantly fewer senior managers than other school boards of comparable size. In spite of the very 'top-down' structure and management style, the first ten years of the Board's life were characterized by innovation, experimentation and organizational energy.

The late 1970s and early 1980s were years of drift. People in the system who wanted to develop new programmes or approaches often did so without too much support from central office. Schools tended to do what they thought was necessary. Teachers' federations, frustrated by the bureaucratic structure, became increasingly adversarial and the school board became less compliant. Conflict among various interest groups came to characterize the system.

By the early 1980s, a new and dynamic director of education was appointed. His mandate from the Board was to 'clean up' the system. This he did with speed, skill and considerable dispatch. Most people in the system who knew the system at its peak applauded his early efforts. His political acuity enabled him to build bridges with the school board, teachers' federations and the community.

Within this context, many system leaders sensed that the schools were out of step with the rapidly accelerating pace of change, and that a vehicle was needed to stimulate a rethinking of schools' purposes and practices and jolt the system out of its complacency. The challenge was to respond to a rather ill-defined need to change, while preserving the best from the system's and schools' previous practices.

The Effective Schools Task Force

To this end, in 1986, as one of a number of renewal initiatives, the Halton board approved the Halton Effective Schools Project to enhance the quality of the system and schools' performance through the application of the characteristics of effective schools. Other change projects such as curriculum and special education reviews resulted from central office leadership. The focus on effective schools, however, came from the initiative of the principals' associations. The Board established the Effective Schools Task Force, composed of a senior manager as chair, nine of the system's most influential principals, three of the most innovative system leaders from central office, and an educational researcher with a strong background in school effectiveness research. This *ad hoc* committee, with its origins outside central

Figure 2.1 Characteristics of effective schools

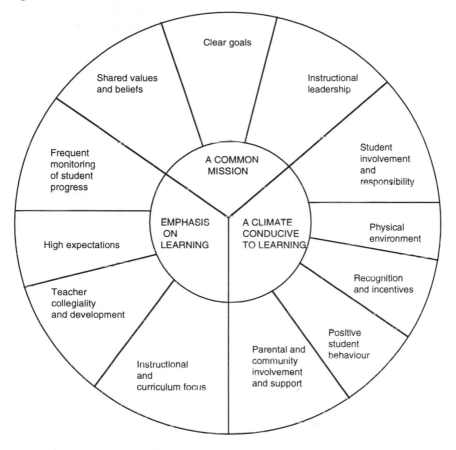

office, was tolerated by the system's bureaucracy because of its quasi-official status and finite lifespan.

The task force reviewed the school effectiveness and school improvement literature available at the time and developed four guiding principles:

1 The focus for the Effective Schools Project would be each school – through a cooperative approach, teachers and schools could 'buy into' the project.
2 The change process would be 'top-down, bottom-up' – the system would provide broad direction and support for schools' own plans.
3 The focus on effective schools would be integrated into existing supervision, planning and managerial systems.
4 The project would not be a 'quick fix'. The plan would take more than five years because 'change is a process, not an event' (Fullan 1982: 41).

In its initial search of the literature, the task force rejected research which defined an effective school as one which raised student test scores on traditional standardized tests. It was most influenced in the beginning by British literature and particularly the research of Mortimore and his colleagues (1988) at the Inner London Education Authority. The task force members combined this body of information with an effective schools model based on the work of Sackney (1986) to develop a model which became the starting point for the Halton effective schools approach (see Figure 2.1).

Twelve characteristics are outlined in this model, which fall into three broader categories:

1 *A common mission,* which is a shared and communicated vision of school goals and priorities. The principal plays a major role in the encouragement of teachers', parents' and students' involvement in, commitment to and responsibility for the vision.
2 *An emphasis on learning,* characterized by teachers who have and convey high expectations to their students. Teachers also use a variety of teaching and monitoring strategies, and work together to create curriculum materials linked to the school goals.
3 *A climate conducive to learning,* where morale and self concept are high, due to active involvement and responsibility on the part of students, recognition and incentives, and fairness and consistency with regard to student behaviour. The learning environment is attractive, with work displays and attention paid to comfort. It is also inviting to parents and members of the community, who are also involved in school life.

Task force members 'taught' this model to each school's staff and waited for wonderful things to happen, assuming that if school staffs knew what made schools effective they would focus their efforts in appropriate directions (Stoll and Fink 1988). They discovered, like many before them, that authentic change is sometimes painfully slow, as described by Sizer's (1985) simple metaphor: 'a good school does not emerge like a pre-packaged frozen dinner stuck for 15 minutes in a radar range; it develops from the slow simmering of carefully blended ingredients' (p. 22).

To enable schools to look at the characteristics within their own context, the task force developed the school growth plan (Halton Board of Education 1988). To do this they drew on models of many other researchers and school districts, particularly those in Britain. The Halton school growth plan was designed to be a systematic means by which an individual school could achieve sustained growth. By taking into account government and school board initiatives, the mosaic of its unique context, and the views of its students, parents and teachers, a school could plan its own development over time.

The school growth plan has four stages of development that correspond to four key questions:

1 Where are we now? (assessment)
2 Where would we like to be in the future? (planning)
3 How best can we move in that direction? (implementation)
4 How do we evaluate the changes we are making? (evaluation)

Nine schools piloted the model in year one, and 25 were added in year two. These schools could apply for small financial grants from an effective schools' budget. The change literature is quite clear; improvement efforts are 're-source hungry' (Louis and Miles 1990). System support in the form of money is crucial to sustain reform initiatives in schools. While Louis and Miles suggest that very large sums of money are necessary to effect change, the most any Halton school received was $1,500. The key to its effective use was to allocate money with 'no strings attached'. The message of trust reinforced the professionalism of teachers. The system received its investment many times over in terms of people's efforts. To argue that large sums of money are vital to change is to provide an excuse for inaction. While resourcing is important, the Halton experience raises questions about the need for large sums of money to effect significant change.

   Task force members spent a considerable amount of time in the pilot schools. They found a wide disparity in planning effectiveness. Some schools had made significant and demonstrable gains to achieve school goals. One large secondary school for instance improved attendance and course completion for non-university-bound students from less than 75 per cent on both dimensions to over 90 per cent attendance and course completion. They found others, however, who mirrored Reynolds and Packer's (1992) description of some Welsh schools in Reynolds's study: 'The knowledge of the rational-empirical paradigm encountered irrationality, emotionality, abnormality and what can only be called personal and group disturbance' (p. 182).

   The task force's analysis suggested that those schools which were successful attended to certain fundamental conditions of planning which enabled them to succeed, whereas schools that foundered often short-circuited the process.

   Attention to the development of shared values, ensuring a climate for change and maintaining a collaborative culture throughout the growth planning process, not only fostered the success of the planning process but also determined the longevity of the changes within the plan. These fundamental conditions, which we develop in detail later in the book, appeared to blend together to create a supportive framework for change. It was important to perceive school growth planning as a process rather than merely a plan in four stages.

   Although a handbook for school growth planning was developed and considerable experimentation with the concept took place in pilot schools, results of surveys showed that the ability of schools to direct their own planning had not become pervasive throughout the system. The unique problems of secondary schools caused by size and organization also became evident. The task force underestimated the need early on for a system-supported staff development programme on the topic. The system therefore, conducted and financed five-day programmes for school growth planning teams which focused on such processes as conflict resolution, decision making, approaches to planning, and assessment and evaluation. Evaluations conducted at the end of the five days revealed the necessity of training for effective school planning as well as the benefit of the team approach to staff development. Assessment by schools of their needs was a real challenge. To help schools, a series of effective schools questionnaires for teachers, parents and students were developed. The system used them to develop baseline data and provided support for schools to use them for self-analysis in the planning process. All schools in the system currently use a school growth plan and report considerable confidence, even in areas where previously they felt unprepared (Halton Board of Education 1992a).

School as the centre of change

As the task force worked through its efforts on school effectiveness and progressed to the next stage of developing processes for school improvement, it became obvious to its members that the work was useful, but was still on the margins of significant change for students. School growth plans tended to focus on non-classroom issues and, with notable exceptions, never challenged traditional approaches to teaching and learning. Murphy (1992) prophesied that ultimately school effectiveness and school improvement would have to address 'fairly radical changes in the design and unfolding of learning experiences' (p. 99), the *why* of change.

By 1994, Murphy's words were being played out in Halton. In effect, eight years after the initiation of a change 'odyssey', a sense of educational purpose had been tied to the insights gained from the work on school effectiveness and school improvement. As the result of links in 1988 to the Learning Consortium (Fullan *et al.* 1990), a school-university partnership with three other large school districts, the Faculty of Education at the University of Toronto and the Ontario Institute for Studies in Education, Halton began to use a different conceptual framework for classroom instruction. This model describes teaching in terms of four interconnected cogs: instructional skills, like time on task; instructional strategies, like cooperative group learning; classroom management; and the curriculum. It helped to reorientate the system's strategic plans and serve as an organizer for staff development programmes.

This system-wide focus on the classroom was facilitated by the appointment of a new director of education in 1988. He came from within the system and had been an early supporter of the task force efforts. As a strong proponent of staff development, he realized to institutionalize change the system must focus and consolidate the various change initiatives which were underway. Perhaps more importantly, he confirmed the notion that real change occurs in classrooms and not district offices. By restructuring the organization and its operating principles, schools became the centre of change rather than the objects of managed change.

His first step was to establish a broadly democratic process to develop a strategic plan in which the system identified a few key priorities and focused its attention and resources on high leverage activities (Halton Board of Education 1989). The system's strategic plan mobilized the entire Halton board to 'zero in' on instructional strategies to meet the needs of gifted students at one end of the spectrum and mentally challenged students at the other. School growth plans were required to have at least one school-wide goal to improve instruction.

The strategic plan listed three targets for the next three years:

1 Instruction – the direction of energies and resources to support the teaching-learning process, through the implementation of a comprehensive model of instruction.
2 School growth planning – the support and encouragement of school-based decision making, consistent with community and board expectations.
3 Staff development – to attract, select, develop and retain the highest calibre staff.

Each of these goals was accompanied by specific objectives, implementation and evaluation plans. In 1993, these directions were reaffirmed and a fourth, which focused on reaching out to the system's various communities, was added. The district was reorganized to model a federal system with implementation decisions made in the schools and broad policy, resource and personnel decisions at the centre. This was the 'top-down' part of the change equation.

Integrating existing structures

With its mandate complete the task force dissolved. Its accomplishments were rolled into the strategic plan. All other system processes were brought into line with the goals and strategic plan for the system. To this end, principal training, promotion, and in-service were revised to be consistent with the system's goals. Similarly, procedures for the hiring, transfer, and appraisal of staff were modified to create consistency for the system's values and goals.

Teacher and principal supervision practices in particular had the potential to be a problem. Schools, their principals and teachers were being encouraged to innovate but were being evaluated on existing expectations: a paradox not uncommon in many educational organizations. To resolve this anomaly and to ensure that existing practices were congruent with new directions, the Halton system undertook a major reorientation of its well-established supervision policies. In the early 1970s, the system had adopted an approach to the supervision of people in leadership roles called 'Education By Agreement' (EBA). The vehicle for agreement on annual goals by system leaders, including principals and vice principals, was the 'Manager's Letter'. Each person in a leadership role developed a Manager's Letter with the person to whom they reported. The process involved the collaborative development of a statement of goals, indicators of success, activities to be pursued and timelines by the partners to the agreement. It was, to use Covey's (1989) phrase, intended to be a 'psychological contract'.

This process was reviewed in 1993 by a committee of principals, to integrate it into the effectiveness model. Each principal, therefore, continues to have a Manager's Letter with a superintendent, and each vice-principal has a Manager's Letter with her or his principal. This personal growth plan contains a few 'high leverage' goals which could extend from six months to three years. It contains goals related to:

- the expectations of principals and vice-principals based on contemporary models of leadership
- the principal's or vice-principal's role in the implementation of the school growth plan
- the principal's or vice-principal's personal growth.

The term 'Manager's Letter' is somewhat dated and perhaps misleading to the outsider. It is, however, meaningful in the Halton context, and an example of how traditional practices and language have been adapted to thread the commitment of system leaders into the fabric of school and system directions.

Similarly, Halton's procedures for the supervision of teachers, Cooperative Supervision and Evaluation (CS&E), were updated and melded into the effectiveness model. Performance appraisal systems walk a fine line between accountability to school boards and the public, and the professional growth of teachers. School board members often want to define principal and teacher roles in narrowly prescribed ways and delineate a review process which is punitive in spirit. A realistic approach to performance appraisals must have sufficiently high expectations to define a truly professional educator and a process of performance review which is not only thorough, but perceived to be rigorous within the larger context of schools and school systems. A representative committee, therefore, updated the expectations for teachers to include understanding gained from the school effectiveness and teacher effectiveness literature, and insights into self concept theory. Through a rather lengthy, but necessary, interactive process with teachers and the school board, the final product received strong professional support as well as political affirmation.

The CS&E process requires each principal to develop an agreement with each teacher every year. The nature of these agreements depend on the age, experience, and goals of the individual teacher. Teacher goals will vary in depth and time commitment. Some will involve a Manager's Letter approach, others require classroom visits and follow-up by the principal. The key word is cooperative. Goals are to be negotiated. If the principal has a serious performance concern the procedure becomes more prescriptive and definitive to ensure 'just cause and due process'. Perhaps the most significant part of this process is the emphasis on providing professional opportunities for teachers' growth. From dialogue between the teacher and the principal, a teacher's personal professional growth plan is developed.

From a principal's point of view, the process provides an opportunity to involve the teacher in the school's growth plan. From a teacher's perspective, if conducted with integrity, it breaks down isolation, provides a vehicle to develop a personal growth plan and a connection to the larger school and system cultures. The review of CS&E resulted in a traditional activity, performance appraisal, becoming tied to the effectiveness model in a meaningful way.

The 'three waves of reform'

Peter Holly (1990), in commenting on the work of Banathy (1988), states:

> in recent times, there have been three waves of educational reform. The first wave of reform entailed 'doing the same, but more of it', the second wave meant doing the same, but doing it better; and the third wave involves the restructuring and redesign of the educational system. It could be argued that the first wave represents the school effectiveness movement, the second wave the drive towards linking it (school effectiveness) with school improvement, and the third wave the pursuit of future excellence.
>
> (p. 195)

The Halton Board's project, which began as a first wave investigation and application of effective schools characteristics, evolved through a second wave process called school growth planning, to the point that today there are major third wave activities within the schools of the Halton system creating significant impact on the classroom. In all of this the school system followed the 'top-down, bottom-up' model of change that differed significantly from its past practices (Stoll and Fink 1994). The school system provided a sense of direction as well as financial and other support for change, but encouraged individual schools to address change and select a focus for it within their own context. This approach created a great deal of energy as well as motivation to effect significant changes within schools.

To this point we have described the top in the 'top-down, bottom-up' change model. The following story not only shows how the bottom interacted with the top, but also how an individual school generated its own change forces.

The Frontenac story

In 1989, Eleanor Adam, a new principal, joined Frontenac Public School, Burlington, Ontario. At this time, staff were not seen to be very involved in decision making, and forward planning was not systematic, with little emphasis on teaching and learning. She interviewed a range of people connected with the school on their perceptions of its strengths and needs. Using Halton's model of effective schools characteristics as an organizer, results of the interviews were shared with staff and parents. Eleanor also worked with staff to analyse results of standardized test scores to determine areas of strengths and those in need of improvement.

Several aspects of climate setting immediately became a focus. These included changes to the physical environment for adults as well as students; greater opportunities for parental involvement; increased teacher involvement in decision making, including hiring of new staff members and development of a behaviour policy; and changes to organizational structures. A timetable was developed to give teachers common team planning time, and assign the principal and vice-principals coverage to support this. Other structural changes were also made to enable further staff collaboration, and recognition and celebration events became frequent occurrences.

Gradually Eleanor met with all grade teams and specialized teaching staff to review plans, and jointly to develop a common planning format which teachers were encouraged, but not required, to use. This format identified learning outcomes, strategies, resources, student activities and evaluation techniques. School-wide themes and cooperative group learning strategies were introduced, and integrated curriculum was incorporated in grades 7 and 8 and collaboratively planned by teachers. Although frustrating, this proved ultimately satisfying, as one teacher noted: 'There were six of us, six people who are real individuals, with very distinctive styles in teaching, and there were a lot of arguments, and yet at the end of the sessions, we were proud of the results and we weren't afraid of differing opinions.'

Staff were requested to submit funding needs and suggestions, and together it was decided that a per pupil amount would be allocated to teams to purchase teaching materials. District funding was obtained and used for teacher release time for collaborative planning or to attend in-service sessions. While there was some direction over staff development choices, when interviewed, teachers reported that they had the opportunity to meet individual needs as well as seeing an increased focus on whole-school or group development initiatives. District consultants also worked with staff, and the principal and vice-principals worked with teams to focus on common goals as part of the CS&E process. Administrators covered classes while teachers observed and coached each other as they implemented new teaching strategies. In addition, staff jointly developed and agreed a set of character-istics of effective teaching to be used by the principal and vice-principals during formal observations. Discussions on curriculum, teaching and learning followed each visit.

In 1990, a school growth plan team was established. Volunteers from each division, the special education team and the principal formed this committee. They first organized a session during which staff began to clarify values and beliefs and to develop a vision of the school in five years' time. A focus statement – 'Together: Learning and Caring' – evolved, and a goal-setting process was initiated. Input to this was also received from parents following a presentation on effective schools research findings. The growth plan team reviewed the statement and goals with staff to ensure they had support. Action plans were then developed by staff, priorities established, and staff volunteered to work on committees to implement the plan. Keeping staff informed of the progress of each committee sometimes presented problems. Each goal area team sought the input of colleagues and incorporated their ideas but committees learned that staff often did not become involved until results affected their work in classrooms. Committees, therefore, decided not only to seek input but also to ask teachers to predict implications and plan solutions for potential blocks.

Conflicts arose when teams worked closely together. Conflict resolution skills were required not only by administrators but also by teachers. Several staff attended a district workshop series on conflict resolution and shared new skills with team partners. Teachers began to report that conflict could be healthy and productive if managed properly. The more they knew each other, the more comfortable they felt in expressing opinions or disagreements.

By 1991 the staff reduced key goal areas to two: 'academics' and 'school community'. The focus of the first was 'a program that meets students' needs'. Cooperative group learning, integrated curriculum and school-wide themes were selected as priorities to achieve this. Also included were student acceptance of responsibility for learning, involvement in decision making, and recognition of learning: all correlates from school effectiveness research. Learning outcomes and corresponding evaluation strategies were incorporated into teaching units. Grade teams reviewed each unit and analysed improvement strategies. By 1992, cooperative group learning strategies were routinely used in all classes. The second area, 'school community', included staff cohesiveness, student discipline and the environment, also school effectiveness characteristics.

In 1991 and 1992, student achievement scores, and teacher and parent survey results were used by Frontenac to focus further work. By 1992 improvements were demonstrated in standardized scores in all curriculum areas, and class averages were now average for the district. Improvements continued, and by 1994 grade scores for standardized mathematics were above the district's norm in 13 out of 17 classes.

In 1991, the effective schools survey was given to all staff and a sample of 100 parents. Results reflected a positive and collaborative school culture. Staff and parents viewed the learning focus and development of positive student self concepts as the school's prime purposes. Of 60 per cent of parental surveys returned, 100 per cent felt that staff worked to improve the school, 92 per cent believed there was a positive feeling throughout the school, 90 per cent thought the principal and vice-principals were accessible to discuss curriculum and instruction, 87 per cent agreed that Frontenac teachers believed all students can learn and be successful, and 85 per cent felt Frontenac students were encouraged to think for themselves.

Conversely, however, staff did not feel totally involved in decision making. Only two-thirds (67 per cent) agreed they participated in shared decision making. Results were fed into the school's development process, and a repeat of the survey in 1994 demonstrated positive changes, with a rise in this percentage to 89. Furthermore, whereas in 1991 82 per cent of teachers thought that 'people in this school work together as a team', 100 per cent believed this by 1994. Changes were also evident in teachers' perceptions of student assessment. While in 1991 only 58 per cent of Frontenac teachers reported that assessment results were used to plan appropriate instruction and curriculum priorities, in 1994 77 per cent reported this to be the case.

When asked why the school was engaged in growth planning, teachers highlighted the need for a focus, goals or objectives and the developmental nature of the process: 'Because I think if we have a focus – a goal that we can see ahead of us – the things we do daily will have more meaning'; 'If you don't do something as a group, then chances are you may all be going off in different directions and you don't have a common goal'; 'You change and adapt as you are going along, but I think having that focus there in the first place is important'; 'It is always a changing thing, but at least we have some direction' (teacher interviews).

By 1994 teachers appeared very committed to the school growth planning process. Most saw planning as a collaborative process, felt parents, students and community members had input, believed that activities throughout the school supported and reinforced the goals, and that goals were reviewed and evaluated.

Conclusion

In times of relative stability it is fairly straightforward for schools to set priorities and stick to them, particularly when they can benefit from district reorganization of support staff and services to meet their planning needs. The years 1992–5 have been unprecedented in Ontario's history. Huge provincial deficits have resulted in massive cuts in educational spending. All public sector wages have been frozen. All Halton budgets have been savagely attacked. Some even speak of a 'slash and burn' mentality. At the same time the provincial government is pushing forward with significant curricular and assessment changes. Thus Ontario, like many other areas before it, is in the throes of considerable change, including movement towards school self-management. 'Turbulence' experienced in Britain and elsewhere is now a reality for Ontario's schools. This combination of pressures provides the ultimate test of 'co-management' in Halton. In spite of fiscal frugality, intemperate remarks by politicians, and simplistic newspaper editorials, the system and its schools continue to work energetically towards improvement in learning for all pupils. In some ways the financial crisis has speeded the process of 'co-management' because downsizing has meant that of necessity more decisions must be made at the school level or by principals' associations. The system and school leadership remain strong and committed. Federations, principals' associations and administration work together to resolve problems created by financial problems and political adversity. The traditional commitment to leadership, hard work and innovation have continued to keep the Halton system energized in the face of unprecedented challenges and change. We would suggest that Halton, and districts that have focused on school self-evaluation and empowerment through growth planning, are better placed than others to deal with the extensive changes they face. Time will tell.

three

SCHOOL EFFECTIVENESS CAN INFORM SCHOOL IMPROVEMENT

The Halton Effective Schools Project was initiated to use the international school effectiveness research to provide direction to school improvement efforts in the district and, more specifically, to make a difference to the lives of pupils in demonstrable ways. Indeed, 'how do we know that what we are doing makes a difference to pupils?' is one of the fundamental questions of school effectiveness that has distinguished it from school improvement. Since Halton's initial efforts, the school effectiveness knowledge base has continually grown. There are now many more ways in which existing school effectiveness research knowledge can inform educators, policy makers, researchers or any other people who are involved or interested in changing our schools. As we learn more about school effectiveness, however, it becomes increasingly important for users of the research to be aware of key current research issues which have a bearing on their appropriate use, because with sophistication comes complexity. In this chapter, therefore, we identify and explain key issues in school effectiveness to assist change agents to employ this research to effect change in schools.

What is meant by school effectiveness?

A discussion of school effectiveness in OECD countries notes that no common definition exists across member countries (Chapman and Aspin 1994). Herein lies a fundamental problem of school effectiveness. What does it actually mean, and does it mean the same thing to different people? One simplistic definition of effectiveness is the production of a desired result or outcome (Levine and Lezotte 1990). The question is, desired by whom? To arrive at a definition of a school as effective, people are forced to choose between competing values. What educators perceive as important outcomes of schooling may not coincide with views of pupils, parents, governors, the local community, government or the media. It is also feasible that any or all of the above groups may have differing perceptions of effectiveness, and that individuals within any of these groups may not agree with each other on a definition. If a common definition cannot be achieved, how can effectiveness be determined? Clearly, at school level, all those concerned need to come to a shared definition and agreement on expected and desirable outcomes.

The emergence of the school effectiveness movement resulted from social science findings that argued that home background had a far greater influence on a child's development than did the school attended (Coleman *et al.* 1966; Plowden 1967; Jencks *et al.* 1972). The interpretation that grew out of such studies was that schools made little difference to pupils' lives. To combat this view, a wide range of research efforts focused on separating the impact of family background from that of the school, and ascertaining whether some schools were more effective than others and, if so, what factors contributed to the positive effects (for example, Brookover *et al.* 1979; Rutter *et al.* 1979). The title of the British study *School Matters* (Mortimore *et al.* 1988) illustrated the intent of school effectiveness researchers to demonstrate that schools, indeed, made a difference.

School effectiveness researchers' aim is to ascertain whether differences in resources, processes and organizational arrangements affect pupil outcomes, and if so, in what way. Ultimately, school effectiveness research seeks to describe what an effective school looks like. School effectiveness is not, however, just defined as quality in outcomes. Edmonds (1979), an early proponent of school effectiveness, blended his definition of quality, in terms of basic skills mastery, with equity: 'I require that an effective school bring the children of the poor to those minimal masteries of basic school skills that now describe minimally successful pupil performance for the children of the middle class' (p. 16).

Edmonds's legacy has continued worldwide; many researchers emphasize equity. Essentially, an underlying belief of the school effectiveness movement is that all children can learn (Murphy 1992).

Recent research broadens the definition of effectiveness. Given the impact of background on pupil attainment (Essen and Wedge 1982), the focus has been switched from outcomes to an examination of progress. Mortimore (1991) summarizes: 'an effective school is one in which pupils progress further than might be expected from consideration of its intake' (p. 9).

Simply, this definition refers to the value added by the school. The term 'value added' describes the boost given by the school to pupils' achievement over and above what they bring in terms of prior attainment and background factors. Thus, statistical predictions, the 'what might be expected' of later levels of achievement can be made on the basis of detailed information about pupils' background and earlier attainment, that is, 'consideration of its intake'. Where pupils exceed these predictions, value added has been demonstrated. This definition allows for intake variations, and therefore attempts to 'level the playing field', which is different from the emphasis placed by Edmonds in his definition. If the word 'all' was added into Mortimore's definition it would help to blend the value added and equity focuses. We discuss the concept of value added in Chapter 11.

The lack of a consensus on a definition can be confusing for those who want to use school effectiveness research. Researchers appear to differ on whether school effectiveness should focus on those pupils 'at risk' or quality for all children. Clearly, a researcher's definition of school effectiveness affects their orientation to its study which, in turn, may impact the results of such a study. In this book, therefore, we choose to define a school as effective if it:

- promotes progress for *all* of its pupils beyond what would be expected given consideration of initial attainment and background factors
- ensures that each pupil achieves the highest standards possible
- enhances all aspects of pupil achievement and development
- continues to improve from year to year.

What outcomes of schooling should determine effectiveness?

Educators may espouse a belief in a broad range of educational goals, but in several countries school effectiveness has become associated with a narrow, back-to-basics orientation. By limiting the scope of effectiveness outcomes and using standardized tests, researchers have derived fairly reliable, inexpensive and easily interpreted data. Such a limited view of educational effectiveness has been severely criticized (Cuban 1983; Brophy and Good 1986; Angus 1993). Many more recent studies, therefore, have variously added pupils' behaviour, attendance, delinquency, attitudes and self concept to information on pupil attainment in order to arrive at measures of school effectiveness (for example, Mortimore *et al.* 1988; Smith and Tomlinson 1989; Teddlie and Stringfield 1993).

Current assessments pay attention to only a fraction of children's skills and ability. It is essential that the diversity of children's abilities and talents is recognized not only in the curriculum on offer, but its associated assessments. This must also apply to choices of outcome measures made by school effectiveness researchers. Furthermore, the world of work now looks for young people who demonstrate flexibility, creativity and problem solving skills, and who are able to cooperate in the workplace – not only those who can spell and count, important as such basic skills may be. If school effectiveness studies wish to reflect this reality of the 1990s, it is essential that researchers use a broad range of outcome measures. Given the changing world identified in Chapter 1, a first imperative for educators must be to identify precisely the range of outcomes they hope to achieve with their pupils. Following from this needs to come a commitment, at the outset, to determine ways to examine the progress, development and achievement of these pupil outcomes. More authentic forms of assessment currently being developed in various countries may provide a way forward, although issues of reliability and expense inhibit more extensive use of non-standardized assessments.

How do design and methodology affect results?

There is a need for users of school effectiveness research to be sensitive to the superficial quotation and use of research results without first examining the quality, appropriateness and applicability of the research design. For example, studies that rely entirely on the collection of quantitative data or snapshots of the school may not tell us enough about its inner workings and processes, whereas mixed methodological approaches, incorporating case-studies as well as 'number crunching' are more likely to be able to explain processes at work. The following questions might help to guide the discriminating consumer:

- Does the research follow pupils over a period of years?
- Does the research use both quantitative and qualitative methodologies, including detailed case-studies?
- Do the studies attempt through multilevel modelling techniques (Goldstein 1995) to assess differences between pupils, classes, year groups, schools and, if appropriate, districts?
- How do the researchers determine causality? Are their conclusions simply correlational or is there evidence to determine the direction of influence? Brophy and Good (1986) highlight this problem: do teachers' high expectations influence pupil achievement or is it that the achievement of pupils influences their teachers' expectations? This is a continuing challenge for researchers.

How do classroom, school and system processes influence effectiveness?

Processes (independent variables) assessed in different school effectiveness studies have also varied. School-level organizational variables have generally been overemphasized in many studies, to the detriment of classroom examination. Inclusion of classroom level process data is particularly important given that analyses demonstrate most of the variation among schools is due to classroom variation (Scheerens 1992). The body of research knowledge built up around teaching effectiveness has been generated through studies carried out by a different group of researchers (for further discussion, see Chapter 8). The question remains, should school effectiveness research study every new technique, text or type of technology in favour at any point in time? Many of these come and go and are superseded by other 'fashions' even by the time the research has been published. The dilemma for researchers is to know on which elements of classroom practice to focus attention.

Despite the need for greater examination of the impact of classroom processes within school effectiveness research, this does not mean that the level of the school should no longer be studied, given the importance of the interface between school and classroom (Fullan and Hargreaves 1991; Stoll and Fink 1994). In some countries, for example The Netherlands, Sweden and parts of Switzerland, the lack of the role of principal as it is known in many other countries may suggest that school-level factors related to leadership are unimportant. From our experience in Halton and Britain, as well as the evidence of other researchers, this is not borne out (see following section and Chapter 7).

One level that is too rarely examined in studies of school effectiveness is that of the district. Rosenholtz (1989) argues the impossibility of fully grasping the nature of schools if the larger environment in which they are embedded is not analysed. She finds a tendency for 'moving schools' to be located in 'moving districts' and 'stuck schools' in 'stuck districts'. Chrispeels (1992), summarizing four North American studies, also attests the relationship between certain district practices and school effectiveness. These practices include clear academic focus and goals, curriculum alignment, analysis of disaggregated test data, staff development that addresses identified needs and leadership training for principals.

Clearly, a movement away from district-level centralization in many countries makes it more difficult to assess the impact of this level on school effectiveness. None the less, there is little evidence to suggest that self-management has a positive impact on pupil outcomes. Multilevel modelling techniques enable examination of the district level, as well as those of the pupil, classroom and school (Riddell 1989).

What are the characteristics of effective schools?

The identification of factors related to greater effectiveness in terms of pupil progress, achievement and, in some cases, social development is a key feature of many effectiveness studies. These, quite naturally, are the results of most

Figure 3.1   Eleven factors for effective schools

1 Professional leadership	Firm and purposeful A participative approach The leading professional
2 Shared vision and goals	Unity of purpose Consistency of practice Collegiality and collaboration
3 A learning environment	An orderly atmosphere An attractive working environment
4 Concentration on teaching and learning	Maximization of learning time Academic emphasis Focus on achievement
5 High expectations	High expectations all round Communicating expectations Providing intellectual challenge
6 Positive reinforcement	Clear and fair discipline Feedback
7 Monitoring progress	Monitoring pupil performance Evaluating school performance
8 Pupil rights and responsibilities	High pupil self-esteem Positions of responsibility Control of work
9 Purposeful teaching	Efficient organization Clarity of purpose Structured lessons Adaptive practice
10 A learning organization	School-based staff development
11 Home-school partnership	Parental involvement

(Sammons et al. 1995)

interest to practitioners and policy makers. While there are some well-known caveats about correlational studies and generalizability of results, there appears to be a surprising amount of agreement across studies and more detailed understanding than was first given in Edmonds's (1979) somewhat simplistic five factors of effective urban elementary schools.

A recent review summarizes British and North American research literature and provides a list of 11 key factors (Sammons *et al.* 1995). These, the authors note, are neither exhaustive, nor are they necessarily independent of each other. They offer, however, a useful synopsis of the most common factors found to be associated with effective schools (see Figure 3.1).

It has been suggested that the school effectiveness characteristics might have outlived their usefulness given a changing world and its impact on education (Murphy 1992; Reynolds and Packer 1992). While this is an understandable argument, our Halton experience suggests that this is not the case. Although school effectiveness research has been criticized for its neglect of curriculum issues, this may have its benefits. Specific classroom practices and materials tend to come and go. Teacher involvement, high expectations, forms of leadership, monitoring of progress, praise and recognition, how-ever, to quote a few examples, are constants. They provide a framework within which the more changing elements of schooling can operate. In essence, they are the foundations for school growth and are fundamental to further reform. They are the roots that enable the branches to grow (Hargreaves and Hopkins 1991) or their life support system. This is not to say that schools and researchers do not need to be future-orientated in the areas they choose to develop or study, but that these areas may well not grow without prior and ongoing attention to their foundations.

Much school effectiveness and school improvement literature ignores the question of resources. This is because, in a number of cases, schools included in any sample have similar levels of funding and – as a result – there is little to distinguish between them on this dimension. This should not be taken as proof that resource levels are not important although such an argument has been robustly presented by at least one American educational economist (Hanushek 1986). A more common view among researchers is that resources help but do not guarantee effectiveness. There is little support for the view that reducing levels of funding will improve the performance of pupils, teachers or schools.

Are there identifiable factors for ineffective schools?

Attempts to improve historically ineffective schools using only factors shown to be present within effective schools have been unsuccessful (Reynolds 1991). It is insufficient, therefore, to describe the characteristics of effective schools and assume that ineffective schools possess the mirror opposite of these factors.

Rosenholtz (1989), who studied the relationship between schools' social organization and pupil outcomes, described two distinctive types of schools: 'moving' or 'learning enriched', and 'stuck' or 'learning impoverished'. What is particularly useful is that, unlike many other studies, this one pinpoints characteristics of less effective, or 'stuck' schools.

The Junior School Project (Mortimore *et al.* 1986) identified factors, both at school and classroom levels, negatively related to pupil progress, achievement and social development. Some of these were less in the control of people within the school, and included changes in the headteacher or deputy head and larger schools. There was also some indication that larger classes and mixed age classes (split grades) were associated with ineffectiveness. These factors may not be solely responsible for a school's difficulties but may put extra constraints on the school.

Teddlie and Stringfield (1993) differentiated characteristics of ineffective middle and low SES (socio-economic status) elementary schools, and Reynolds (1995) has reported preliminary results of unsuccessful interventions in two failing schools. By combining the results of these four efforts we can begin to see the shape of factors which predict ineffectiveness.

Lack of vision

Ineffective schools not only possess a 'maintenance mentality', the teachers hold little attachment 'to anything or anybody' (Rosenholtz 1989). Reynolds (1995) argues that the school staffs of his failing schools lacked knowledge of their context, the change process, and even their own school's culture.

Unfocused leadership

Rosenholtz's (1989) 'stuck schools' were characterized as routine and having 'a numbing sameness', unaided by principals who mostly assumed 'the posture of a burrowing animal'. Teachers experienced 'a string of broken promises' that led to a loss of faith and sometimes despair. Teddlie and Stringfield (1993) found that in their ineffective schools principals' academic expectations were lower than those of teachers; principals devoted more energy to other aspects of student development than academic skills; and principals' actions had little impact.

Dysfunctional staff relationships

In the 'stuck schools', Rosenholtz (1989) described staff relationships as 'listless', 'self-reliant' and resistant to asking advice. This resulted in a lack of a coherent staff development policy, demonstrated in random and indiscriminate choices of in-service. Reynolds (1995) described relationships in his failing schools as irrational, 'reactive' and 'fractured'. Bradshaw (1988) provides the lens of the dysfunctional family through which we might view staff relationships in ineffective schools. He describes a body of covert rules that operate unconsciously and create distress:

- Control – the major defensive strategy for shame, control gives family members a sense of power, predictability and security. Hence, at all times it is necessary to be in control of all interactions, feelings and behaviour.
- Perfectionism – it is essential always to be 'right' in everything that is done, and to avoid what is bad, wrong or inferior: 'No rule leads to hopelessness more powerfully than this one. The ideal is a mental creation. The ideal is ideal, rather than real. The ideal is shameless since it disallows mistakes' (Bradshaw 1988: 81). Fear of failure is a common feature of ineffective schools.
- Blame – when anything does not turn out as planned, members blame themselves or others, and thereby avoid deeper feelings. Both Reynolds (1995) and Rosenholtz (1989) reported that deflecting blame for failure was a pervasive staff strategy. Evidence of failure merely confirmed their views on the inadequacy of the parents and pupils.
- Denial of the five freedoms – feelings, perceptions, thoughts, wants and imaginings are denied, especially negative ones like fear, hurt, rejection and dependency needs.
- No-talk rule – negative feelings, thoughts and experiences are not discussed openly.
- Myth making – a mask of brightness is used to distract others from the distress that is really happening: 'The system remains closed and rigid. Anyone rocking the boat would upset the status quo' (Bradshaw 1988: 82) Reynolds (1995) talks of 'clingons', where people carry on doing things because they have always been done that way, and of how problems presented for advice are often masks for real problems of morale, competence and feelings of failure.
- Incompletion – the same fights and disagreements are continued for years, either through unresolved chronic fighting or 'enmeshment and confluence', that is, agreeing never to disagree.
- Unreliability – reliability in relationships is not expected. No one is trusted and, therefore, no one gets disappointed.

Ineffective classroom practices

Mortimore and colleagues (1986) and Teddlie and Stringfield (1993) have identified a number of ineffective classroom practices:

- Inconsistent approaches to the curriculum and teaching, with generally low expectations for pupils in low SES schools.
- An emphasis on supervising and communicating about routines, connected with a range of uncoordinated activities, low levels of work discussion and a lack of challenge or clear framework within which pupils can work.

- Low levels of teacher–pupil interaction, with the teacher engaged in 'housekeeping' activities, several periods when pupils are left unattended, and low levels of pupil involvement in work.
- Pupil perceptions of teachers as people who did not care, praise, provide help, or consider learning important.
- High classroom noise levels and considerable non-work-related movement.
- Frequent use of criticism and negative feedback.

Recent summary comments on ineffective classroom situations resulting from external inspections in Britain tend to confirm these themes (OFSTED 1995).

Teachers in low SES schools in Teddlie and Stringfield's (1993) study, in particular, reported less satisfaction with teaching (a finding in common with that of Rosenholtz 1989); a lack of teacher ownership for their ability to influence student outcomes; and greater teacher absence and desire to work in another school. Clearly we have only touched the surface in the area of ineffectiveness characteristics. More work is needed on understanding the nature of school and classroom processes in ineffective schools if internal and external change agents are to develop improvement strategies which can promote improvement for all pupils.

What is differential effectiveness?

While other aspects of school effectiveness research focus on differences between schools, differential effectiveness focuses on differences within schools. It is often assumed that an effective school is effective for all of its pupils. Evidence, however, suggests that some pupils may do better than others within certain schools. When this occurs, the school is displaying differential effectiveness. Evidence of schools' differential effectiveness has been found (at secondary level) for pupils with different prior attainment levels, boys versus girls and pupils of different ethnic and social class backgrounds; and for prior attainment only at primary level (Sammons *et al.* 1993).

Issues of consistency are concerned with whether schools are effective for their pupils all of the time across classes, departments or subject boundaries. Much of the evidence is limited to comparisons of language and mathematics (Sammons *et al.* 1996). The evidence to date is inconclusive. In a study of differences in pupils' General Certificate of Secondary Education (GCSE) results, taken at the end of compulsory schooling in Britain, Sammons and colleagues (1994) found that the variation *between* schools in their effects on pupils' performance in some subjects was greater than that found in an overall measure of GCSE performance: that is, some departments were more effective than others in promoting better results. It may, therefore, be too simplistic to describe the dimensionality of schools' effects in terms of whole-school effectiveness or ineffectiveness. The implications are that broad measurements of overall effectiveness are inadequate and that progress and development data must be analysed subject by subject.

Are findings from one context generalizable to different contexts?

Generalizability of school effectiveness research findings has been questioned because of the different contexts in which studies have been carried out. It has become increasingly clear that what works in one context may lack relevance in others. Context can be generally defined under the following headings:

- location – within a country: inner city; urban; rural
             – between countries
- background of pupils
- phase of schooling or grade levels.

Studies of schools serving students from different social class backgrounds have shown student SES to have an effect on the success of strategies used to make schools more effective (Hallinger and Murphy 1986; Teddlie *et al.* 1989), and international attempts to replicate one country's findings elsewhere or examine the same factors have also faced difficulties. This could be because research instruments do not translate well from one cultural context to another, and interpretations of concepts may also differ from country to country (Reynolds *et al.* 1994).

Similarly, some uncertainty has been expressed whether characteristics identified in effective elementary schools have the same relevance in secondary settings (Levine and Lezotte 1990). The review of key characteristics of effective schools outlined earlier, however, concluded that the 11 factors identified appear to be generic (Sammons *et al.* 1995). Indeed, the authors originally intended to produce separate lists for the two sectors, but found the degree of overlap repetitious. Further study is needed to understand the precise nature of primary and secondary school differences. Context in terms of pupils' social class background and school location (inner city, urban or rural) must also be considered in any application of the characteristics. The implications are that listings of generic school effectiveness characteristics such as those already outlined may be insufficient.

Are school effects stable over time?

Although estimates of the stability of school effects vary over time, it is generally agreed that a school's effectiveness should be considered over a period of several years. Even value-added estimates of effectiveness in one year do not provide sufficient knowledge as to whether the school is able to sustain its effectiveness over time. By examining progress over several years, the weight given to the results of any single year in making sense of school effectiveness can be established.

A rare study following schools' effectiveness or ineffectiveness over eight years was carried out by Teddlie and Stringfield (1993). Their interest lay in the processes whereby schools at both ends of the continuum retained their status or changed. While much concern is expressed about the difficulty of improving an ineffective school, it is reasonable to assume that it is easier for a school to deteriorate than to improve.

The lasting impact of schooling is another important issue. Sammons and colleagues (in press) identified continuing effects of primary schools on attainment in GCSE examinations, taken at age 16. They suggest that more effective primary schools may help to raise pupils' later achievement by raising their sense of self-efficacy. What is clear from this research is that it is too late to leave it until secondary school to 'get it right'.

What is the size of school effects?

Currently, most studies have identified that between eight and 14 per cent of the total variance in pupils' achievement is attributable to the school. This does not sound like very much but it may turn out to be the crucial difference between success and failure. The question is, have researchers studied every relevant aspect of schooling, especially at the classroom level? To what extent might it be possible to explain more of the variation between schools? Two avenues to explore are the research findings of studies carried out in developing countries and the use of international studies. Research in developing countries demonstrates the importance of resources and teacher quality variables (Lockheed 1995). While school effectiveness and resource management are studied in developed countries, not all of the other facets of school and classroom practice commonly the focus of effectiveness studies are currently examined. A greater integration might increase effect sizes. Furthermore, as variation in teacher training length, quality and operation increases through government reforms, effect sizes in developed countries may increase through incorporation of such variables found to be significant in developing countries (Reynolds *et al.* 1994).

Do we have any theories of school effectiveness which help us to understand what works and why?

Given the large number of effectiveness studies and their applications, there has been surprisingly little theory on how and why processes lead to successful outcomes. As Slater and Teddlie (1992) note, despite criticisms of school effectiveness on a range of issues, 'no one has ever accused it of being too theoretical' (p. 242). Various models have contributed pieces to the theory puzzle but no single theory is sufficiently comprehensive to incorporate all the variables which affect school effectiveness. A review of the evolution of school effectiveness theory confirms the need for better understanding of the field and, in particular, connections with and implications for school improvement. Our attempt at such a model will conclude this book but here we briefly examine other models and review key contributions from those that impinge on our own model.

Five-factor model

Edmonds's (1979) well-known and simplistic model lists five factors. It was argued that if they were adopted by a school, educational achievement would follow. While this model established the importance of equity to school effectiveness, its usefulness was constrained by its emphasis on achievement in basic skills, its assumption of causality based on correlational evidence, the independence and locus of the factors, and the tautology of relating an emphasis on basic skills to achievement in basic skills.

Input-process-output model

The economic production ideal of inputs and outputs was adapted by various school effectiveness researchers. Controlling for pupils' backgrounds and previous attainment levels, longitudinal studies that examine the processes that lead to output, pupil progress, attainment and social development are implicit models (for example, Rutter *et al.* 1979; Mortimore *et al.* 1988; Tizard *et al.* 1988). Often, school and classroom processes are combined, although some research teams study the processes separately and use multilevel models to examine different levels within the school.

Integrated model of school effectiveness

The analytic systems model was refined by Scheerens (1992) into an integrated model of school effectiveness. The model incorporates contingency theory (Mintzberg 1979), in that a school's effectiveness can depend on situational or contextual conditions. While productivity or output is viewed as paramount, resource acquisition, stability and control in the organization's functioning, and cohesion and morale among its members also play roles dependent on contingency factors. A multilevel framework is used that identifies pupil, classroom and school characteristics, as well as environmental and contextual influences.

A typology of school effectiveness and leadership

Slater and Teddlie (1992) set the scene for further theoretical development through a typology that also highlights schooling's context (contingency). In addition, however, it addresses process (stage). Three main elements of effectiveness are identified: principal appropriateness at the school level; teacher preparedness at the classroom level; and pupil learning readiness at the pupil level. The interaction between any two of these three elements comprises 'context'. Based on contextual differences in school effectiveness research findings, different strategies, for example, may be necessary where staff that are motivated, skilled and confident rather than when they are not.

Under 'stage', the authors posit that schools go through stages of effectiveness. First, schools will deteriorate if left to themselves. Second, schools can be improved by recruitment (selection) or development (socialization). Given that the latter is more likely, time is a consideration. Third, the smaller the component within the school, the easier it is to change. For example, one principal is easier to change than 40 teachers.

Interactive model of the transformative process of school effectiveness and improvement

External influences are considered in Chrispeels's (1992) model. She takes Hanna's (1988) description of open systems as her starting point. Open systems incorporate many facets of models already described, and are characterized by seven specific elements: a permeable boundary, enabling two-way interactions; purpose and goals defined by multiple players; inputs in terms of people and other resources; a transformative or 'throughput' process; outputs related to the purpose that shapes the transformative process; feedback about accomplishments; and the environment within which the school, in this case, is nested, including the system and the community.

Comprehensive model of educational effectiveness

Creemers (1994) argues that the basic idea behind all school effectiveness models is to distinguish between educational levels, the higher levels contributing to lower ones. Based on Carroll's (1963) model of school learning, the model specifies characteristics of quality, time and opportunity at the student, classroom, school and context levels that are facilitated by characteristics at higher levels, leading to consistency, cohesion, constancy and control at higher levels and achievement in basic, higher order and metacognitive skills at the student level.

In summary, while school effectiveness models, few though there are, have become more sophisticated, they still do not explain how processes fit together. They are more attempts at path modelling than at middle range theory building. They also do not address adequately the process by which a school might develop itself (Chapter 5), the influence of culture (Chapter 6) and interconnections with external agencies (Chapter 9). Clearly there is need for theory that is sufficiently practical that it can be applied and tested. It is notable that only recently have more comprehensive school effectiveness models appeared that begin to recognize the process and context implications of school effectiveness. There is room for further models of school effectiveness, but these must pay attention to the practical needs of educators and the processes of school improvement.

How can school effectiveness research be made accessible to educators?

One of the reasons for the limited use of research results by educators may be the traditional inaccessibility of researchers. Both in the written and spoken word, many researchers turn teachers off with their use of complex language to explain relatively simple phenomena. For this reason, many educators have become attracted to ideas such as the five-factor theory of effectiveness, notably developed by an educator (Edmonds 1979). Unfortunately, five-, seven- or 12-factor theories tend to be boiled down by educators to single sentences that denote the key thrust of each characteristic.

Educators have little time to read books, even when they are written in accessible language. Shorter summaries of key findings would be helpful, without loss of the research findings' essence. Teachers could read these and teach them to each other using cooperative group learning techniques (Aronson *et al.* 1978). Use of effective schools questionnaires is another way to bring the research findings to teachers because the indicators within them give more detail on the concepts. It is important, however, that teachers understand that such questionnaires are not blueprints for effectiveness nor to be used merely as checklists to denote what a school is or is not doing. Rather, their purpose in individual schools is as a basis for discussion and reflection regarding both what is happening related to what the research says happens in more effective schools, and teachers' experience within their own context.

More important is the need for researchers to work closely with schools, introduce the research findings to them in meaningful ways, and work with them using action research to try out, reflect on and evaluate the findings in projects tailored to schools' unique contexts.

Can the effective characteristics be implemented?

Rutter and colleagues (1979) demonstrated that the combination of all of the characteristics of effectiveness in their study into an overall concept of ethos was more powerful than the impact of any individual characteristic. This might suggest that it is necessary for a school to work on all the characteristics at one time. Our experience, however, suggests that it is necessary to focus improvement efforts on a few key goals at one time. Furthermore, as each school is unique, it is the best judge of the time, order and way in which it will choose to implement the characteristics. Thus, the characteristics can be implemented but this implementation cannot be mandated or managed from outside. It has to be sequenced according to the school's needs and will be interpreted by each school in a unique way. There are, however, some characteristics that appear to be fundamental conditions for successful improvement and many of these set the stage for later work on other characteristics (see next chapter).

Conclusion

School effectiveness remains a dynamic research area with evolving methodology, new insights and increasing attention to theory building. From the perspective of teachers and principals, school effectiveness research will be little more than an interesting intellectual activity unrelated to the daily work of schools and of little significance in the various reform agendas unless it is tied to proved approaches to effecting change in the structures and cultures of schools. Fortunately, the rich field of school improvement has evolved separately but simultaneously. While different in theory, methodology and purposes, in many countries it has only been in recent times that school improvement has been linked with school effectiveness to bring about meaningful change in schools and school districts. In the next chapter we begin our exploration of linkages between the two research areas by examining school improvement.

four

THE POSSIBILITIES AND CHALLENGES OF SCHOOL IMPROVEMENT

These days, everybody has something to say about school improvement. To use an ice cream metaphor, it is definitely 'flavour of the month'. Different ideas are put forward on what motivates improvement and routes to achieve it. The word 'improvement' itself has a somewhat negative connotation, bringing to mind less than satisfactory reports from our own school days, and suggesting a deficit model of improvement. We do not, however, decorate our homes because they are falling down. School improvement is, or should be, the business of every school. A school is either improving or it is getting worse. It cannot stand still because its context is constantly changing. What is school improvement and how does it occur? What is its relationship with change? Are there particular conditions that promote improvement and others that inhibit it? In this chapter we address some important issues related to improvement, and examine some attempts to link it with school effectiveness.

What is improvement?

Although people have approached change in many ways, a widely accepted definition of school improvement emanates from the 14-country International School Improvement Project (ISIP). It is 'a systematic, sustained effort aimed at change in learning conditions and other related internal conditions in one or more schools, with the ultimate aim of accomplishing educational goals more effectively' (van Velzen *et al.* 1985: 48).

This definition highlights the importance of careful planning, management and continuity even in the face of difficulties. It also emphasizes a teaching and learning focus as well as the need for supporting organizational conditions. Additionally, the intricate relationship between school improvement and change is signalled, and while improvement occurs within schools, their location within a larger educational system is indicated. The range of school improvement goals includes those related to pupils, teachers and school organization. School improvement's ultimate aim, however, is to enhance pupil progress, achievement and development. This is the bottom line. A more recent improvement definition also emphasizes pupil outcomes as well as change management capacity (Hopkins *et al.* 1994).

Drawing on our experience and earlier definitions, in this book we define school improvement as a series of concurrent and recurring processes in which a school:

- enhances pupil outcomes
- focuses on teaching and learning
- builds the capacity to take charge of change regardless of its source
- defines its own direction
- assesses its current culture and works to develop positive cultural norms
- has strategies to achieve its goals
- addresses the internal conditions that enhance change
- maintains momentum during periods of turbulence
- monitors and evaluates its process, progress, achievement and development.

School improvement is unique to each school because each school's context is unique. This means that schools will address these processes in different ways and no blueprint can be proposed for all schools. Ultimately, school improvement comes from within (Barth 1990) and cannot be externally mandated. This does not mean that the outside world is ignored; far from it. Rather, the school is part of its external environment and is connected to it, but it moves in its chosen direction.

School improvement has been around since the 1960s when it focused on organization, curriculum, and pupil-orientated outcomes (Reynolds *et al.* 1993). Lack of teacher commitment to government-initiated 'top-down' reforms led to a new improvement paradigm in the 1980s, that celebrated a 'bottom-up' approach through use of practitioner rather than exclusively external knowledge. Its focus was shifted from the school to the teacher, although the improvement attempt was whole-school orientated. It emphasized the notion of school self-evaluation or school-based review. The outcomes of schooling, rather than being accepted as given, were seen as problematic and open for debate, as the movement shifted in orientation towards the process of change. This process-orientated 'journey', however, did not always lead to actual improvement and by the late 1980s there began to be a return towards a focus on the evaluation of processes and outcomes.

Understanding change

Although not all change is improvement, all improvement involves change. Fullan (1992) emphasizes the intricate relationship between school improvement and change: 'successful school improvement ... depends on an understanding of the problem of change at the level of practice and the development of corresponding strategies for bringing about beneficial reforms' (p. 27).

The need to understand the complexity of change when engaged in school improvement is all too often downplayed. Here we will examine phases of change and assumptions about it.

Change phases

The change process has been seen to include three broad phases. The first, initiation, incorporates the process that leads up to the decision to change. Drawing on the work of Miles (1986) and others, Fullan (1991) argues that initiation depends on three Rs:

- *relevance* of the improvement innovation in terms of need, quality, practicality, clarity and complexity
- *readiness* of the staff to become involved
- *resource* and support availability, including time.

Other factors also influence whether initiation occurs. These include existence and quality of existing innovations, access to innovations, advocacy from teachers or external sources, new policies and funds, and a problem-solving orientation.

The second phase, implementation, consists of early experiences of putting reforms into practice. Successful implementation is influenced by many similar factors, including characteristics of the change, school and external factors. Miles (1986) highlights the importance of:

- clear responsibility for orchestration
- shared control over implementation
- a blend of pressure and support
- sustained staff development
- early rewards for teachers.

The third phase, institutionalization, describes whether or not innovations are built into ongoing practice. This, Fullan (1991) summarizes, is achieved through:

- mobilization of broad support
- principal commitment

- embedding into classroom practice through structural changes and incorporation into policy
- skill and commitment of a critical mass of staff
- procedures for ongoing assistance, especially for newcomers
- removal of competing priorities
- inbuilt evaluation
- assistance, networking and peer support.

An additional, and important, phase is outcome. This refers to a variety of results, whether pupil, teacher or organizational, but generally focuses on the extent of improvement according to specified criteria. This state is further elaborated in Chapter 11 when we look at measuring change.

Assumptions about change

In school improvement efforts, a key capacity that differentiates more and less successful schools is understanding of the change process. In this respect, Fullan's (1991) 'do' and 'don't' assumptions for those who attempt change have been useful to us and to schools with whom we have worked. We have added to them to offer our best current understanding of key change process issues:

- There is not only one version of what the change should be. A main purpose of the process is for all involved to exchange realities and continue to develop ideas.
- People have to understand the change and work out their own meaning through clarification, which often occurs through practice. Changes in teacher behaviour may, therefore, precede rather than follow changes in belief.
- Change is a personal experience. It is necessary to recognize and attend to individuals' concerns. Stress and anxiety are common early emotions.
- Change is approached differently by each school. Innovations are, and need to be, modified to suit the school's own context.
- Conflict and disagreement are inevitable and fundamental. There is always an 'implementation dip'. If everything goes too smoothly, it is likely that not much is happening (Huberman and Miles 1984).
- A mix of pressure and support is needed. People need help and encouragement when relearning is at stake. Particularly important are assistance, training in new skills, and follow-up help.
- 'Top-down, bottom-up' change engenders more commitment and continuation than either an autocratic, centralized approach or a *laissez-faire* decentralized approach.
- Change rarely involves single innovations. Several ideas and activities are involved simultaneously and need to be blended. Sarason (1990) describes

a rippling effect: 'what you seek to change is so embedded in a system of interacting parts that if it is changed, then changes elsewhere are likely to occur' (p. 16).

- Effective change takes time, therefore persistence is essential. Even moderate change can take three to five years, while complex organizational restructuring may take much longer.
- A school cannot always be developing otherwise it runs out of steam. Change involves times of relative activity and consolidation periods.
- There are many valid reasons why people do not implement change; it is not just resistance to all change.
- It is not realistic to expect all people to change. As an ex-colleague of ours used to say, 'don't water the rocks!' If you spend an inordinate amount of time on a few people relative to time spent on everyone else, is it fair and always worth the effort?
- It is necessary to plan based on these assumptions.
- No amount of knowledge ever makes totally clear the action needed to be taken. Development is evolutionary. It is not beneficial to lay down precise plans. Rather, it is important to get started and constantly make amendments. This requires people to 'trust the process'.
- The real agenda is changing school culture, ensuring whole-school development rather than implementation of single innovations.

Initiating change

Where should schools start? There is no single best route. Schools get into improvement in different ways. Joyce (1991) used the metaphor of doors to describe different approaches educators choose to take to initiate change. We have adapted and updated his list to include doors currently being opened in schools. Some are opened from *inside* schools. These doors include:

- Research – studying and using research findings on school and classroom effectiveness and school improvement.
- Self-evaluation – collecting and analysing school and pupil data, target setting, action research in classrooms and self-generated appraisal.
- Curriculum – introducing self-chosen curricular or crosscurricular changes or projects.
- Teaching and learning – studying teaching skills and strategies, using various staff development strategies. Increasingly, classroom improvement is seen as a fundamental lever for whole-school improvement.
- Leadership – arrival of a new principal can trigger innovation. Another stimulus might be the principal's participation in a degree or other course.

- Partnerships – voluntary activities and projects that link schools with one or more external partners in joint pursuit of improvement.
- Problems – issues which require prompt attention can lead to improvement processes. Pupil fights in the playground, for example, might lead to a problem-solving work group.
- School development planning – involving needs assessment; priority setting; decisions about responsibilities, timelines, staff development needs, required resources and success criteria; implementation activities; and monitoring and evaluation strategies.

Other doors are opened by those *outside* the school:

- National curricula – the assumption is that need to master subjects promotes curriculum development.
- Published test and examination results – the rationale is that growth is stimulated by placing schools in competition with each other to attract pupils through publishing raw, rank-ordered performance tables. Many school systems provide schools with assessment information adjusted to take account of prior attainment, background factors or both. This enables schools to see to what extent they have boosted progress of their pupils.
- Inspection – an external inspection visit highlights improvement areas to be addressed, sometimes through a published action plan. Difficulties arise when the school does not know how to address identified improvement areas.
- Governing bodies or school councils – increasingly, such bodies are seen to have a role in strategic school improvement decisions. Barber and colleagues (1995b) argue that a governing body 'should focus on where it can add most value – that is, in helping to decide the school's strategy for improvement' (p. 2).
- Teacher appraisal and evaluation – frequently externally mandated by governments or districts, teacher evaluation systems are introduced to promote teachers' personal and professional development, with the aim of contributing to school development.
- Quality approaches – emanating from business and industry, approaches include Total Quality Management and Investors In People. These take a quality assurance orientation and are based on a set of principles or standards (Bowering-Carr and West Burnham 1994).
- High reliability organizations – based on businesses that do not tolerate failure, for example air traffic control, this approach emphasizes standard operating procedures that detail what participants should do; intensive training based on data provision; alertness to minor and trivial 'flaws' which, unattended, cascade; and mutual monitoring (Stringfield 1995).

Proponents who mandate or recommend external doors are convinced of their ability to achieve improvement. While opening mandated doors will certainly get people's attention, there is little evidence that they engender commitment on the part of people who have to implement the change. It is through opening as many internal doors as possible that authentic change occurs. Opening any doors, however, whether internal or external, without attention to the deeper culture and organizational conditions of the school is unlikely to lead to improvement. For example, a school lacking a collaborative culture may select computer technology as a goal. Despite whole-school training, computer usage may not increase because it is not the norm for people to work together, try out ideas and discuss difficulties with each other. Simultaneous focus on the content and culture of change can be likened to seeing the world through bifocal spectacles. Both lenses are necessary for perceptual clarity and coherence. We discuss the power of school culture in Chapter 6.

The focus for school improvement

The focus for improvement must be core to the school. Change has to be meaningful, and teachers derive most meaning from work with pupils in the classroom (Lortie 1975). Consequently, their commitment to classroom rather than school processes is greater. School effectiveness research also suggests that classroom actions account for more of the variation in schools' effects on pupil outcomes than does school-level activity (Scheerens 1992). Curriculum, teaching and learning focuses are, therefore, fundamental to improvement efforts. Indeed, Brown and McIntyre (1993) argue that any serious attempt to change classrooms has to begin from where teachers are and how they construe their own teaching, their pupils and what they hope to achieve. It appears clear that 'improvement efforts which duck the question of what's in them for teachers are likely to fail' (Gray and Wilcox 1995: 250). We address teaching and learning, the purpose of schools, in Chapter 8.

Strategies for school improvement

While models of school improvement exist, there is a preference for frameworks, processes and guidelines, many of which are variants on the school development planning process described in the next chapter. Fullan (1991) comments:

> We do know more about the processes of change as a result of the research of the 1970s and 1980s, only to discover that there are no

hard-and-fast rules, rather a set of suggestions or implications given the contingencies specific to local situations.

(p. 47)

Strategies mobilize action. They are the logistics of school improvement and need to be carefully thought out. Strategies might include creation of cross-role improvement teams, peer observation in classrooms with subsequent feedback, parental or volunteer involvement in hearing pupils read, use of computers, to give a few examples. Strategies will depend on the specific context. The two following examples demonstrate different improvement strategies. The first is from a Halton school, the second a larger-scale American project.

General level project

A group of department heads and administrators in a traditionally academic, 850-student Halton high school developed an action plan to improve instruction and curriculum in general level courses (for non-university-bound students) in grades 9 and 10 and in the core subjects. A team of many of the school's best teachers and department heads, most of whom traditionally taught more academic courses, were selected and agreed to participate. The team included the guidance and special education department heads and a vice-principal. Team members were timetabled a common lunch and/or spare period to facilitate twice weekly meetings. In addition, they occasionally participated in longer professional development sessions, school visits, and other activities. Regular progress reports were given to staff through department and staff meetings.

The project specifically addressed effective teaching and learning strategies; suitable teaching and learning materials; preferred student learning styles; curriculum review and development; evaluation of achievement; motivational strategies; behaviour management techniques; special education needs; and social-emotional needs. Intended student and staff outcomes were defined. At the end of the school year target students were considerably more positive than before, demonstrated in results of a follow-up to an earlier survey. The project continued in subsequent years with ongoing positive student attitudes and increased performance in course work and examinations.

Success for All

The many different school improvement programmes in the United States include The Comer School Development Programme (Comer 1988), Sizer's Coalition of Essential Schools (Sizer 1989), Glickman and colleagues' League of Professional Schools (Glickman *et al.* 1994) and Success for All (Slavin *et al.* 1994). This latter project initially focuses on early elementary level. Its basic principles are prevention and immediate intensive intervention. Strategies include daily individual reading tuition for individual students with difficulties; additional classroom reading support; ability-grouped whole-class teaching of reading; eight-weekly reading assessments; a concurrent preschool and kindergarten programme; a family support team of social workers, parent liaisons and counsellors; a full-time programme facilitator to oversee project operation, help classes, provide staff development, and coordinate family support team and teacher activities; and an advisory committee. Evaluations demonstrate consistently increased reading achievement and reduced special education placements and retention rates.

Internal conditions

Strategies alone do not ensure improvement. Concurrently, schools need to address internal conditions that maintain and support improvement. Without these, improvement efforts are inhibited particularly when the going gets tough, which it inevitably does. The conditions need to be in place for real improvement in terms of pupil outcomes to occur, but they are continuing conditions to be adapted as needs arise. Earlier we mentioned readiness. The readiness for change and capacity to take ownership are vital to school improvement but harder to achieve in some schools than others. In these schools facets of their climate may need attention very early on before people feel able to participate actively in improvement efforts and concentrate on the real agenda. We have summarized these prerequisites within the overall heading of 'climate setting'.

Climate setting

Some schools appear to be unable to focus on teaching and learning until they have dealt with underlying climate issues and have adequate maintenance systems in place. More successful schools devote considerable time to establish trust and openness between staff, pupils and the community before they embark on substantive changes. Recognition of teachers and celebration of their successes is emphasized, and humour encouraged. A school's readiness for change depends to a large extent on individual teachers. Their psychological state may have an impact. Reynolds and Packer (1992) maintain that neglect of interpersonal and psychological processes may lead teachers to behave defensively to protect themselves from innovations that might expose their inadequacies. The valuing of individuals as people and their contributions to others enhances teachers' self-esteem and builds trust.

Addressing such issues as improvements to the physical environment, school behaviour policy development and establishment of communication lines and decision-making procedures are also climate-setting features. Attention is required to behaviour and attendance procedures: two notoriously popular and recurring themes, particularly in secondary schools. Developing a positive image for the school and building closer links with parents and the community (see Chapter 9) are also important.

Adam (1987) visited secondary schools in London with recently-arrived headteachers and asked them about the first change they implemented when they came to the school. Almost all made some deliberate change to the physical environment as a statement of their arrival. Often this change was for the benefit of teachers rather than pupils. Obviously, schools do not have the luxury to engage in climate setting before they make changes. The point is, without attention to these prerequisites at the earliest opportunity, real lasting changes that will improve teaching and learning are highly unlikely.

We now turn to continuing conditions that enhance school improvement efforts. In our experience, certain conditions exist in more successful schools in terms of development planning, meaningful focus on teaching and learning, and ultimate enhancement of pupil outcomes. These fundamental conditions often build up over a long period. Some conditions are the subject of later chapters.

Vision

> Nothing so professionalizes work in schools as educators who create within the schoolhouse visions of good education. Everyone who works in a school is not only entitled to a unique and personal vision of the way he or she would like the school to become, but has an obligation to uncover, discover, and rediscover what the vision is and contribute it to the betterment of the school community.
>
> (Barth 1990. 159)

The importance of vision to school improvement has been frequently stressed. Vision helps schools to define their own direction and to develop an attitude that says 'we're in charge of change'.

Vision can be seen as the shared values and beliefs of a group of people, whereas mission is the articulation of these values in goal setting and, sometimes, a statement of purpose (Block 1987). A difficulty of developing a whole-school vision is that while teachers enter teaching with a personal vision of what they believe is good education, due to pressures, demands and overload of school life, these visions become 'deeply submerged, sometimes fragmentary, and seldom articulated' (Barth 1990: 148). It is not possible even to attempt to come up with a shared vision if people are not clear about their own vision. Thus an important first step is to help teachers articulate and question their own values and beliefs and then consider how these might relate to those of others. Louis and Miles (1990), in their study of five urban high schools, found a preference for planning first, because the evolutionary nature of planning allowed teachers to reflect on their beliefs and subsequently articulate them more clearly. They described visions as 'a complex braid of the evolving themes of the change program' (p. 237). In their schools, vision building was a dynamic process that started with a small group of people but spread throughout the school.

Joint planning

Louis and Miles (1990) view good planning as essential for positive change, but note that because of changing external pressures or internal disagreements over priorities, no specific plan can exist for long. In schools in their study, planning was evolutionary, with 'many twists and turns as unexpected events occur along the way' (p. 193). Similar ideas have been proposed in the business sector, where Kanter (1989) encourages the attitude of 'learning by doing'. The concept of school development planning is related to evolutionary planning in that while detailed plans are constructed for one year, longer-term priorities are only sketched, to allow for changes that arise from differing needs or external initiatives. School development planning is described in Chapter 5.

Among the more successful schools in the development of school-based initiatives are those who spend time to facilitate staff planning together. Collaborative cultures appear to be closely related to school improvement (see Chapter 6).

Leadership

We have already described leadership as one possible route into improvement. Most research also highlights that it is a fundamental continuing condition of school improvement. Leadership is further described in Chapter 7. Effective principals also build opportunities for others to assume leadership roles through involvement and empowerment.

Involvement and empowerment

Commitment to change is more likely when those involved in implementation of school improvement are also consulted and involved in making decisions. Decentralization of decision making in schools is not always straightforward, especially when principals have traditionally been used to making all the decisions; many teachers still expect this. Additionally, the principal carries the ultimate responsibility for school-level decisions and, therefore, must know they can be defended. Shared leadership also involves extra time commitment for all concerned. None the less, the literature is replete with evidence confirming the importance of teacher ownership for commitment.

Teachers must be motivated and interested to make a change. In short, they must possess the will to make school improvement succeed (Miles 1987). This will is generated by increased empowerment. Rosenholtz (1989) found that teachers' sense of optimism, hope and commitment was associated with workplace conditions where they felt professionally empowered. Louis and Miles (1990) outline five specific strategies for involvement: power sharing, rewards for staff; openness and inclusiveness; expanding leadership roles; and patience.

What of pupil involvement? Pupil engagement and involvement in school life is critical. Improving schools involve pupils in the decisions that affect them. The ramifications of non-involvement of pupils in classroom and school experiences are worrying (see Chapter 9).

Partnership

Outside assistance or stimulation has been shown to have the greatest influence on implementation when it is integrated with local support efforts. We dedicate Chapter 9 to this key topic.

Monitoring and evaluation

Successful school improvement is linked to systematically planned and executed monitoring and evaluation of process and final outcomes. The monitoring of the change process is as important as measurement of outcomes. We examine monitoring and evaluation in more detail in Chapter 11.

Problem seeking and problem solving

The process of school improvement is not without problems. Successful schools do not have fewer problems than other schools. However, they cope better with their problems, by applying 'deep' and 'shallow' coping styles as appropriate (Louis and Miles 1990). Deeper coping styles include creation of new roles, redesign of ideas, and provision of extra assistance and time. The ability to deal with problems actively, promptly and in some depth was the single biggest determinant of the success of school improvement programmes in Louis and Miles's study. Active searching for potential problems or blocks is an essential part of the problem-solving process, and is vital to maintain momentum, as is the next condition.

Staff development and resource assistance

Reporting on their study of school improvement, Huberman and Miles (1984) commented: 'Large-scale, change-bearing innovations lived or died by the amount and quality of assistance that their users received once the change process was under way' (p. 273).

This statement is well supported by other research. Staff development can be misapplied, however, unless it is understood in relation to the meaning of change and the change process. 'One-shot' strategies are of little assistance. Staff development strategies within the school, for example mentoring, coaching and action research, have all been found to aid classroom and school improvement. Teacher development is included in Chapter 10.

Louis and Miles (1990) found that improving schools needed a variety of resources and that change could not be managed with the regular resource level. These resources included money, time, space, equipment, personnel, 'big ideas' – for example school effectiveness knowledge – and materials. They also concluded that some schools were better than others at resource location, acquisition and use. Our own research highlighted the need for instructional follow-up support, facilitation of aspects of the growth planning process and analysis and interpretation of assessment data.

Adapting management structures

Leadership has to be supported by good management practices. When school improvement efforts are underway, it is frequently necessary to restructure existing arrangements that obstruct the change process. This might include:

• adapting timetables
• creating new policies
• amending roles and responsibilities
• developing clear lines of authority and responsibility
• providing time for people to meet
• linking existing and new aspects of the culture, for example weaving appraisal into the school development planning process
• hiring new staff to 'fit' and help steer the changing direction of the school
• facilitating coordination of the process.

Creativity

Schools require flexibility to accommodate external ideas within their own context and needs. Even within an externally determined framework, more successful schools are able to pursue their own areas of interest. This relates back to a sense of shared vision, but it is more than this. The school, rather than the government, ministry or district is in the driver's seat, setting its own direction and adapting mandates creatively to fit its vision. Creative schools have an ownership mentality. They are the schools that define their own direction, irrespective of external demands.

Ongoing work on the conditions of change is vital to resolve inevitable challenges to improvement.

Challenges to improvement

Improvement is notoriously complex and considerable barriers get in its way. As we work with schools and try to understand the factors that lead to improvement and effectiveness, we face issues that challenge schools and us. Many have frustrated practitioners and researchers engaged in different projects. It is not possible to come up with a cookbook of answers for every situation. What is important is awareness of the potholes in the road and, through problem solving and seeking, coming up with creative solutions to fit the particular circumstance.

Mobility of teachers and principals

A high level of turnover causes obvious problems of continuity, commitment to goals and school vision, and can disrupt momentum of the improvement process. In some instances, once a principal left a Halton school it was unclear whether the growth plan had been the entire staff's or only the principal's. Given that the leadership role of the principal is key to the change process, it can have a profound effect on school improvement when a new leader arrives with a different perspective and none of the school's joint history. Sometimes this is a benefit, but in other cases problems can ensue.

The difficulty of sustaining commitment

In some ways this is related to the previous challenge in that new staff may not be committed to particular goals and, in sufficient numbers, may influence other colleagues. The issue, however, is broader. The problem of sustaining commitment 'is endemic to all new programs irrespective of whether they arise from external initiative or are internally developed' (Fullan 1991: 89). Continuation requires ongoing coordination, problem solving, negotiation, support, communication and sharing of new knowledge.

Micropolitical pressures

Micro-political issues significantly challenge school improvement. Sarason (1990) maintains that educational reforms continuously fail because attention is not paid to the alteration of power relationships. Schools are places in which control is a key issue. Principals are faced with the problem of maintaining control while trying to generate enthusiasm and commitment (Ball 1987). Some have difficulty in finding this balance and in involving teachers in decision making. It is difficult for teachers to create and sustain the conditions conducive to pupils' development if these conditions do not exist for teachers themselves (Sarason 1990). There are ramifications for pupil involvement if teachers control their pupils in the same way they are controlled by their principals (McNeil 1988; Holly and Southworth 1989).

Decentralization

There are many benefits to schools having increased control over their own destinies. A drawback, however, is that while more effective schools, free from constraints, can move in their chosen direction without being held back by district policies, less effective schools are left to flounder without system-level 'checks and balances' to ensure they do not decline. Given that such schools often do not realize their difficulties until too late, many do not seek help to improve. Often, in voluntary projects set up by districts and higher education, volunteers tend to be those who least need support. With limited external capacity for resources to be offered as an incentive, uninvolved schools are often those least aware and most needy of support and stimulation. It brings to mind parents' evenings when parents who do not appear are those teachers most want to see. We do not only refer to schools with difficulties; complacent schools are also at risk. The challenges are how to raise awareness of, engage interest in and commitment to school effectiveness and improvement in all schools.

The difficulty of linking direct outcomes with improvement

School effectiveness knowledge suggests that we should measure success of improvement efforts through pupils' achievement, progress and development. None the less, causality is extremely difficult to infer, and within each school any improvement initiative is only one of many different activities in which the school is currently involved. Thus there is the complication of trying to separate out the effects of one of many innovations. Schools need to set their own success criteria. For those that take a focus on language or mathematics, the use of baseline and outcome data is more straightforward. This is not the case for schools that choose a broader focus, for example flexible learning strategies or a particular crosscurricular teaching technique.

Maintaining the distinction between means and end

While it is often difficult to measure outcomes of improvement efforts, it is essential to keep them in mind. We have observed some schools, albeit with the best of intentions, become bogged down in the improvement process for its own sake. It is necessary to remember ongoing monitoring and evaluation of self-selected success criteria.

The implications of projects

The advantages of improvement projects can include pump priming, bringing together people on the same focus, support and status, and the project or Hawthorne effect, whereby improvement occurs because of being involved in a project. By describing such programmes as 'projects', however, there is a possibility that schools see their involvement as an add-on activity rather than informing and being fully integrated within whole-school development. Where the project is linked to centrally provided funding there is a danger of it having a finite lifespan and thus becoming an event rather than a process. In both cases, strategies to help schools maintain and build on the process are essential.

Concurrent agendas

Schools are busy places. At the same time that they are involved in development work, they also maintain their focus on other commitments and respond to external directives. In England and Wales, advanced knowledge of, preparation for and, sometimes, the aftermath of Office for Standards in Education (OFSTED) inspections has proved to have a particularly strong impact on school improvement. During the lifetime of one project, four of eight participating schools underwent OFSTED inspections (Myers 1996). The immediate reaction to schools receiving notification of an inspection is often that all efforts must be devoted to preparation for it and nothing else can be considered until it is over. Indeed, we have observed 'development paralysis' in some such schools, often for many months. This reaction must be countered if school improvement is to have meaning and impact.

Contextual differences: does one size fit all?

A problem of generic knowledge about school improvement is insufficient detail in attention to variations in improvement conditions and strategies in different types of schools. How to address contextual differences between schools is one of the greatest challenges for school improvers. Different change strategies, leadership styles, and communication networks may be required to effect change. Indeed, as no two schools are the same, there may be no single best way to approach school improvement, which is likely to frustrate those who seek simple solutions. Schools can also be grouped in terms of other contextual characteristics that influence school improvement:

- Phase or level of schooling – change is more complex in secondary schools due to diversity of purposes and objectives, size, department structures and 'looser coupling', leading to greater decentralization of authority (Louis and Miles 1990).
- SES composition – different improvement strategies are necessary for low SES and high SES schools (Brown *et al.* 1996).
- Location – schools in rural or isolated areas with less access to and knowledge of outside ideas, resources and stimulation may require a different approach to schools in big cities.
- Schools with effective outcomes that exhibit different leadership patterns (Galloway 1983) – even among effective schools, different strategies may work because of each unique context.
- Current effectiveness and improvement capacity – in 'historically ineffective settings' (Reynolds *et al.* 1993) or 'stuck' schools (Rosenholtz 1989), the sort of support often provided within the scope of improvement projects may be inadequate to help such schools set their own change priorities, take ownership of process, and focus on teaching and learning.
- Differences within schools – departments may differ in their improvement orientation, as may teachers of older and younger primary pupils.
- Speed of current improvement – will the same improvement approaches work in schools currently improving at different rates?

It is generally agreed that schools facing difficulties require more external support than those starting from a solid base. The closure of schools in difficulty is a measure only to be used in the most extreme cases, when all other supportive attempts have clearly failed. As we have argued, attention to climate setting is a vital early step that, we believe, precedes a whole-school emphasis on teaching and learning. This does not mean that individuals or groups who are ready for change should be held back. Far from it. In Chapter 6 we propose a typology of different school cultures; we discuss in that chapter and the subsequent one, approaches that might be taken in schools that vary in terms of effectiveness and improvement.

Increased links between school effectiveness and school improvement

Despite different orientations on the part of school effectiveness and school improvement researchers (Reynolds *et al.* 1993), practitioners are increasingly intolerant of intellectual 'navel gazing' and, knowingly or unknowingly, have linked the two fields for some years (Stoll 1996). Their use of school effectiveness research, however, has evolved from top-down approaches to efforts that pay greater attention to school improvement and change knowledge bases. In 1988, schools in 41 per cent of America's school districts (approximately 6,500) were engaged in effective schools programmes (General Accounting Office 1989), half of which were mandated, the remainder voluntary. Within the last few years, there have been many other concerted attempts internationally to link the two, particularly by members of the International Congress for School Effectiveness and Improvement (ICSEI). In brief, these include:

- Canada's Saskatchewan School Improvement Program (Hajnal *et al.* 1994)
- the Dutch National School Improvement Project (Houtveen and Osinga 1995)
- Israel's 30 Communities Project (Bashi 1995)
- Australia's Effective Schools Project (McGaw *et al.* 1991)
- Sweden's Researching Effective Improvement (Grosin 1995; McNamara 1995)
- Hong Kong's Towards a Better School Movement (Cheung 1995)
- Improving the Quality of Education for All (IQEA), established by Cambridge University's Institute of Education in Britain (Hopkins *et al.* 1994).

For further details, interested readers are referred to the journal *School Effectiveness and School Improvement*, Reynolds *et al.* (1989), Creemers *et al.* (1989), Bashi and Sass (1992) and Creemers and Osinga (1995).

Three British projects in which one of us has been involved are now described in more detail.

Schools Make a Difference

Schools Make a Difference – in Hammersmith and Fulham Local Education Authority in London – started in 1993 (Myers 1996). All eight of the LEA's secondary schools chose to participate. Project principles were based on school effectiveness research findings. A project manager worked with schools and LEA personnel to establish structures and procedures. She visited schools, took senior management teams to visit interesting schools around the country, and organized in-service. Schools appointed project coordinators, who were awarded 30 half days cover to carry out project-associated work, attend in-service and visit other schools. Project working parties were established in schools with representation from a wide range of stakeholders.

Each school produced a plan based on criteria agreed by headteachers for expenditure of a centrally offered budget. These were developed through wide consultation, and included a focus based on schools' development plans. Schools engaged in various forms of staff development to help introduce new teaching and pupil study methods. This included mutual classroom observation and acting as each other's 'critical friends'. The project also funded school-based revision centres during vacations. An external evaluator interviewed participants, and LEA research staff collected data on examination results, attendance and delinquency. Schools were also involved in self-evaluation.

Lewisham School Improvement Project

The Lewisham School Improvement Project is a partnership between schools in Lewisham in London, Lewisham Local Education Authority and the London Institute of Education (Stoll and Thomson 1996). Commencing in 1993, it draws heavily on school effectiveness and improvement findings, including those from Halton. It has four broad aims:

- to enhance pupil progress, achievement and development
- to develop schools' internal capacity to manage change and evaluate its impact at whole-school, classroom and pupil levels
- to develop the LEA's capacity to provide schools with data that will strengthen their ability to plan and evaluate change
- to integrate the above with the system's ongoing in-service and support services to form a coherent approach to professional development.

The project has four dimensions:

1 Leadership development – a voluntary workshop series for headteachers and deputy headteachers, focusing on effectiveness and improvement issues.
2 School projects – ten (primary, secondary and special) schools identified a teaching and learning improvement focus. Cross-role teams attended workshops to refine focus areas and examine practical implications of school effectiveness and school improvement research. The schools agreed to nine effectiveness and improvement 'ground rules':
   - to focus on achievement in its broadest sense
   - manageability – 'start small, think big'
   - team leadership and general ownership
   - teams that represented a range of stakeholders and experience
   - teams as agents of change
   - school responsibility for project management
   - systematic monitoring and evaluation
   - support from the LEA and Institute
   - dissemination to system colleagues.

Individual schools' focuses include developing structured group work to improve individuals' achievement, raising achievement in non-fiction writing, underachievement of black boys, reading and specific curriculum areas. Strategies incorporate developing and testing new teaching and assessment techniques, mutual observation, keeping diaries, open meetings, inviting external 'critical friends' to provide feedback, pupil surveys, and in-service sessions run by school improvement teams for colleagues.

3 Indicators creation – identification and development by a voluntary cross-role staff group of whole system indicators of change, achievement and development for special educational needs pupils.

4 Evaluation – monitoring and evaluation. Schools collect data, develop and measure success criteria, and engage in ongoing evaluation. LEA staff monitor project progress and impact. Institute staff interview participants to elicit insights into the change process. Dissemination of findings occurs throughout the LEA.

Improving School Effectiveness Project

Funded by the Scottish Office Education Department, this two-year collaborative venture between the University of Strathclyde and the Institute of Education in London involves 84 schools throughout Scotland, and focuses on three particular approaches to improvement: school development planning, teaching and learning, and developing a 'moving' school ethos (MacBeath and Mortimore 1994). It is unusual in that it blends:

- examination of school effectiveness outcomes, using multilevel modelling techniques to establish the value added by 84 schools
- in-depth qualitative examination of the processes of improvement in 24 case-study schools
- intervention and support in these 24 schools.

Conclusion

Many efforts to effect school improvement over the past 20 years have failed. In the 1970s, it was believed that if a school or a system adopted a particular change somehow it was magically implemented. It was often assumed that the mailing date from the source of the change was the implementation date as well. The failure of reform in the 1970s led in the 1980s to school effectiveness, which tended to be imposed as a 'top-down' change strategy, and school improvement, which attempted to draw lessons from unsuccessful attempts in the past to effect change. A high proportion of school effectiveness efforts worldwide have collapsed because of resistance to the imposition of change. Unfortunately, this entire area of research, which once had been seen as promising, has suffered because it is seen as having delivered very little. In effect the message was damaged by the way the message was sent.

Similarly, many school improvement projects have suffered because of a lack of focus on the important purposes of schooling, pupil outcomes and an inability to show 'results'. By combining the two fields, however, we have joined an outcomes orientation with a process to achieve change in our schools. Much of what has been described in this chapter are conditions necessary to deal with the irrationality of and resistance to change in order to create a setting for more rational approaches to change. With such conditions as vision, empowerment, readiness, partnerships and problem solving (among others) at least addressed, a school can more effectively approach school development planning. The next chapter provides a rational way to combine school effectiveness and school improvement while suggesting strengths and limitations of such planning.

five

SCHOOL DEVELOPMENT PLANNING: A PATH TO CHANGE

For those who believe in the need to link school effectiveness and school improvement, a key challenge has been to discover the mechanisms by which these two bodies of knowledge can be interwoven to help schools produce successful change and enhanced outcomes for all pupils. School development planning appears to offer a vehicle to connect the two fields, and also illustrates a way to open improvement doors simultaneously. Forms of planning are not new to schools. School development planning can be seen in various guises, and carrying different names, throughout the world. It derives from various origins, notably school self-evaluation and school-based review, curriculum development and the push for greater accountability. This latter theme has influenced the spread of development planning in Britain, for while there remains no government legislation that requires schools to have a development plan, most government policies are premised on their existence (MacGilchrist *et al.* 1995), including judgements in the inspection framework used by the Office for Standards in Education. In Britain, at least, what was intended by early proponents as voluntary guidelines to be adapted in a process of internal development (McMahon *et al.* 1984) has increasingly become associated with external accountability.

In this chapter we explore the purposes of development planning and summarize its process before discussing issues raised in our own and other research.

The purposes of school development planning

Most proponents agree that its ultimate aim is to improve the quality of pupil learning. MacGilchrist (1994) suggests, however, that other purposes appear to be means by which control can be exerted over the work of schools or by which the school can control its own work. The purposes can be summarized as:

- improving teaching and learning
- incorporating and interpreting external policy requirements
- empowering schools to take charge of their own development
- meeting government legislation commitments to parents
- a monitoring and accountability device for school districts
- a means to coordinate district support
- a management tool for principals to control their budgets.

The purposes send mixed messages of development and accountability to schools. This is reality, however, in a changing educational world. Schools must balance increased school autonomy with national, provincial or state government controls to deal with the demands made of them, while at the same time not being controlled by these demands. In essence, they must know where they are headed which, in school effectiveness and improvement terms, is towards better learning experiences and outcomes for pupils.

The process of development planning

Halton's growth planning model was based particularly on British models. The four stages (outlined in Chapter 2) are now briefly described and analysed. The terminology adopted is largely that used in Halton, although complementary ideas have been drawn from other sources (for example, Loucks-Horsley and Hergert 1985; Caldwell and Spinks 1988; DES 1989; Hargreaves and Hopkins 1991; Skelton *et al.* 1991; Davies and Ellison 1992; MacGilchrist *et al.* 1995).

Assessment

The assessment stage, often referred to as audit, occurs before planning. In most schemes this is when the school gathers and analyses information to provide an objective assessment of where it is now. An important feature of assessment is moving away from a 'cardiac approach' (Glickman 1991) – gut reaction to selecting development priorities – to one based on more systematic evidence. For this, various methods might be used, including informal observations, interviews, discussions, notes of activities, surveys and results of assessments, tests or examinations. To guard against inequity, information collected not only needs to be examined for overall trends, but also disaggregated to examine differences among pupil groups.

   This stage frequently is mismanaged and school staffs express considerable uncertainty about what it is most important to audit. This is compounded by anxiety over collecting large amounts of data, due in part to lack of knowledge about data analysis and interpretation. If there is a lack of focus, too much data may be collected. This can lead to uncertainty about how to organize and bring meaning to it. This was demonstrated in one Halton secondary school, where an exiting principal issued homework surveys to students, parents and teachers, and a student attitude survey. The incoming principal interviewed all teachers. He subsequently sent out a 'report card' survey to parents, administered a staff collaboration survey and asked the staff to generate a list of accomplishments and concerns. The result was an anxious call to the researcher in central office because the school felt swamped! This cautionary tale points to the importance of collecting only a manageable amount of information and the need for data interpretation training.

Planning

During planning or construction, assessment information is used to establish a plan with specific priorities or targets generated from results of the audit. The action plan includes responsibilities of staff members for specific activities; timelines or target dates by which they should be completed; and staff development and resource needs, with requests for help from people both within and outside the school. The action plan also crucially includes success criteria, because the question is asked for each priority: 'how will we know this has made a difference?' Staffs decide what criteria to use to assess the goal's effectiveness, and agree how and when it should be assessed. In practice, this has proved extremely difficult for many school staffs.

Implementation

Implementation is often a neglected part of the whole planning process and guidelines in this area are often noticeably short. Yet it is during implementation that the school has to follow through with the plan and carry out all actions necessary to ensure its fulfilment. This is a long-range process that requires periodical review and monitoring to see whether activities have taken place as planned and if they appear to be having the intended effect. In some schools what goes on in the classroom bears little relation to what is set down in the school's plan (MacGilchrist *et al.* 1995). Implementation is thus the translation of rhetoric into reality, and depends on staff, pupils and any other people involved understanding the plan's contents and being committed to their roles in the process.

Support is particularly crucial at this stage. In Halton, we found an increasing need to provide strategies to help staff who were involved in the initiation of change and development. These included forums where staff could share skills and strategies acquired through in-service, release time for teachers to plan together, coaching, consultation or peer problem solving and time for reflection. As with all implementation efforts, schools also faced their fair share of problems. This meant that the development of a comprehensive staff development support system was all the more important. Support for development planning is described in a later section.

Evaluation

In most schemes, the final stage of development planning is evaluation. To describe it as the final stage does not do it justice because, in reality, it plays a major role in every phase of development planning and, as such, its impact is felt much earlier. To measure change, success criteria need to be set, evaluation methods planned early on and relevant baseline assessments carried out. Furthermore, formative evaluation needs to occur during implementation. Thus evaluation weaves its threads throughout the entire process. Evaluation is fundamental. If development is measured by pupil learning, ways must be devised to know whether selected priorities are being met. Not only, however, is it important to know the degree to which objectives have been achieved, schools should also assess whether activities have been completed and if the plan itself has been useful. Unfortunately, this phase of planning is still neglected in many schools.

Monitoring of the plan is ongoing. During the final evaluation, decisions are made about each target. A report is prepared about the main stages of the plan so far. This might also include information about external initiatives likely to affect the next year's planning. The report is then often shown to the governing body or school council and, in some cases, a copy is required by the district. Final discussions revolve around changes introduced, and whether the development should be continued and/or extended. After reviewing targets, the whole process is repeated. For continuing objectives, further planning, implementation and evaluation occurs. Successfully accomplished goals also need to be maintained and become a regular part of the school's norms and practices. Unfortunately, this does not always occur (Stoll 1992; MacGilchrist *et al.* 1995). Sometimes, schools 'complete' a goal then turn to other key initiatives without a backwards glance.

School development planning issues

Our work in Halton and subsequent experience of development planning, particularly in Britain, have led us to suggest twelve issues for consideration by anyone engaged in such activity.

1 Coordination of the process

It is neither manageable, possible nor a good use of teachers' time for everyone to be involved in all of the finer details of development planning. Levine (1994) warns that plans which specify that most or all teachers will participate to the same extent in the same innovation are a signal of no more than 'organizational maintenance' or the 'politics of efficacy' (Fraatz 1988). In Halton's more successful schools we observed that teachers were aware of all the goals and participated in related school-wide staff development. However, they were not expected to be involved in all of them at a high level. Rather, they participated to a greater or lesser degree according to their level of interest and comfort. A balance between whole-school development priorities and the personal, professional development and autonomy of the teacher is essential. Teachers are more likely to view involvement as worthwhile if they participate selectively (Hargreaves and Hopkins 1994).

In Halton, many schools had growth planning teams that varied in size according to school size. Membership selection and roles varied. In some schools teachers volunteered; in others they were co-opted or requested by the principal. Some schools were only represented by those in responsibility positions, for example department heads. Other schools had much wider representation. This promoted a broader perspective and, consequently, greater commitment, as did principals who took a lower profile role on the team rather than those who directed all activities. These teams had a shared leadership role and, through participation in specifically designed training, developed their capacity as change agents (Fullan 1993).

Sometimes, team members expressed initial concern they might be perceived as an élite. Ongoing communication between these people and other teachers was essential to develop trust and commitment. Planning teams can include broader representation, particularly parents and pupils. The opening-up of the team, we found, often took adjustment time. In some schools anxiety was expressed about involvement of parents in this process. It appears that teachers are not eager to include parents or pupils until they themselves feel adequately involved.

Part of coordination involves building commitment of colleagues through joint decision making. A London teacher attending a school development masters degree course told one of us, with much amusement and some cynicism, that on the school's last 'Baker Day' (professional development day), 'while we teachers were "being developed" the head and senior management team went off to write the development plan!' A deputy headteacher of a London secondary school has also reflected on her school's early experience of development planning:

In effect the real development plan was in my head. Given that my senior colleagues operated in much the same way, it could be said that the school development plan was in the minds of the senior management team rather than in the hearts of the staff.

It is not shared decision making *per se* that is significant but, rather, the feeling of control that ensues. This is particularly important in times of externally mandated change and overload where internal control of the change process can offset turbulence caused by innovation (Wallace and McMahon 1994). A greater sense of control, therefore, appears to lead to greater confidence in the process and individuals' feeling of empowerment to take charge of change.

2 Attention to fundamental conditions of school culture

Observations of Halton schools involved in growth planning suggested that there appeared to be fundamental conditions to the process that required attention to promote a better planning experience. In addition, an understanding of and ability to enhance school culture underpinned successful school growth planning efforts. In Halton it appeared that more successful schools moved from a vision of a more attractive future to total staff commitment to a mission. This, in turn, drove the growth plan. There were three features in this process:

- development of a shared vision leading, in some cases, but not all, to a mission statement
- climate setting
- promotion of staff collegiality and continuous improvement.

These are described in more detail in Chapters 4 and 6.

3 Commitment to a few key goals

One of the most challenging features of the school development planning process is the ability to keep the plan to a realistic and manageable size. Schools face so many competing external demands, as well as their own areas of interest, that it is hard for them to decide on a few key priorities. In guidance on development planning in Britain, curriculum, resources and staff development are always included, and one scheme recommends incorporation of up to eight dimensions of a school's work (Davies and Ellison 1992). In choice of priorities, schools need to consider both manageability and coherence of sequence. MacGilchrist and colleagues (1995), drawing on Hargreaves and Hopkins (1991), recommend three strategies to avoid selection of an unrealistic number of targets. Balance is necessary between:

- Small (one-year) priorities and those for the medium or long term, which can be sketched out.
- Maintenance and development priorities, such that schools should always work on new initiatives, but need to plan for the maintenance of past practice and sustenance of recently implemented priorities.
- Root and branch priorities, whereby the roots provide the foundations for growth of the branches. Structures and policies would be examples of roots.

Where Halton's growth plan differs from Britain's school development plan is that it does not attempt to perform both maintenance and development functions. In common with the South Australian plan (Cuttance 1994), it focuses exclusively on development, while various processes are set in place separately to ensure that maintenance occurs. Without these, tension is likely to occur between continuation of earlier priorities and current needs. Teachers also need to pursue areas of their own interest. The major function of the growth plan, however, is to select a small number of areas and engage in school-wide development of them. A growth plan is not expected to contain everything the school is involved in or else it becomes an indiscriminate list. Schools that chose three or four goals, depending on the school's size, found more teachers became involved in more goals and that it was easier to monitor the progress of implementation and to focus staff development. Furthermore, teachers, students and parents were also more likely to be aware of and committed to the goals. In his study of organizational development, Senge (1990) suggests that the best results come from smaller, more focused efforts. Schools with prior experience of planning tend to become more realistic the second time around and identify priorities that represent a balance between those that are easy to accomplish and those that are more difficult (Mac-Gilchrist 1994).

Two British school effectiveness and improvement projects, Schools Make a Difference and the Lewisham School Improvement Project (Stoll *et al.* 1995) are based on the 'start small, think big' (Fullan 1991) premiss. In both, priorities have been selected that are key to the school and relate to its development plan. Furthermore, the fundamental conditions outlined previously are emphasized, and attempts are made to embed roots on which branches can grow.

The number of priorities selected depends on the extent to which every member of staff needs to be involved in each target and the extent of external intervention. An era of increased accountability and legislated governmental innovation limits the luxury of choice. It appears, however, that certain schools are able to steer the course in their own preferred direction. This may require compromise in terms of ensuring consonance with external reform pressures (Hopkins *et al.* 1994) or creativity (see Chapter 2). Some schools focus on the opportunities offered by reform and turn it to their own advantage.

4 Engagement in an ongoing, dynamic process

School improvement has been likened to a journey. Thus the planning process becomes the vehicle to reach the destination and the plan itself the map. It should not be overlooked, however, that the quality of ongoing discussion and reflection is of considerably greater importance than the plan. If the plan itself becomes a substitute for school improvement or its intended outcomes, the whole process will become a pointless paper and pencil exercise.

Change also takes time. In Halton, each cycle of the growth planning process lasted approximately three years, to enable sufficient time for implementation of individual goals. It has been suggested that schools and school systems are not rational (Patterson *et al.* 1986) and that the turbulence of schools' environment requires a more flexible approach because it does not lend itself to the neatness and rigidity of annual planning cycles (Wallace 1994).

Despite relative stability in Ontario at the time of our study, Halton schools rarely developed neat linear growth plans. Rather they evolved and changed as schools made ongoing goal adaptations to meet students' needs. While it appeared that there were conditions for successful growth planning, they did not always occur before planning started. Indeed, the changing, meandering nature of goal development and implementation was somewhat evolutionary, and similar to that described by Louis and Miles (1990) in their urban high school study. On the basis that change takes at least three years for a single innovation and five to ten years for more substantial reforms (Fullan 1991), it would be highly unlikely that amendments would not be made to innovations over that period of time, given external pressures, societal change, internal monitoring and changes in interest. Furthermore, changes in personnel will also impact a school's processes and development. Consequently, the approach taken by many schools mirrored the philosophy espoused by a business executive cited by Peters and Waterman (1982): 'ready, fire, aim'. This does not mean, however, that schools cannot control the process, but that flexibility needs to be built into the approach.

Development planning is a living and active process; the plan has to be implemented. It is the responsibility of all involved to see that this occurs. There is a fundamental difference between rhetoric and reality. The written part of the plan is far less important than the ideas within it, and there is also a danger that planning can become an activity in its own right, separate from the main purpose of the school (West and Ainscow 1991). This was illustrated for us when we asked one teacher, 'Will your growth plan make this a more effective school?' In her answer, 'If it gets off the paper', she emphasized the need to focus on substance rather than packaging. One London deputy headteacher has also mused: 'We gave no thought to the process of development planning and regarded the plan as an end in itself. Preparing the plan was seen as an unenviable, laborious task relating to external accountability rather than to internal development.'

The gap between the written plan and its implementation is often the weakest aspect of development planning (Hargreaves and Hopkins 1991). The deputy continues:

> At strategic points during the next two years, copies of the curriculum and assessment plan were brought out at heads of department meetings so that we could review progress in achieving 'our' targets. On these occasions I was perturbed to notice glazed eyes and quizzical looks from around the room . . . Even as a partial participant I realized that I could not recall any of the developments proposed in other parts of the plan. In retrospect it seems incredible that, during a period of rapid innovation and reform, we failed to seize the opportunity to take collective control of the process of change.

Development planning is not just a means to an end. Impact on teaching and learning needs to be demonstrated in classrooms, and yet this occurs too infrequently.

5 Getting a fix on current reality

As schools set their own directions through the development planning process, they need to be aware of their particular context and needs. This is achieved through an audit that needs to include information about current pupil outcomes as well as the school and classroom processes used to attain these outcomes. In Halton a questionnaire was designed to help schools assess themselves in relation to the characteristics of school effectiveness (Stoll 1992). They were also encouraged to collect other student achievement and social development data and specific contextual and external information. Inevitably, the completion of surveys, in itself, did not lead to positive change. Schools who made use of the results, however, found their efforts to be more focused.

The prime purpose of the survey was to start discussion within schools. As a needs assessment instrument, data from which would be used for future planning, it was necessary for a school to examine both the current position and its importance in creating an effective school. As schools analysed the gap in their responses between what they believed to be important and what they perceived to be happening currently, they were able to identify strengths and areas of need. In Halton, these surveys were available to schools as only one part of their assessment and self-evaluation process. Because each school was unique, spaces were left for schools to add five issues special to their own context, and background information was later included to enable analysis of differential effectiveness. Schools compared their own results with those of a system-wide sample collected at the same time.

While school effectiveness research findings provide one source of attitudinal information for a needs assessment, they are not the only source. The importance of obtaining the views of a wide range of stakeholders on a variety of issues is increasingly recognized (see, for example, Coleman *et al.* 1993; MacBeath 1994; Townsend 1994); state departments and universities in many countries have developed surveys to seek their input.

6 The significance of monitoring and evaluation

School self-evaluation is complex. Formal and informal data collection is an important and vital part of the school development planning process, and yet, as we have noted, gut reaction is still often used to determine areas of need and evaluate the success of goal-setting endeavours. Ongoing monitoring of implementation of goal strategies needs to be stressed to ensure that the process works well and that it achieves its intended outcomes. A headteacher in one British primary planning project talked of the need to spend time in classrooms to observe the actual effect of the plan on the children (MacGilchrist 1994). Interestingly, none of the teachers in this study identified a specific monitoring or evaluation role for themselves. This is a common problem, although we found in Halton that questions to teachers about the evaluation of specific priorities in which they were involved produced more evidence of evaluation:

> The children did a research project. We developed criteria for how we would mark that. We have a sheet for each child on the different aspects of the research and how well they did at each stage. We gave them a test for knowledge. We also relied a lot on observation of the skills that the children developed working in cooperative group activities and how well they could relate and use their information.
>
> (teacher interview)

There is a danger, if priorities are not properly evaluated, that the school will just move on to another priority with no systems in place to ensure that the current priority is embedded into the general work of the school and receives the necessary maintenance support.

Schools need to believe that the most important purpose of data collection and use is for the development of school goals aimed at growth and improvement and for self-evaluation or self-accountability (Stoll 1991), rather than for external school evaluation. Without this belief schools are reluctant to become involved in the sharing of school-based data that can be valuable in the determination of future directions. Certainly, in the British context of external inspections, there is a danger that headteachers might respond to requirement of access to the school's development plan in a managerial and bureaucratic manner. Hargreaves and Hopkins (1994) caution:

> when accountability is seen as the major instrument for promoting school effectiveness, development planning, originally designed to assist schools in their growth towards greater effectiveness, could lose all its potential as a means of school improvement.
>
> (p. 3).

7 A focus on teaching and the improvement of learning

The central purpose of development planning as expressed by a report of a committee of the Inner London Education Authority (1985) was that it be construed in terms of improvements in children's learning. In the 'moving' or 'learning enriched' schools in Rosenholtz's (1989) study of Tennessee school districts, teaching and learning were also central: 'shared goals, beliefs and values led teachers through their talk to a more ennobling vision that placed teaching issues and children's interests at the forefront' (p. 39).

School development planning as a process in itself is insufficient to engender meaningful teacher commitment because teachers generally derive meaning from their work in the classroom. Since educational change depends on teachers' commitment, teacher involvement is essential to the success of a change effort. In Halton when the strategic plan was developed, instruction was one of three strategic directions. In the event, it both provided a key focus for the school growth plan and the meaningful link for teachers. Indeed, the majority of schools focused most of their goals on classroom improvement although, as already noted, early attempts at growth planning included many climate and collegiality issues. When interviewed, teachers in Halton and in the London primary planning study (MacGilchrist 1994) were more likely to mention priorities that impinged directly on the classroom.

By offering voluntary workshops and institutes on effective teaching models and techniques, Halton was able to influence schools' decisions to focus on instruction without mandating any particular approach. For example, as a result of the system's focus on cooperative group learning, several schools subsequently chose this particular strategy for further development. In this way, the system offered 'menus rather than mandates' (Fullan and Hargreaves 1991). At the same time, the district also encouraged individual schools' own choices for development. District support staff sometimes found that schools knew more about a particular teaching technique than they did, which required professional development on their part to keep pace with these schools.

8 Recognition that each school is unique

Schools are like small societies. If school development planning is viewed as a sociopolitical process rather than a rational management practice (Dempster *et al.* 1994), planning processes depend on each school's political dynamics and motivations: planning recipes become inappropriate. Demonstrations of this in Halton and in Britain have been seen both in schools' choices and individual interpretations of government and district policies, and in varied approaches taken by different schools to development planning, vision building and mission development. Some more traditional Halton secondary schools balked at the 'Halton jargon'. In these schools, administrators often initially presented new ideas in their own language. For example, several schools had a 'school plan' rather than a 'school growth plan'. There is no single best way to approach school improvement. From our experience, schools approach planning in different ways, according to their particular context and culture. Past and present culture clearly supports or inhibits a school's planning process and can be, in turn, influenced by the process (Hargreaves and Hopkins 1991). This being the case, 'one size will not fit all'; individuality within a broad framework is inevitable.

The situation becomes more complex in schools that are struggling. Without prior attention to climate setting, attempts at shared leadership, decision making and parental involvement can prove disastrous: 'in troubled school circumstances, school development planning can lead to staff/administration or school personnel/parent schisms that defy healing in all but the long term' (Dempster *et al.* 1994: 4)

9 The reality of multiple innovations and the need for interconnections

Much of what we know about change has resulted from study of implementation of discrete innovations, for example a particular approach to reading or a teaching strategy. In reality, however, schools and school systems balance multiple innovations (Wallace 1991). Normally districts do not interrelate and coordinate their policies, so that any given project, no matter how good it is in its own right, fails to make a sustained impact (Fullan and Miles 1992). Indeed, Sarason (1990) maintains that educational reform has persistently failed because educators have dabbled in innovations one at a time.

Within schools, teachers are faced with a multiplicity of initiatives. In order to make the learning experience more coherent for pupils, some means to integrate these initiatives is necessary. Fragmented solutions are often a short-term response to the problem of overload (Fullan and Hargreaves 1991). Halton schools noted, however, that the school growth plan, through its focus on a small number of key priorities, provided a way of dealing with multiple innovations and overload. It gave them the opportunity to say no to further demands from the system as, indeed, the more successful schools did.

Schools cannot only be concerned with their own individual context. They are not islands and should not become isolated even though they are, and should be, the locus of decision making. Schools need to be located at the centre of change, with links to their outside environment and antennae sensitive to the local and national context in which they are situated. This, of course, has implications for development planning. On one hand schools are autonomous and set and steer their course of direction. On the other, local or national governments prescribe specific paths for them to take. In Halton, the link with the district provided accountability in terms of the system's broad directions, but also support according to individual schools' expressed needs. The action plan demanded of English schools after an external inspection also needs to be connected to the existing development plan. This may prove a dilemma for schools where there is commitment to development plan targets, but different priorities are highlighted by inspectors. In times of prevailing external government mandates, the ability to make connections appears to be an important part of a school's ability to integrate internally and externally generated priorities into a coherent plan.

10 The benefits of a support infrastructure

When teachers plan together and become more involved in school-level decisions, staff development in group process skills and other knowledge and skills necessary to implement development plans become necessary. Principals also require training in these skills, given that for some, at least, to relinquish complete control of the school's reins causes anxiety and may be seen as a threat. As growth planning was developed in Halton, it became evident that availability and accessibility of human resources and information to support growth planning was vital to enhance the process and reduce later problems, as was a regional staff development plan that would respond to in-service needs related to school growth plans. One Halton principal observed, 'School improvement can be more satisfying if the principal and teachers involved have been trained effectively to cope with educational change.'

A parallel plan was therefore developed for system support for school growth planning. This incorporated a range of staff development activities, development consultancy, research support and resources. Our experience suggests that there is a need for someone with research skills to develop or locate assessment strategies, coordinate data collection and analysis, and provide related in-service to schools. This might include the design of a value-added analysis system as described in Chapter 11, development, analysis and feedback of surveys similar to those outlined earlier or analysis and disaggregation of a school's own surveys.

11 *The fundamental question of impact*

The question a school effectiveness researcher asks of any initiative is: 'does it make a difference?' The key question in relationship to development planning is: 'is it really necessary for a school to have a development plan?' This is an impact question, and relates to the purposes of development planning, in particular enhancement of pupils' learning. If there is little or no impact, why waste time on the whole exercise? A countrywide primary school planning project in Australia (Dempster *et al.* 1994) found little direct evidence of impact of school development planning on students' work and achievement. The researchers conclude: 'The question of how a school plan influences a teacher's classroom plan and how this in turn, is transformed into improvements in outcomes for children is a complex one' (p. 5).

All too often the many purposes of school development planning appear to go unquestioned as lists of its benefits are glibly cited. Much guidance assumes that development plans will make schools more efficient and effective. Even if the development plan is an efficient management tool, this does not automatically lead to greater effectiveness.

From the experience of more successful Halton schools and a minority in one British primary planning study (MacGilchrist *et al.* 1995), the answer is a 'yes, it does make a difference', but this is qualified. Given the importance of a school's culture to its capacity for change, attempts to improve classroom teaching and learning without attention to culture and the conditions outlined above are likely to be superficial and short-lived. Halton's school growth planning process, because of its emphasis on participatory decision making, flexibility and respect for schools' contexts and individual teachers' comfort level, was intended to address the school's culture while at the same time providing a focus on teaching and students' learning.

Improvement inside the classroom is dependent on improvement outside the classroom. That is, there has to be a focus on 'the total school' (Fullan and Hargreaves 1991). When successfully operated, the development planning process attends to the total school and, in its focus, allows teachers to concentrate on issues of importance to them. These are directly related to the classroom and pupils' learning. Only through careful monitoring and evaluation can the impact of planning and its goals be seen.

12 The developmental nature of development planning

The evidence suggests that learning can be derived from engaging in development planning. MacGilchrist and colleagues (1995) differentiate four types of plan according to the extent of shared ownership, purpose, leadership and management of the process. These plans and their processes are perceived to lead to different outcomes:

- The rhetorical plan – characterized by weak leadership and management, lack of shared ownership and purpose, the plan is not a working document, teachers feel minimal control over the process and lack confidence in ensuing benefits. There is no link with finance or staff development, poor monitoring, and the result is teacher frustration, disillusionment and distance from the headteacher.
- The singular plan – used to improve management efficiency and school organization and provide accountability, the head alone leads, manages and feels ownership and purpose. Staff control over the process is limited. The plan is not a working document, and there is little or no supportive finance and professional development, weak monitoring and evaluation. While improved management and organization ensues, staff and pupils are not affected.
- The cooperative plan – partially 'owned' by teachers, who willingly participate, the working document emphasizes efficiency, effectiveness and teacher professional development. The headteacher is responsible for leadership, but key staff share management. Finance and staff development support implementation, and growing confidence and control exist. Monitoring and evaluation, however, lack rigour. Positive impacts are observed in management, organization, relationships and classroom effectiveness, but evidence of improvements for pupils is limited.
- The corporate plan – focusing on teaching and learning, effort to improve is united, with shared ownership, staff involvement and attempts to involve others. The open, working document emphasizes effectiveness and efficiency. Control, confidence and responsibility ensue from leadership shared among senior management and whole-staff involvement in management. Finance and professional development are linked, and sound monitoring and evaluation strategies used. Pupils' learning opportunities are improved, and links are observed between schools', teachers' and children's development, with increasing evidence of a learning community.

While the plans are seen to represent a continuum from least to most effective according to their impact, it is not a linear, developmental process. For example, a school with a cooperative plan previously had one that was rhetorical and one with a corporate plan started with a cooperative plan. Despite this, all the headteachers reported having learnt lessons and made a variety of changes as a result of their previous planning experience. Hargreaves and Hopkins (1994) also note a learning process, identifying 'a fairly predictable sequence of stages through which a school passes as it engages with and understands the process' (p. 17). The characteristics of these stages relate to some identified in the primary study. Hargreaves and Hopkins's three stages are:

1 Attention to the plan as a document, exemplified in such questions as, 'what does a plan look like?'
2 Recognition that the process, rather than the plan itself, is central, with commensurate identification of appropriate priorities and strategies, a system for consultation and involvement, and staff development opportunities.
3 Realization that the quality of the management of planning is key to its success. This includes the management arrangements (Hargreaves and Hopkins 1991) of frameworks, roles and responsibilities and working together. Review and potential change to fundamental structures and the culture of the school may thus be required. It is only with this that 'immediate impact on pupil achievement can be anticipated' (p. 17).

Achieving the necessary quality of management arrangements may, however, take time. This suggests that there might be a further stage in the process once this is attained. Cuttance (1994) reports on South Australia, where school development planning involves a wider group of stakeholders. One year after its introduction, a review of support (Education Department of South Australia 1991) found schools to be at one of four stages in their planning. This study's categories of planning share common features with the work of MacGilchrist and colleagues (1995) and Hargreaves and Hopkins (1994) but also particularly highlight involvement of other stakeholders, for example parents and students.

The positive ends of all three schemes highlight an increasingly complex process, rather than simply a written plan, involvement and management, and monitoring and review. Such complexity also featured in more successful growth planning experiences in Halton. With all the knowledge about shared leadership and management, monitoring and evaluation, flexible approaches and staff development needs for implementation, must schools still work through different development stages? Under many circumstances it may not be necessary, but we are not convinced that a corporate planning experience is immediately possible in an ineffective school. The context in which development planning takes place not only influences teachers' orientation to the process but also the plan's content. Until climate and collegiality issues receive attention, teachers in schools experiencing difficulties often show little interest in development of teaching and learning strategies. Such schools may need to go through two phases in development planning consistent with

Hargreaves and Hopkins's (1991) description of root and branch innovations:

1 In the early phase, more attention will be focused on prerequisites, for example, pupil behaviour, physical environment, parental involvement, communication and collaboration, although there will be teaching and learning objectives. The climate issues are, for some schools, necessary evils that have to be given attention but do not engender much excitement. Indeed, in many secondary schools in particular, these are seen as issues that are really the responsibility of senior managers and those in official leadership roles.

2 The later phase of development planning can see schools more actively engaged in teaching and learning issues, using techniques derived from earlier efforts, for example collaborative planning, to enhance their newer focuses.

Conclusion

Without careful consideration, school development planning can easily be a bureaucratic management strategy that does not affect the lives of teachers and pupils. Conversely, with serious attention to the issues we have raised, we have known many schools for whom it has made a positive difference. One of the most complex challenges to school development planning, however, is school culture. It is to this important topic that we now turn.

six

THE POWER OF SCHOOL CULTURE

School culture plays a powerful role in changing our schools. While a school effectiveness orientation concentrates on formal, organizational structures of schooling, it tends to neglect its cultural and informal dimension. As Rosenholtz (1989) argues,

> Among the most important conceptual issues is that student learning gains have been associated with a handful of school characteristics without convincing rationales and empirical support for how these specific characteristics actually came to affect the internal dynamics of schools.
>
> (p. 2).

School improvers have focused more closely on processes that a school goes through in its search for effectiveness. They too, however, have devoted inadequate attention to these areas. Herein lies a fundamental problem because

> the school as a workplace proves extraordinarily powerful. Without denying differences in individuals' skills, interests, commitment, curiosity, or persistence, the prevailing patterns of interactions and interpretations in each building demonstrably creates certain possibilities and sets certain limits.
>
> (Little 1982: 338)

Put more bluntly, 'When culture works against you, it's nearly impossible to get anything done' (Deal and Kennedy 1983: 4). Typically, those who introduce educational reforms or restructure educational systems pay scant attention to the social organization and contexts in which these changes are introduced. Any attempt to improve a school, however, that does not address the underlying organizational conditions can be viewed as 'doomed to tinkering' (Fullan 1988).

Understanding school culture is a vital part of school improvement. So what is school culture? How does it influence the way a school operates and how is it influenced? Should we talk in terms of cultures rather than just one culture? These are questions that have perplexed many others and continue to challenge us. In this chapter we summarize our understanding of different facets of this complex concept by posing and attempting to answer a series of questions, and add illustrations from our work with schools in Halton and elsewhere.

What is school culture and what does it do?

Culture is difficult to define. Schein (1985) notes various interpretations: observed behavioural regularities, including language and rituals; norms that evolve in working groups; dominant values espoused by an organization; philosophy that guides an organization's policy; rules of the game for getting along in the organization; and the feeling or climate conveyed in an organization. While Schein agrees that these meanings reflect the organization's culture, he does not believe they are its essence. This, he argues, is 'the deeper level of *basic assumptions* and *beliefs* that are shared by members of an organization, that operate unconsciously, and that define in a basic "taken-for-granted" fashion an organization's view of itself and its environment' (p. 6).

More simply, organizational culture can be viewed as 'the way we do things around here' (Deal and Kennedy 1983). It is elusive and hard to capture because it is largely implicit and we only see surface aspects. Often we only begin to know a school's culture when we break one of its unspoken rules. Cultural rules and rituals abound within schools. We have visited several schools and been offered coffee, only to be told in forbidding terms as we pick up a cup, 'that's *Jane's* cup'! Metaphor, customs, rituals, ceremonies, myths, symbols, stories and humour are all facets of school culture. In one Halton elementary school, the new principal removed a table tennis table from the staffroom and hid it. This, she noted, was 'a big mistake'. Her first impression of the table had been negative, denoting a lack of work during planning time. In retrospect, she saw it as a symbol of togetherness, rarely used. After two months, the table reappeared, in her office, put there by teachers as a joke. The principal commented: 'I knew by that time that . . . my interpretation was really incorrect, so it went back in [to the staffroom] and everybody laughed. They folded it up and didn't use it very often.'

There are various roles in the cultural network (Deal and Kennedy 1983) that make schools seem more like locations for a thriller or spy novel: priests or culture bearers, often assistant principals, guardians of the culture's values through their behaviour and speech; whisperers, unseen powers behind the throne (often found in the secretary or custodian's/ schoolkeeper's office!); spies, who keep their fingers on the organization's pulse; heroes and heroines, who are revered; storytellers, who play the role of interpreter; and culture founders (Schein 1985; Nias *et al.* 1989), often principals, whose contribution or responsibility is the change of school culture by installation of new values and beliefs. Schein (1985) argues the possibility that the 'only thing of real importance that leaders do is to create and manage culture' (p. 2).

How does something starting at such a deep level find its way to the surface? Nias and colleagues (1989) work backwards from the surface to describe the process:

> Action, we could see, was governed by norms which were, in turn, an expression of values, in that they expressed staff members' views on the differential worth and utility of particular artefacts, opinions, activities, lifestyles and so on. But these values themselves appeared to be an expression of beliefs to which it was very hard for an outsider to gain access because, being shared and understood, they were seldom voiced.
>
> (p. 10)

They continue with a description of how one member of their team 'became' a member of staff:

> First, he learnt, by watching and listening attentively, what were the acceptable ways for an adult to speak and act in that school. Then, as through appropriate behaviour he demonstrated his capacity to 'fit in', he gradually came to understand the reasons for the norms he was following. In turn this enabled him to apprehend the principles on which these norms were constructed and the silent agreements which underlay them. Acceptance of these gave access to the shared language in which they were expressed and to the realization that he was able to hear what he called the 'secret harmonies' of the school. He was able at last to experience from inside what the staff described as 'the Sedgemoor way'.
>
> (p. 10)

Culture describes how things are and acts as a screen or lens through which the world is viewed. It defines reality for those within a social organization, gives them support and identity and 'forms a framework for occupational learning' (Hargreaves 1994a: 165).

What influences school culture?

Schools are shaped by their history, context and the people within them. Schools are also influenced by external political and economic forces and changes in national or local educational policies. Changes in society pose challenges to a school's culture, whether related to learning, the pupil population, organizational management, rapid technological developments or the changing role of women (Dalin 1993). Each of these raises questions for traditional modernistic schools, yet frequent responses come from the comfortable cultural paradigm:

> Schools and teachers are being affected more and more by the demands and contingencies of an increasingly complex and fast-paced post-modern world. Yet their response is often inappropriate or ineffective – leaving intact the systems and structures of the present, or retreating to comforting myths of the past.
>
> (Hargreaves 1994a: 23)

Schools need to be able to meet society's demands and challenges. Clearly, traditional cultural response patterns are no longer appropriate. We heard the story of a parent who was concerned that his son's school did not teach the important lessons he learnt when he was at school. The teacher replied: 'I have to make a choice. I can either prepare your son for your past or his future. Which would you prefer?' There is a message here for some governments! With such rapid change, of course, this means that a school needs to be adaptable. The question therefore arises, is school culture flexible or, once established, is it fairly permanent?

Is school culture fixed?

Some writers suggest that once an organization's culture is formed it becomes fixed. Bolman and Deal (1991) view culture as both product and process: 'As product, it embodies the accumulated wisdom of those who were members before we came. As process, it is continually renewed and re-created as new members are taught the old ways and eventually become teachers themselves' (p. 250).

If new members have no means to influence culture but merely learn the old ways, this could be taken to imply that an organization's culture rarely changes. We agree with those who take issue with such an opinion (Nias *et al.* 1989; Hopkins *et al.* 1994). Because culture is created by its participants, it inevitably changes as participants change, although it can also be a stabilizing force, particularly for longer-standing members. It presents, therefore, the paradox of both being static and dynamic. In many schools, although not necessarily all, the process of development planning can change a school's culture as can a new principal. This is not to say that changing a school's culture does not take time, but rather that it constantly evolves. A traditional Halton secondary school with a new principal illustrates this point. For many years the school carried the American confederate flag to sporting events as its symbol. The new principal felt that values the flag represented were inappropriate and decided to change it. The furore created surprised the principal, with complaints expressed by students and teachers alike. For them, the flag symbolized their school; they never associated it with any other meaning. To the new principal, a newcomer with no understanding of the flag's inherent tradition, its message was entirely different. It took several months of consultation, film viewing, discussion and negotiation with the students' council and staff members for agreement to change the symbol and for students to create a new one.

The extent to which culture is dynamic may also be influenced by the type of norms involved. Rossman and colleagues (1988) distinguish between 'sacred' and 'profane' norms. The former, defined as 'unquestionably true', give life meaning and are described as less likely to change than the composition of people who share them. They are, like Schein's (1985) basic assumptions, immutable and enduring. In contrast, the latter are based on beliefs held less dear and are, as such, more open to debate, refinement and change. The case of the flag would be an example of a challenge to profane norms.

What is the relationship between culture and structure?

It is impossible to examine school culture in isolation because it is inextricably linked to structure. In many ways they are interdependent. Culture, however, can only be affected indirectly, whereas structures can be changed. The difficulty arises that in changing structures without changes in school culture, change is likely to be superficial, which is a danger with all externally generated educational reforms. Culture is so subtle that if one tries to infer a school's culture from existing structures, it is often impossible to decipher the underlying assumptions that led initially to those structures (Schein 1985). In other words, two schools with similar structures could have different cultures. This is not always so, because cultures can be formed within and framed by particular structures (Hargreaves 1994a). Cultural change, therefore, is at least in part achieved through structural change, as illustrated in the Frontenac story (see Chapter 2).

Are there different types of school culture?

Several typologies have been created that describe and label different idealized types of school culture. These may serve as valuable tools to help educators identify their school with a particular type and analyse its implications for school development. It should be borne in mind that such typologies cannot capture subtle nuances of individual schools and possible subcultures within schools. Despite this important caveat, we have found such typologies useful and have developed our own based on two other models. Rosenholtz's (1989) 'moving' and 'stuck' schools model is powerful because it conveys stark contrasts. You can visualize two schools next door to each other, with similar intakes, in the same school system, facing the same external government mandates, and yet they are emotionally different. The moving school feels 'freedom to' focus on its priorities, the stuck school seeks 'freedom from' outside demands. Rosenholtz's dimensions have been expanded by Hopkins and colleagues (1994) into 'four expressions of school culture'. They have created two continua; one of effectiveness and ineffectiveness in terms of outcomes and the other representing the degree of dynamism of the improvement process, from dynamic to static.

Our own model develops these ideas. We have argued that school improvement can be powerfully influenced by school effectiveness research. We have also indicated that schools are either getting better or they are getting worse, because the rapidly accelerating pace of change makes standing still impossible. These two concepts allow us to look at school cultures on two dimensions, effectiveness–ineffectiveness, and improving–declining (see Figure 6.1).

Figure 6.1 Effectiveness and improvement typology of schools

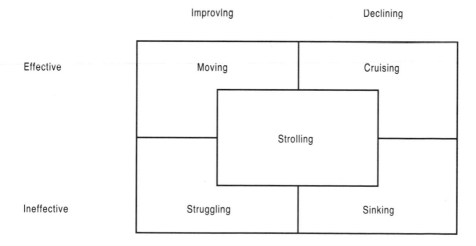

Moving schools are not only effective in 'value added' terms but people within them are also actively working together to respond to their changing context and to keep developing. They know where they are going; they have systems and the 'will and the skill' (Louis and Miles 1990) to get there.

Cruising schools are perceived effective by teachers, school community and outside inspectors or district administrators and appear to possess many of the qualities of an effective school. They are usually located in higher SES areas where the pupils achieve often in spite of teaching quality. League tables and other rankings based on absolute achievement rather than 'value added' often give the appearance of effectiveness. If, however, schools are to be effective for all children we must raise the ceiling as well as the floor. These are the 'good schools, if this were 1965'. Schools which are smugly marking time and not seeking to prepare their pupils for the changing world into which they are going are doing them a disservice.

Strolling schools are neither particularly effective nor ineffective. They are moving towards some kind of school improvement but at an inadequate rate to cope with the pace of change which threatens to overrun their efforts. They have ill-defined and sometimes conflicting aims which inhibit improvement efforts. In many ways these would be considered very average schools. They may not show up on league tables or other similar indicators as 'disasters', but none the less they seem to be meandering into the future – to the detriment of their pupils. It is these kinds of schools that require stimulation from an outside inspection, a new principal, governors or a school council.

Struggling schools are ineffective and they know it. They expend considerable energy to improve. While there may be considerable unproductive thrashing about as they determine the what and how of the change process, there is a willingness to try anything that may make a difference. Ultimately they will succeed because they have the will, despite lacking the skill. These are the schools that outside consultants or networks can have an impact on because the school staff recognize that the school is ineffective and change is necessary.

Sinking schools are failing schools. They are not only ineffective; the staff, either out of apathy or ignorance, are not prepared or able to change. They are schools which display characteristics of ineffectiveness described previously – isolation, self-reliance, blame and loss of faith – powerful inhibitors of improvement. They will often be in lower SES areas where parents are undemanding and teachers explain away failure by blaming inadequate parenting or unprepared children. Such schools need dramatic action and significant external support. One option is to close all such schools – 'the unthinkable alternative?' (Gray and Wilcox 1995) – and reopen new schools on the same site. While extreme on the surface, in a few situations it may have to be the last resort, for the sake of the pupils (Barber 1995).

D. Hargreaves (1995a) offers a different but interesting model which should be considered in examining school culture. It is based on two dimensions: the instrumental domain, representing social control and orientation to the task at hand; and the expressive domain, reflecting social cohesion through maintenance of positive relationships. Four types of school cultures sit in different and extreme places on the two dimensions:

- traditional – low social cohesion, high social control – custodial, formal, unapproachable
- welfarist – low social control, high social cohesion – relaxed, caring, cosy
- hothouse – high social control, high social cohesion – claustrophobic, pressured, controlled
- anomic – low social cohesion, low social control – insecure, alienated, isolated, 'at risk'.

Hargreaves points out that these are ideals rather than real cultures because real schools 'move around' and, indeed, departments within schools may fall within different parts of this model. He proposes a fifth culture, that of an effective school:

- effective – optimal social cohesion, optimal social control – fairly high expectations, support for achieving standards.

In this typology there are a variety of ways to be an effective school and many ways of being ineffective. As Hargreaves accepts, however, it is hard to place any particular school on the model with any accuracy. Such models are useful, though, as a discussion starting point to help teachers consider the different facets of their school's culture. One of these facets is likely to be the existence of subcultures.

Do schools have subcultures?

Most models of school culture and related literature assume that the environment and cultural world of teachers in the workplace is 'a school level phenomenon' (Siskin 1994). School culture has been viewed by some as more of an agglomeration of several subcultures (McLaughlin *et al.* 1990; Huberman 1992). Various cultures within one school may differentiate themselves: those of the teachers, pupils, administrators, non-teaching staff and parents. Such subcultures may form around interests pertinent to the particular group and create the potential to pull a school in several directions. There may be one dominant culture, often embodied in the principal's actions, and one or more smaller subgroups, each with their own, different set of beliefs, attitudes and norms. Alternatively, particularly in large secondary schools, smaller, closer 'webs' are formed by subsets of colleagues who have common interests and are influenced by a desire for social relationships

(Siskin 1994). Departmental divisions can prove powerful barriers to whole-school communication and collegiality. Hargreaves (1994a) considers teacher subcultures in his model:

- Individualism – bounded in metaphors of classrooms as egg crates or castles, autonomy, isolation and insulation prevail, blame is avoided, as is support. Individualism is often an active choice related to psychic rewards of working with young people (Lortie 1975). Individualism is distinguished from both individuality – the power to exercise independent, discretionary judgement – and solitude – 'a withdrawal to delve into one's personal resources; to reflect, retreat and regroup' (Hargreaves 1994a: 180).
- Collaboration – teachers choose, spontaneously and voluntarily, to work together, without an external control agenda. Forms vary from comfortable activities, such as sharing ideas and materials, to more rigorous forms, including mutual observation and focused reflective enquiry.
- Contrived collegiality – in contrast, teachers' collaborative working relationships are compulsorily imposed by administrators. Fixed times and places may be set for collaboration, for example planning meetings during preparation time. The intention of such collegiality is that its outcomes are predictable, although this cannot always be guaranteed.
- Balkanization – in this form of collaboration, teachers are neither isolated nor work as a whole school. Smaller groups form, for example within secondary school departments, between infant and junior teachers, primary and junior divisions, class teachers and resource support teachers, or teaching and non-teaching staff. Small-group collaboration *per se* is not a problem. Balkanized cultures, however, are characterized by insulation of subgroups from each other; little movement between them; strong identification – for example, seeing oneself as a primary teacher or chemistry teacher, and with views of learning associated with that subgroup; and by concern with micropolitical issues of status, promotion, and power dynamics.

Hargreaves' fifth cultural form is proposed to meet the needs of restructured schools and the postmodern world:

- The moving mosaic – drawing on Toffler's (1990) metaphor, Hargreaves promotes the notion of teachers flexibly and creatively engaged in different problem-solving tasks. Their orientation is one of continuous learning and improvement. They are characterized by collaboration, opportunism, adaptable partnerships and alliances. Thus membership of groups overlaps and shifts over time to meet the needs of the circumstance and context.

This model focuses on teacher cultures. What of other subcultures? The specific role of pupils in school culture is neglected in much of the literature.

While pupils have been questioned on what they think of school, little is known about what they think about educational change. They can, however, be a block to change if they do not understand the reason for it or are given no involvement in the decision-making process (Sarason 1990). Rudduck (1991) cautions:

> where innovations fail to take root in schools and classrooms, it may be because pupils are guardians of the existing culture, and as such represent a powerful conservative force, and that unless we give attention to the problems that pupils face, we may be overlooking a significant feature of the innovation process.
>
> (p. 57).

Adolescents, in particular, can form their own subcultures, related to key facets of their current state of development. These can include physical, emotional, social and intellectual changes; the need to belong to a peer group; conflicts, inconsistencies and alienation as they face new possible identities and values; a need for independence; a concern with and need to cope with complexities of the wider world surrounding them; gender, ethnic and social class influences; and reactions of adults to them (Hargreaves *et al.* 1996). Consideration of cultural change neglects pupil subcultures at its peril.

How does cultural change happen?

Cultural change occurs in different ways and for different reasons. Rossman and colleagues (1988) identify three cultural change processes that represent a continuum according to the degree of explicit, conscious focus on cultural change. *Evolutionary* change is implicit, unconscious and unplanned. Over time, norms, values and beliefs are introduced as others steadily fade. *Additive* change may or may not be explicit, as norms, beliefs and values become suddenly modified when new initiatives are introduced. *Transformative* change, in contrast, is explicit and conscious, with deliberate attention to changing norms, values and beliefs. In terms of planned effectiveness and improvement efforts, cultural change is likely to be of the second or third kind. The school that decides to embark on a particular improvement project or to introduce a specific teaching strategy may find itself involved in additive change. Frequently, however, school improvement efforts only focus on change of behaviours or technology and, therefore, do not touch the cultural core of the school. If a conscious decision has been made to work on participants' cultural norms and assumptions, however, transformative change is more likely to occur. Transformative change might also result from the actions of a new principal or unsuccessful result of an inspection. The age of the organization can equally affect cultural change. The developmental stage of the organization and the degree to which it is 'unfrozen' and ready to change underpin the perspective taken by Schein (1985), who identifies three significant developmental periods in the life of an organization. Whilst Schein's work is based on business organizations, parallels can be drawn with educational organizations. Depending on the growth stage, cultural function changes, as do mechanisms likely to bring about change.

Birth and early growth

In the early years of a new school dominant values emanate from its founders and the school makes its culture explicit. It clarifies its values, finds and articulates a unique identity and shares these with newcomers, whether teachers, pupils or parents. Culture is the glue that holds everyone together, and can be seen as a positive development force. As time passes, the culture moves into a succession phase where differences occur between conservative and liberal forces and new people take leadership roles. Four possible change mechanisms are identified during birth and early growth:

- Natural evolution – similar to evolutionary cultural change, refinement and development naturally occur, and adaptations are made to meet the needs of the particular pupil intake.
- Self-guided evolution – the self-motivated school in particular engages in self-assessment to identify the strengths and weaknesses of its culture. If high motivation exists, considerable shifts in beliefs can occur, but 'organizations sometimes have to get into real trouble, however, before they recognize their need for help' (Schein 1985: 280).
- Managed evolution through hybrids – accepted insiders with slightly different values take on new leadership roles, for example the assistant principal becomes principal or a respected teacher is appointed assistant principal.
- Managed 'revolution' through outsiders – particularly relevant in struggling and strolling schools, where a new principal with new values is hired. This, of course, is no easy task because structures, recurring processes, age-old symbols and myths have to be weakened before a new leader can introduce their own values.

Midlife

The school is well established but must continue on a path of growth and renewal. Changes may have occurred to its external and internal contexts, altering strengths and weaknesses. The most important aspects of the culture are now embedded and taken for granted, and culture is increasingly implicit. Subcultures have also sprung up. 'Unfreezing' occurs if the school in some way does not meet its goals or if rivalries develop between subgroups. Change becomes much more difficult because of less consciousness of the culture; it is harder to articulate and understand. None the less, this is the phase when careful internal diagnosis and understanding of cultural issues bears most fruit. Within midlife four different change mechanisms might operate:

- Planned change and organization development – use of an organizational development approach to deal with conflicts between and among various subgroups and culture founders.
- Technological seduction – additive and transformative processes are relevant, as new materials or schemes are introduced either as part of a general improvement effort or, specifically, to change teacher behaviour causing re-examination of beliefs and values.
- Change through scandal, explosion of myths – if a school develops myths and stories about the way it operates, conflicting with what actually occurs, reality could be exposed by external events or internal leaks. The precipitated crisis forces participants to re-examine values.
- Incrementalism – consistent use is made of every opportunity and decision to influence the school in a particular direction. Changes are slow and incremental.

Maturity and/or stagnation and decline

This stage is most problematical from the cultural change perspective. It is reached if the school has ceased to grow and respond to its environment, for example, sinking and cruising schools. Dysfunctional elements have surfaced, but challenge of old assumptions is resisted. Change processes in this situation become more radical and complex:

- Coercive persuasion – 'the right incentives' are used to make it hard for certain teachers to leave. Meanwhile old values are consistently challenged, and rewards and support given to those who take on new assumptions. 'If psychological safety is sufficient, members of the group can begin to examine and possibly give up some of their cognitive defenses' (Schein 1985:294).
- Turnaround – many of the other mechanisms are combined, once the school has been coercively persuaded to understand the difficulties associated with past values, norms and actions. Turnaround requires participation of all groups; again, psychological safety is important.
- Reorganization and rebirth – this represents the traumatic process of school closure, by which it is assumed that the old culture will be destroyed. If a new school was to open, participants would start to build a culture of their own.

Which cultural norms underpin successful school improvement?

Another route into understanding school culture is through exploring cultural norms (Saphier and King 1985), one of the pieces that make up the culture puzzle. Because basic assumptions and values are so deep-seated, it is hard to uncover them. If we peel off the next layer of the onion, norms, we see they underlie most aspects of behaviour in schools. If norms are an expression of deeply held values and influence workplace action, it would be fruitful to consider norms that appear to underpin more successful improvement efforts. From our experience in Britain and Canada, and from our understanding of the literature, we propose ten cultural norms that influence school improvement. To a great extent they are interconnected and feed off each other. Many are also basic to human rights of equity and respect. They do not just represent a snapshot of an effective school that it is impossible to emulate if you are currently in a struggling school. They focus on fundamental issues of how people relate to and value each other. Because norms are frequently unspoken, we have added catchphrases to articulate their core messages.

1 *Shared goals – 'we know where we're going'*

A shared sense of direction places teaching, learning and pupils' interests front and centre, and drives everyone in the school to pursue the same vision. Rosenholtz (1989) claims:

> If there is any centre to the mystery of schools' success, mediocrity, or failure, it lies deep within the structure of organizational goals: whether or not they exist, how they are defined and manifested, the extent to which they are mutually shared. Indeed, the hallmark of any successful organization is a shared sense among its members about what they are trying to accomplish.
>
> (p. 13)

Such a shared sense can only be derived from ongoing talk among participants about what is important and from value clarification, leading to a common understanding and language. Louis and colleagues (1995) argue that shared norms and values 'are the bedrock upon which all other aspects of professional community are built' (p. 28). Halton teachers discussed the importance in their school of having a joint focus, and how it brought with it a sense of security and self-efficacy: 'if you don't do something as a group, then chances are you may be all going off in different directions and you don't have a common goal' (teacher interview). 'Because . . . if we have a focus – a goal that we can see ahead of us – the things we do daily will have more meaning' (teacher interview). Examination of values and purposes that leads to goal setting, however, is not a one-off event, but part of an ongoing process of self-evaluation and development.

2 Responsibility for success – 'we must succeed'

There is a belief that everyone can and must make a difference, underpinned by a fundamental tenet of school effectiveness: all children can learn. Joyce and Murphy (1990) highlight the danger inherent in disbelief:

> The frustration in Ron Edmonds' famous question, 'How many do you have to see?' may point to some of the real issues in the struggle to change the culture of the school. School improvement efforts depend on the belief that curriculum, instruction, and social climate affect student learning. If the culture of a school is permeated with a belief that the causes of student learning lie largely outside the school, in the genes and social background of the students, school improvement efforts may appear hopeless and even ridiculous.
>
> (p. 248)

The all-too-common reaction to difficulty within an improvement effort – a tendency to give up, back off or assume that the innovation is bad and that it would be better to try something different – is combated. Responsibility for making a difference is also tied to a personal sense of accountability rather than perceived external accountability, but is made more powerful by the collegial belief of 'being in it together', leading to collective responsibility (Louis *et al.* 1995). This responsibility is also communicated:

> The kids know that on all levels we support them and we expect the best from them and we give them the best that we have. Parents know that. The parents get a report card every six weeks at this school. Teachers are in contact quite frequently with parents and home either over marks or over attendance so they know that the teachers' interest is definitely there.
>
> (teacher interview)

Pupil success becomes paramount, and linked to high expectations. Teachers convey to pupils their belief in pupils' ability to learn and challenge them with appropriate teaching strategies.

3 Collegiality – 'we're working on this together'

'. . . difficult to spell, hard to pronounce, harder to define' (Barth 1990: 30), this much-used but complex concept involves mutual sharing and assistance, an orientation towards the school as a whole, and is spontaneous, voluntary, development-orientated, unscheduled and unpredictable. Little (1990) identifies four types of collegial relations, the first three of which she views as weak forms: scanning and storytelling, help and assistance, and sharing. It is the fourth form, joint work, that is most likely to lead to improvement. Examples of joint work include team teaching, mentoring, action research, peer coaching, planning and mutual observation and feedback. These derive their strength from the creation of greater interdependence, collective commitment, shared responsibility, and review and critique.

In a London secondary school, collegiality underpins a cooperative group learning project:

> In a sense our main aim is to change our classroom practice supported by our colleagues, and as a major part of that we want to be able to observe each other in the classroom, to be able to have someone who can be what we are calling a 'reflective friend' to whom you can talk afterwards about the things that went well, the things that didn't go so well.
>
> (teacher interview)

4 Continuous improvement – 'we can get better'

No matter how effective the school is deemed to be, there is an assumption that more can always be achieved. Collegiality, *per se*, is seen as insufficient. Teachers constantly seek and try out potentially better practices, 'pursuing connections between teaching and learning with aggressive curiosity and healthy scepticism rather than taking as self-evidently effective tactics that sustain some measure of interest, achievement, and decorum among a reasonably large number of students' (Little 1982: 339). Innovation does not, however, occur simply for its own sake. One Halton elementary teacher reflected: 'The people here are up on research; they are using current ideas; they try new things. There is a lot of very good modelling. . . and everyone is looking at how they themselves could get better and not how the system could treat them better' (teacher interview).

Continuous improvement also involves understanding that there are, and should be, 'down times'; it is not necessary or wise to develop everything all of the time.

5 Lifelong learning – 'learning is for everyone'

There is a fundamental belief that learning never stops; there is always more to learn and pupils can only learn alongside adults who also learn, because 'When teachers stop growing, so do their students' (Barth 1990: 50). The initiative for learning comes from the teachers themselves, as in this interview with a teacher about her colleagues: 'There has been a large emphasis on trying to improve our instruction techniques through cooperative group learning . . . that was a case of teachers who decided that they wanted to learn more'.

Frequently the learning is school based and involves teachers sharing areas of expertise with colleagues, which challenges them to consider their own ways of working:

> The presentation we're doing tomorrow is essentially how to create a workable group atmosphere, how to be evaluated, how to set up groups, how to monitor groups' progress and individuals', so it is very much instruction-oriented . . . It has helped me to better articulate my beliefs on student evaluation for myself as well, and to slow down and rethink the stages that you go through.
>
> (Halton teacher interview)

6 Risk taking – 'we learn by trying something new'

Experimentation, trial and error and learning through failure are essential parts of growing. A teacher at Sedgemoor describes how 'In the other schools I've taught in you didn't fail' (Nias *et al.* 1989: 68). There is always an element of uncertainty when trying out a new practice or strategy, and a distinct possibility that it will not work. If there is no safety net that 'it's OK if you don't get it right', it becomes too risky to shift from tried and tested, faithful old practices to something new. Psychological safety plays an important role here, particularly in schools facing difficulties. The ability to admit to oneself and to colleagues that a particular lesson, session or course needs adaptation is important, as is feeling safe, as one of the London teachers involved in joint observation attested: 'A "reflective friend" is someone who you can feel safe with, you can describe things to, and hopefully they're going to be able to give you some sort of support or criticism which is going to allow you to develop' (interview).

The principal can play a role by encouraging and modelling risk taking. One Halton elementary school was let down by an external facilitator at its professional development retreat. The principal persuaded the staff development committee to organize and run the event themselves. Subsequent reports from other teachers suggested greater benefits were derived from this experience than if an external person had organized the retreat.

7 Support – 'there's always someone there to help'

While collegiality refers to work-related interdependence, this norm is more concerned with personal availability, kindness and caring, where teachers and administrators make time for each other, even when very busy. Several principals explained how they took all paperwork home to be available to teachers during the day. We all know individuals who, despite being busy, seem to have time for other people. In some schools this is much more the norm than in others. Giving time, the ability to listen and the public visibility of the principal and vice-principal were viewed as important by Halton teachers:

> If you need to see her [principal], she's there right away . . . She's always there when you need her. She's a good listener and she's very supportive.

> (teacher interview)

> — was the first principal I ever saw at football games that I coached. He tries to show up at some of these important events and — [vice-principal] has always been supportive because of her involvement with the community and the library and — [vice-principal] was good that way too. When they were around they tried to be visible and promote things and support things. That helps the atmosphere of the school, no question about it.

> (teacher interview)

8 Mutual respect – 'everyone has something to offer'

Diversity is perceived as a strength; there is freedom for individuals to realize shared goals in different ways. Groupthink (Fullan and Hargreaves 1991) is discouraged and people listen to each other. In British primary schools where individuals were valued 'as people', Nias and colleagues (1989) found respect had many guises, including a lack of status consciousness, opportunity for newcomers to be heard, right to privacy, tolerance, sympathy, consideration and out-of-school relationship networks. In addition, differences between people were seen as 'a mutually enriching source of strength' (p. 57). In more successful Halton schools, the respect of the principal for teachers appeared to be vital:

> She shows that she cares about her staff and the commitment and effort and time that is put into our teaching. I have never worked for anyone like her and I think she is terrific. She really makes you feel that what you do is important.

> (teacher interview)

> He has a lot of really good and talented people on staff, and he allows them to be that way.

> (teacher interview)

The development of a high level of trust is also linked to respect, and respect for pupils is a norm. One Halton secondary teacher described the president of the student council who runs the most efficient meetings of any person I've ever seen and so I watched him for the first two or three meetings and picked up all kinds of tips, so from my point of view it was like sitting in another class and watching a teacher who was an expert manage a group.

(teacher interview)

9 Openness – 'we can discuss our differences'

The ability to speak one's mind and voice concerns publicly in school rather than outside in the car park is valued. Criticism is viewed as an opportunity for self-improvement rather than a threat; negative emotions and dis-agreements are an acceptable part of adult communication. Teacher disagreement is critical in a collegial support group. This is when learning takes place and people's paradigms are challenged: 'This school, before I got here, would never listen to criticism of this place . . . Just the opposite should be happening. We should be encouraging so that we hear it, channel it, and then respond to it' (Halton principal interview).

10 Celebration and humour – 'we feel good about ourselves'

Recognition of pupils and adults and celebration are highlighted, and teachers talk of feeling valued. In several Halton schools, flowers, thank-you notes, food at staff meetings and professional development activities, public and private recognition and 'treats' are frequent occurrences:

> This is the first school I have been at where there are continuing notes of appreciation, some recognition for the fact that you . . . have worked hard at something. I find the staff happier than they were.
>
> (teacher interview)

> He [principal] is very aware of saying and doing things that make you feel good about your job, and makes you feel good about being here.
>
> (teacher interview)

People also enjoy each other's company, and celebrations provide opportunities to focus on key values:

> One of the things that's really special to this school is how positive people are with the children. It's something that we've developed because it works and children like to know that they're cared about, and on a Monday morning we celebrate that side of things and that assembly celebrates what we feel in this school is really important, which is being positive about children.
>
> (British primary headteacher interview)

Humour serves many purposes in schools (Nias *et al.* 1989). It reduces tension, maintains a sense of belonging, highlights shared meanings, enables difficult issues to be openly discussed and, at a basic level, can make work and collaboration fun:

> It's a very personal place, a very upbeat place. Humour is rampant and I believe that is a very important strength or characteristic. I think that makes all the other things easier.
>
> (Halton teacher interview)

> It's a family. There's a lot of humour, a lot of kidding around, and this goes from the custodian to the secretaries.
>
> (Halton teacher interview)

How do these norms relate to more and less effective schools?

All schools are unique and may possess few, some or all of these norms. Furthermore, in balkanized schools some subcultures may emulate norms foreign to other subcultures. It is only through consideration of its individual circumstances and context that any particular school might identify which norms have more significance. The ultimate aim of any school should be that practice be underpinned by all of these norms. We would anticipate, however, that those with an interest in the improvement of struggling schools would focus initially on development of different norms than those in strolling schools, and that these, again, would vary from those in moving schools. In the next chapter, we propose several structural changes leaders might make in different types of schools. Here, we discuss further approaches to changing cultural norms. Work on the norms of school culture in any school, of course, occurs concurrently with work on structures and conditions of improvement.

Moving schools – all norms influence the school's work. Goals are regularly re-examined to ensure they meet the needs of pupils and a changing external environment. New ways of teaching are practised in an environment of trust, collegiality and support. Increasingly, risks are taken as input and reactions to the learning process are sought from pupils, parents and other partners. External inspections are viewed as confirmation, feedback and further growth opportunities. The hiring process can also be used to ensure that newcomers understand and are committed to the espoused values of those within the school.

Cruising schools – such schools do not demonstrate they have added significant value to their pupils. In this sense, they share many similarities with strolling schools. Ongoing discussions are needed to clarify goals, with specific reference to the needs of current society and employers. Complacency, a danger in 'effective' schools, could not occur if norms of continuous improvement, lifelong learning and risk taking were embedded. Ways to enhance these, therefore, are particularly important, as is assurance that teachers respect what pupils bring to the learning process. Academic results are disaggregated for different groups of pupils to demonstrate any inequities in opportunity to learn.

Strolling schools – some people-related norms might need further examination and promotion. At this stage attention is focused particularly on clarification of a shared direction that emphasizes need for continuous improvement and adult learning, through collegial efforts, backed by supportive colleagues. Gradually, teachers are encouraged to take more risks and experiment with new ideas, in particular those that promote self-reflection. Teachers more comfortable with such ways of working are supported as they increasingly open their classrooms up to colleagues' scrutiny. Particular attention is paid to understanding of pupil cultures and how they might be addressed to enhance participation. Celebration is ongoing. Opportunities for professional development are offered and timetables adapted to enable people to work together.

Struggling schools – people-related norms are a particularly important first step, emphasizing respect, celebration and support, in order to rebuild trust, confidence and self-efficacy, leading to greater openness. Concurrently, a bolstering of ideas around responsibility for success and high expectations occurs. There is a gradual increase in discussion about values related to teaching and learning. Where 'moving' subcultures exist, participants are reinforced and supported in development or maintenance of the more learning-orientated norms, and encouraged in attempts to draw in other colleagues, and given time to work with each other.

Sinking schools – similar to struggling schools, but the first steps take longer. Any learning achievements are celebrated. In-class support is offered to any teacher who wishes it. 'Moving' subcultures are encouraged and enabled to continue developing.

What are the implications for changing school culture?

From the previous discussion, it can be seen that culture is extremely subtle and yet powerful in the way it permeates the life of a school. So how do you go about trying to change school culture? We already know that culture is not fixed and that it is intertwined with amendable structures, so should culture be approached through restructuring? The unsatisfactory answer is, it all depends, because schools differ from each other in so many ways that 'standardized formulas make no sense' (Lieberman 1990: 532).

Practical guidance is offered by Deal and Kennedy (1983), who propose three steps for schools that take into account their individual nature:

1 Get to know your culture – ask teachers, pupils, parents, non-teaching staff and other involved participants what the school really stands for; note how people spend their time; find out who are the heroines, spies and other roles in the cultural network, and reflect on the values they represent.
2 Consider how the school culture encourages or inhibits pupil progress, development and achievement, and the accomplishment of school goals. Examine people's values to see whether they are the same or whether there is a mismatch between groups.
3 Arrange opportunities where people can discuss and re-examine their values.

This third step appears simple, but is frequently neglected. Structures can be adapted, but without concurrent discussion about values, change is likely to be superficial. One of us was working with the entire staff of a traditional secondary school to discuss the results of effective school questionnaires completed by teachers, students and parents. As they encountered differences in response both within and between groups, highlighted in step two above, they were forced to confront their own values and assumptions about school and teaching processes and relationships. Several longstanding teachers commented that this was the first time they had discussed such issues.

Conclusion

Fullan (1991) argues that 'educational change depends on what teachers do and think – it's as simple and as complex as that' (p. 117). What they do and think is fundamentally influenced by their beliefs, assumptions and values, which in turn shape norms. In terms of change, underlying values are much more difficult to reach than surface behaviours, and yet it is vital to understand them and how they motivate norms and actions. This is particularly important in that norms, beliefs and values also influence teachers' perceptions and definitions of what it means to be effective. Culture, therefore, defines effectiveness (Rossman *et al.* 1988). The leadership of the principal in shaping culture is highly significant. Our next chapter examines leadership for changing schools.

seven

INVITATIONAL
LEADERSHIP

Good leadership is one of the key features of successful schools. This has been emphasised time and again . . . It has always been the case, particularly in Britain where heads have a powerful role, but the major changes which are affecting schools will make even more significant demands.

(National Commission on Education 1993: 229)

There is no shortage of similar statements extolling the need for quality leadership for schools of the future. There is, however, considerable disagreement as to what is good leadership. Do good leaders attend primarily to forces of continuity or forces of change? Are good leaders effective managers, change agents, leaders of the educational programme, politicians, facilitators, supervisors, administrators, moral authorities? Do good leaders share leadership with others? The answer is probably, 'yes, but it depends on the circumstances'. Our experience in attempting to bring about change suggests that effective leadership is a key determinant in deciding whether anything positive happens in a school or a school system (Stoll and Fink 1988, 1989, 1994). We have arrived at a place in our own thinking, however, which suggests that traditional descriptions of leadership which tend to sort leaders into categories or typologies are inappropriate for the postmodern age and the challenges it brings to educational leaders.

In this chapter, we first look at society's ambivalence towards leadership and how it has affected education. We then briefly outline how research in school effectiveness and school improvement has contributed to an evolving concept of leadership, with particular emphasis on the leadership of the school principal. We end the chapter by adding to this leadership dialogue by suggesting that changing social forces will require a reconceptualization of leadership. We offer a leadership model which focuses on the humanistic side of education rather than one which merely promotes a bureaucratic corporate agenda designed to promote individualism, competition and standardization. Our model, we believe, is appropriate for leadership at all levels, both formal and informal.

The leadership paradox

To the paradoxes we have described previously, we now add the leadership paradox. There is an abundance of literature which describes types of leaders necessary to lead western societies into the twenty-first century. The new leader is an entrepreneur, a risk taker and a visionary who inspires loyalty and commitment while 'managing by walking around' (Bennis and Nanus, 1985). Management advice is one of the fastest-growing information fields in many countries. Management gurus receive huge per diem rates to share their wisdom with managers around the world.

Ironically, at a time when so much time, energy and money is being expended on promoting new conceptions of leadership, the public appears to hold a profound distrust, if not antipathy, towards many of its leaders. In the face of incomprehensible changes, people find their leaders impotent to resolve pressing issues. Saul (1993) argues that this cynicism is produced by bureaucratic élites who control most leadership roles in the public and private sectors in western societies and, therefore, control the real power in society. These anonymous and rather faceless technocrats, he contends, confront the forces of postmodernity armed with the philosophy and techniques of modernity. This is the leadership paradox.

Using the obscurantist language of expertise, and their skills of intrigue and manoeuvre, these élites have successfully clouded citizens' understanding of the issues in the name of rational problem solving. In the process, other ways of knowing – creativity, imagination, history and intuition – are demeaned. Bewildered as these corporate-thinking leaders are by forces they do not understand, they look for scapegoats for their own failures. Schools have become easy and safe targets.

This interest in education has produced a new fundamentalism supported by corporations and political and religious élites which holds, as an article of faith, that schools, and particularly state schools, have failed. To succeed, educational leaders must adopt business strategies, market measures and focus on the bottom line. While the evidence that these strategies improve schools is far from compelling, evidence is really unnecessary because the agenda has now become an article of faith. The historian Barbara Tuchman's (1984) description of Philip II of Spain captured this leadership mind-set. 'No experience of the failure of his policy could shake his belief in its essential excellence' (p. 7).

Giroux (1992) describes this position when he states:

> There is a strong propensity in this view of leadership to abstract leadership from ethical responsibility, to subordinate basic human needs to narrow market measures, and to downplay the importance of creating support systems that name, address, and help students who are caught in the spiraling web of unemployment, poverty, racial discrimination, and institutional abuse.
>
> (p. 7).

Traditional leadership at the school and district level has often mirrored this technocratic model and has, unfortunately, proven incapable of responding to the legitimate concerns of parents and the community about what and why things are happening in schools. Attempts to respond to this community unease through policies of decentralization and school-based management have obliged leaders to operate from a 'political model' (Sackney and Dibski 1994). When one adds the challenges of direct political involvement at the school level, reduced budgets, the changing demographics of schools resulting from inclusionary policies for special needs and socially maladaptive students, *and* the demands created by centralized curriculum and assessment policies to the already burdensome load of system and school leaders, the need to reconceptualize leadership becomes crucial.

Conceptions of leadership

Busher and Saran (1994) provide a succinct and useful summary of five leadership models which have at various times influenced thinking about leadership. These paradigms provide a context for a discussion of a leadership model which we suggest will travel well into the 1990s and beyond:

- Structural functional – the traditional rational model which focuses on roles, role differentiation and hierarchical structures. Senior managers define the purposes of the organization, mobilize support for the directions, and make sure everyone is 'marching to the same drummer'.
- Open systems – focusing on 'the effect of the sociopolitical environment on the organization and how this is accommodated by boundary management' (p. 5). The role of the formal leader is to mobilize subordinates to achieve organizational goals.
- Cultural pluralism – attempting to shape people's personal and professional values to organizational policy development, leaders promote –

or, to the more cynical, manipulate – the culture to achieve organizational goals.

● Interpersonal – a derivative of the cultural model, leaders in this model use interpersonal skills to build a consensus in support of organizational goals. The key to leadership is the development of followership (Kouzis and Posner 1987). This is usually the style of the very charismatic leader.

● Political – leadership is observed from a micropolitical perspective. The leader in this model is somewhat of a broker between and among various internal and external political forces.

While agreement on the importance of leadership to effective schools is a consistent feature of British and American school effectiveness literature, there is limited agreement among researchers and policy makers as to which of these models is most appropriate to develop effective schools. An American government publication states that effective principals:

> scrutinize existing practices to assure that all activities and procedures contribute to the quality of the time available for learning. They make sure teachers participate actively in the process . . . effective principals are experts at making sure time is available to learn, and at ensuring that teachers and students make the best use of that time.
>
> (United States Department of Education 1987: 64)

This is a control and direct structural functional model of leadership. Frederick Taylor and other proponents of scientific management would applaud. It is the leader's vision; he obliges compliance; he ensures participation. We choose the pronoun 'he' purposely, because most leadership research, until recent years, has looked at men's behaviour. Individualism, competitiveness, and self-actualization are important components of the model which has enabled males to progress in organizational hierarchies. Prior to the 1980s, to succeed, women had to demonstrate to male superiors their ability to make tough decisions and be more efficient than male counterparts. This model of leadership suggests that teachers, like children, must be directed, influenced and, if necessary, coerced. Behind this view is an implied hint of sanctions for non-conformers. The focus is on outputs, 'the bottom line', as measured by 'intellectual accounting methods', standardized tests.

Instructional leadership

Mortimore and colleagues (1988) describe the purposeful leadership of the staff by the headteacher as one of the key factors in school effectiveness in British junior schools:

Purposeful leadership occurred where the headteacher understood the needs of the school and was involved actively in the school's work, without exerting total control over the rest of the staff . . . effective headteachers were sufficiently involved in, and knowledgeable about what went on in classrooms and about the progress of individual pupils.
(pp. 250–1).

This research began to view the leader as an instructional leader who could work with teachers to promote classroom learning. Smith and Andrews (1989) took this concept further and determined that instructional leaders possessed four sets of competencies: the leader as a 'resource provider', an 'instructional resource', a 'communicator' and a 'visible presence'.

Transactional leadership

This evolving leadership model is what Leithwood and others would call transactional. In this open systems model, leadership is:

based on an exchange of services (from a teacher, for example) for various kinds of rewards (salary, recognition, intrinsic rewards) that the leader controls, at least in part. Transactional leadership practices some claim, help people recognize what needs to be done in order to reach a desired outcome and may also increase their confidence and motivation.
(Leithwood 1992: 9)

The emphasis on transactional leadership is primarily about management of school structure. It involves focusing on purposes of the organization, developing plans, ensuring task completion, facilitating information flow, and working well with the various school groups, particularly teachers. These factors are necessary to maintain effectiveness. Many effective leaders in our work carry out these continuity functions very well. When the purposes of change are clearly defined, such as a curriculum modification, a procedural change, or the introduction of a new textbook, transactional leaders are very effective.

There is, however, a great deal of murkiness and confusion created by international restructuring or reform movements. Complex changes – such as market-driven policies designed to improve standards, site-based management, elaborate testing procedures, teaching for understanding and school councils – have not only energized schools and leaders but also brought confusion, tensions and instability (Her Majesty's Inspectorate 1992). In this postmodern climate of diversity, complexity, indeterminacy and instability, '"commitment" rather than "control" strategies are called for' (Leithwood 1993: 5).

Transformational leadership

This view suggests that transformational leadership, rather than transactional leadership, is the leadership style of choice in unstable and uncertain times. Such leadership

> arises when leaders are more concerned about gaining overall co-operation and energetic participation from organization members than they are in getting particular tasks performed . . . effective leadership requires an approach that transforms the feelings, attitudes, and beliefs of their followers . . . Transformational leaders are 'people oriented'; rather than focus on tasks and performance, they build relationships and help followers develop goals and identify strategies for their accomplishment.
>
> (Mitchell and Tucker 1992: 32)

This model of cultural pluralism is more consistent with school improvement literature and its emphasis on process and school culture. Successful principals exhibit a feel for the change process, engage teacher commitment to a shared vision, and model their cultural beliefs through leadership by example. Transformational leaders not only manage the structure; they purposefully impact the culture to achieve school development.

Conceptually, we see an evolving concept of leadership in which managerial or instrumental approaches to leadership are superseded by transactional or instructional leadership to be subsumed within a construct called transformational leadership. While these conceptions of leadership are the subjects of research and journal articles, reality in schools is significantly different. Southworth (1994), observing leadership in British primary schools, concluded: 'While these categories help us to classify heads as transactional or transformational, they do not capture the character and nature of leadership in action. They are too abstract and omit the vigorous quality of headteachers at work' (p. 18).

The reality

Research conducted in Ontario secondary schools by King and his colleagues (1988) supports Southworth's views, painting a very different picture of leadership from that of the image of the instructional or transformational leader. Principals reported that they spent over 30 per cent of their time in administrative tasks, disciplining students and looking after the physical plant. They spent only six per cent of their time in curriculum planning. When asked the most stressful aspects of the job a principal replied: 'Expectations in terms of the number of things one is expected to do and be expert in exceed the amount of time available' (p. 71). Another indicated that stress came from 'dealing with "burned out" teachers near retirement' (p. 71). Yet another principal expressed concern with 'staffing in a situation of declining enrolment; inadequate staff to deal with a student body with vastly increased personal and social problems' (p. 71).

What emerges is a picture of school leaders who must staff schools, meet pupils' needs, attend to staff personal and professional problems, keep open lines of communications to parents and the community and, of course, handle the paperwork, all within the constraints of time and energy. We see evidence of the interpersonal and political models of leadership described previously. Much of the principal's time appears to be consumed by necessary maintenance or continuity issues. Management issues do not go away.

Bennis and Nanus (1985) have discriminated between managers and leaders. 'Managers are people who do things right and leaders are people who do right things' (p. 21). Managers operate from a transactional stance and leaders from a transformational stance. These dichotomies, as the preceding discussion suggests, fail to capture the role of educational leaders in the past and certainly the type of leadership required in the future. Effective educational leaders attend to both structure and culture, continuity and change; they are both managers and leaders; they are both transactional and transformational. It would appear that no single leadership model adequately describes the expectations and reality for contemporary educational leaders. Furthermore, because each school's culture is unique, being successful as a leader in one school does not automatically predict a similar experience in the leader's next appointment (Brighouse 1991).

Louis and Miles (1990) found that leadership and management are difficult to separate in the daily life of schools. They state that 'school administrators need both leadership and management skills to deal with change and "ordinary" circumstances' (p. 21). Indeed, often 'the seemingly ordinary and "little stuff" of management is the vehicle for the leader's messages' (Southworth 1994: 19).

Ball (1993) illustrates the impact of the corporate agenda on leaders in Britain:

> The time, energy and attention that headteachers now devote to the budget, income generation and public relations and the new employer/ employee relationship with teaching (and other) staff can seriously diminish the possibilities and viabilities of the head's educational leadership in the school.
>
> (p. 227).

While the models and conceptualizations of leadership described to this point have contributed significantly to our understanding of leadership, they provide little guidance to principals in dealing with the types of issues discussed by Ball, and the paradoxes we have described. What is required is a leadership model which synthesizes existing leadership models while providing sufficient scope to encourage the imagination, creativity and intuition of school leaders.

Invitational leadership

Reynolds and Packer (1992) refer to the failure to embrace psychology in school effectiveness research. Our view of leadership offers a conception based on the perceptual tradition of psychology. This tradition starts from the premiss that human behaviour is the product of how individuals view the world. Perceptual psychology sees each person as a conscious agent who gives meaning to sensory stimuli: 'These meanings extend far beyond sensory receptors to include such personal experiences as feelings, desires, aspirations, and the ways people view themselves, others, and the world' (Purkey and Schmidt 1987: 27).

Between interpretations of a stimulus and response, individuals have a conscious choice of how to behave, based on their knowledge and perceptions. To say, therefore, that one person can motivate another is to deny free will. A leader can create a context in which a person is inclined to act in preferred ways, but – from the perceptual point of view – cannot motivate someone, any more than one can oblige love or any other human emotion. When a person says, I am angry, or depressed, or exhilarated, or motivated, that person has chosen that response to a situation or context.

Viktor Frankl's (1984) inspiring book *Man's Search for Meaning* makes this point most poignantly. Frankl was a Jewish psychiatrist who, unlike his entire family, survived a Nazi concentration camp. He tells of men who gave their last morsel of bread so that others might survive. They too survived, whereas others who gave up on themselves and others died very quickly. From his experience he wrote:

> The experiences of camp life show that man [*sic*] does have a choice of action ... Man can preserve a vestige of spiritual freedom, of independence of mind, even in such terrible conditions of psychic and physical stress ... everything can be taken from a man but one thing: the last of the human freedoms – to choose one's attitude in any given set of circumstances, to choose one's own way.
>
> (p. 86)

We have the choice to act or react, to behave responsibly or irresponsibly. It is a far more accountable view of behaviour. We cannot blame others for our failures. The most important perception we develop is a perception of self. We develop this concept based on the myriad of positive and negative interactions we have with significant others over time. Since change in organizations is about change in people, attention to their perceptions of reality and particularly their sense of self is a key to successful 'change agentry' (Fullan 1993).

Purkey and Novak (1990) use the metaphor of an invitation or disinvitation to describe the positive and negative interactions which shape one's concept of self. People, they contend, behave in ways consistent with their concept of self, regardless of whether it is helpful or hurtful to themselves or others. Invitations, therefore, are messages communicated to people which inform them that they are able, responsible and worthwhile. Disinvitations are the messages to people, whether intentional or unintentional, which are uncaring, demeaning, devaluing, intolerant or discriminatory, and hurtful. Not only are invitations and disinvitations communicated through interpersonal interaction but also through institutional policies, programmes, practices and physical environments.

Leadership is about communicating invitational messages to individuals and groups with whom leaders interact in order to build and act on a shared and evolving vision of enhanced educational experiences for pupils. Invitational leadership is built on four basic premises. The first is *optimism*. People have untapped potential for growth and development. People need to be affirmed of their present worth and, under the right circumstances, can realize their potential. This view is not 'polyannish'. People choose their behaviours. The leader can, therefore, hold high expectations for others.

Secondly, leaders *respect* the individuality of each human being. This respect is manifested in such behaviours as civility, politeness, courtesy and caring (Purkey and Schmidt 1987). Respect manifests itself in the encouragement of vigorous discussion and dissent.

The ideal of a civil society within a school is built on the third component of the invitational stance, *trust*. Since humans are interdependent, trust becomes 'the highest form of human motivation' (Covey 1989: 178). If one accepts that behaviour is based on individual choices and people are able, worthwhile and responsible, then invitational leaders trust others to behave in concert with these preconceptions. In turn, invitational leaders through their relationships, policies and practices behave with integrity.

Invitational leaders operate from a purposefully invitational stance. Their actions are *intentionally* supportive, caring and encouraging. Their support, care and encouragement are not instrumental or situational to convince, coerce or manipulate preferred behaviours from others. Invitational leaders support policies, practices, programmes and structures, based on these principles, which intentionally create an environment and provide opportunities for all pupils to function fully as citizens in the postmodern world. To this end, we suggest that there are four categories of leadership activities which, when taken together, comprise invitational leadership.

Dimensions of invitational leadership

In our work with 83 Halton schools we have observed, talked to and worked with well over 100 school leaders. Relatively few leaders we observed could or would succeed in all settings within the system. There were, however, a significant number of principals in whom the senior management of the system had sufficient confidence to place them with any school in the assurance they would succeed.

These successful leaders functioned on a very clear set of principles or set of beliefs, which guided the choices that they made. Within our invitational philosophy, they had invited *themselves*, personally and professionally. They operated from an invitational stance of optimism, respect, trust and intentionality. In effect, they might have behaved situationally as a manager, facilitator, counsellor or change agent depending on circumstances, but they remained steadfast in their stance with themselves and others.

They also had developed the skills of communication, decision making, conflict resolution, among others, that enabled them to invite *others* both personally and professionally. More important, they had taken the time to understand the perceptions of others so that the invitations they offered were appropriate.

They lived by Covey's (1989) maxim, 'seek first to understand and then to be understood' (p. 235). In effect, these successful leaders employed many of the strategies described in the literature as instructional leadership or transformational leadership, but did so in ways which united colleagues in the pursuit of higher goals for themselves and their pupils. The invitational approach is open-ended. There is no fail-safe list of invitational strategies to invite others to do things differently. The following outline of the dimensions of invitational leadership provides an introduction to its possibilities.

Invitational leaders invite themselves personally

A common workshop strategy, which obliges people to address what they really cherish or value in their lives, is to ask participants to write their own obituary. They are first asked to imagine that they have six months to live and it is their task to arrange for speakers at their own funeral. Then they write what they would like a family member, a work colleague, a neighbour, a friend, or other people who represent their life's various roles to say about their lives. Finally, they are invited to think about how close what they have written fits with reality. The purpose is, of course, to have people see how balanced their life is. Few people on their death bed, for instance, say I wish I had spent more time at the office, but many leaders let office demands dominate other aspects of their lives. What this exercise does is to begin the process of developing a personal vision of what one would hope to be and to achieve, and at the same time initiates an internal dialogue about current reality.

Leaders, to invite others, must first invite themselves, physically, intellectually, socially, emotionally and spiritually. The challenge, when we all play so many roles, is to stay in balance as a professional, spouse, parent, citizen or community contributor. The leaders we observed who could succeed in any environment tended to be very 'centred' people. They had a realistic idea of who they were and what they wanted to achieve both personally and professionally. They reflected the strengths of the invitational approach in which each role in their lives was grounded in the four dimensions of optimism, trust, respect and intentionality.

Since we are the product of the interactions between our decisions and our conditions, we each invite ourselves by the kind of personal maps we develop. Senge (1990) talks about personal mastery as one of his five disciplines which contribute to learning organizations. A discipline is 'a series of practices and principles that must be applied to be useful' (p. 147). Personal mastery is the 'discipline of personal growth and learning' (p. 141). To invite ourselves personally we need a sense of purpose or a vision. George Bernard Shaw in the preface to *Man and Superman* (1946) expressed this idea:

> This is the true joy in life, the being used for a purpose recognized by yourself as a mighty one . . . the being a force of nature instead of a feverish, selfish little clot of ailments and grievances complaining that the world will not devote itself to making you happy.

A vision, as Block (1987) suggests, is a 'dream created in our waking hours' (p. 107) of a preferred future. Invitational leaders dream dreams of more beneficial futures for themselves and others. A corollary of a personal and professional vision is to have a very clear sense of reality. The gap between one's vision and one's knowledge of current reality can excite creative tension or, if too great or unrealistic, anxiety and psychological stress which leads to burn-out. The resolution of this tension, whether creative or pathological, is either to lower one's vision or move current reality towards the vision.

Leaders invite themselves personally by devising means to determine the truth about personal and professional relationships. Perhaps the easiest strategy is to ask a third party, who is trusted by the leader and the staff, to conduct a simple survey about the leader's behaviour which asks three questions: what should the leader stop doing? what should the leader continue to do? and what should the leader start to do? This can be a risky business. Given the opportunity the staff may, as in the fable, tell the emperor or empress that he or she is wearing no clothes.

An important personal invitation is to examine one's mental model. 'New insights fail to get put into practice because they conflict with deeply held images of how the world works, images that limit us to familiar ways of thinking and acting' (Senge 1990: 174).

We all carry mental models of how the world works. We have our rituals, our etiquettes and habits. Without them life could be rather bewildering. The problem arises when a person's model becomes the only one possible. A mental model or paradigm based on optimism, respect for others, trust and intentionality promotes shared visions and wise decisions.

To invite oneself personally, one must, as Fullan (1991) suggests, 'practise fearlessness and other forms of risk taking' (p. 167). We are not talking about stupid risks but, rather, calculated risks backed by personal competence. Block (1987) states that leadership choices are between maintenance and greatness, caution and courage, and dependence and autonomy. The successful leaders we observed had an uncanny sense of the moment. They seemed to know when to be cautious and when to be courageous. Perhaps as significant, they were well prepared before they practised 'greatness, courage and autonomy'. Part of that preparation was to mobilize the various stakeholders in the pursuit of common goals. This competence and preparation came from leaders who invited themselves professionally.

Invitational leaders invite themselves professionally

The professional obligation of each leader is to choose to grow professionally. Invitational leaders invite themselves professionally by reading, relating, reflecting and researching. Shaping one's professional vision and providing the leadership necessary to enrol others in the pursuit of a shared educational vision requires informed thought. The dramatic increase in the quality and quantity of educational research in the last ten years has challenged, in fact condemned, many of the accepted mental models of teaching and learning. Leaders, therefore, must stay current with the educational literature to have the credibility to promote organizational learning.

The well-known Peter principle postulates that you rise to your level of incompetence. There is corollary which has been called Paul's principle; if you were competent at one point in your career and you have failed to keep abreast of the changing nature of your job, then you become increasingly incompetent. If leaders, like schools, are not getting better, they are getting worse. There are too many examples in education, like most professions, in which people have 20 years of experience, which is in reality one year of experience repeated 20 times.

We learn powerfully from our peers. A basic principle of adult learning is that adults learn effectively in groups. Invitational leaders build networks through attendance at conferences and workshops, writing to colleagues and joining networks. Teachers' unions, principals' associations, leadership centres and curriculum councils are also useful avenues to make contacts which enable leaders to enhance their professional competence.

Reflective practice as popularized by Schön (1983, 1987) and others is also a vital part of inviting oneself professionally. Reflection is the practice or art of analysing one's actions, decisions or products by focusing on the process of achieving them. Meaningful reflection requires data or 'friendly facts' (Waterman 1988).

Senge (1990) uses the example of a frog to illustrate the need for constant reflection on practices. A frog, if placed in boiling water will immediately jump out. If, however, one places the frog in lukewarm water and gradually raises the temperature to boiling point, the frog will adapt until it becomes groggy and unable to jump out of the pot. Even though there are no restraints, the frog will sit in the water and boil to death. Invitational leaders remain aware of when the 'temperature' is changing by constantly monitoring the school's context. Leaders need answers to such questions as, what do colleagues, teachers, pupils and parents say about the leader's performance? What do the parents think of the leader's school?

A derivative and more in-depth form of reflection is research. Few teachers and principals actually undertake small-scale research projects in their school or classroom, but this is a useful way to direct or redirect practice. Action research by the school principal can prepare the leader professionally to respond to the real needs of the school and not just the issues of the most vocal.

Few leadership theories attend to the personal and professional preparation required to function in an unstable and often irrational environment. Most organizations spend little time or effort to help their leaders develop 'personal mastery' (Senge 1990).

Invitational leaders invite others personally

Preparedness for leadership roles through personal and professional invitations are fundamental to working effectively with others. Decentralization of responsibility will require principals to interact more intimately with a broader spectrum of involved and interested people. In addition to staff, pupils and parents, the principal will need to enrol business leaders, governors or school council members, local politicians and representatives of social agencies – to mention but a few – in support of a vision of school growth.

Naisbett and Aburdene predicted in *Megatrends 2000* (1990) that 'the most exciting breakthroughs of the twenty first century will occur not because of technology but because of an expanding concept of what it means to be human' (p. 16).

Leaders who invite others personally build the kind of relationships that create supportive school cultures and communities. It is the principal's and, through the principal, the school's responsibility to reach out to its various communities by listening to their voices and understanding and responding to their points of view. Invitational leaders, therefore, not only articulate a vision; they share power and authority in order to invite others to share and develop the dream.

Helgesen (1991) speaks of augmenting the concept of vision with that of voice. Vision is a one-way process. As a vision, it may exist alone in the mind of a single human being, but a voice requires someone to hear it. Voice, therefore, is interactive. The metaphor becomes more accurate if one considers vision as the ability to look into the distance and determine an appropriate path. Without the concept of voice, however, it becomes a solitary trip. Invitational leaders possess a vision and encourage voice. Helgesen advances the view that women leaders are more focused on people's perception than are men. One might argue that to invite others personally is to adopt a female style of leadership. Shakeshaft (1993b) summarizes a number of studies concerning differences between male and female leadership styles:

> Women spend more time with people, communicate more, care more about individual differences, are concerned more with teachers and marginal students, and motivate more than do men . . . Building community is an essential part of a woman administrator's style . . . Women involve themselves more with staff and students, ask for and get higher participation, and maintain more closely knit organisations than do men.
>
> (p. 49)

The leader, whether male or female, who is optimistic, respects others, trusts others and acts with intentionality builds the kind of relationships which result in truly collaborative school cultures.

Leadership is not just about leaders; it is about followers. As Franklin Roosevelt said after a public outcry in 1937 against his attempt to warn the United States of the threat of fascism, 'It's a terrible thing to look over your shoulder when you are trying to lead – and to find no one there' (Roosevelt public papers quoted in Leuchtenburg, 1963: 226).

Kouzis and Posner's (1987) research on what followers in the business community looked for in leaders included the following qualities in order of frequency of response: honesty, competence, forward looking and inspirational, which they define as inspiring confidence in the validity of the vision. The parallels to the 'dimensions' of invitational leadership are striking. Combining the research by Kouzis and Posner with the invitational stance, we have developed a sequential set of questions that leaders who intend to invite others personally must answer for the individuals in their various

Figure 7.1   Questions for invitational leaders

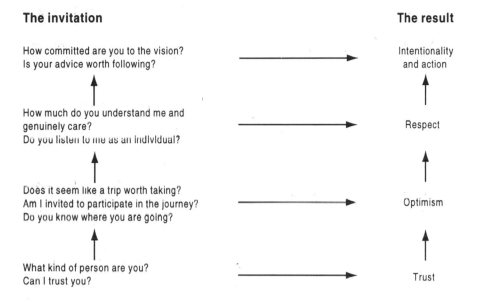

The invitation

How committed are you to the vision?
Is your advice worth following?

How much do you understand me and
genuinely care?
Do you listen to me as an individual?

Does it seem like a trip worth taking?
Am I invited to participate in the journey?
Do you know where you are going?

What kind of person are you?
Can I trust you?

The result

Intentionality
and action

Respect

Optimism

Trust

communities (see Figure 7.1). Regardless of the instability and irrationality of the postmodern age, the leader who can respond to these questions with integrity has the prerequisite qualities to invite others professionally.

Invitational leaders invite others professionally

The theory of invitational leadership presented here suggests personal and professional preparedness by leaders is a necessary precondition to their facilitating personal and professional growth in others. The nature of professional invitations varies depending on school context. Widcen (1994) points out that what contributes to change in any particular school depends on its own unique factors. To illustrate, we use the typology introduced in Chapter 6 to suggest some ways to invite professional growth in different contexts. This discussion makes two assumptions: first, the principal is not the source of the problem; second, the principal is prepared personally and professionally for the challenge.

Moving schools are both effective and improving. The most challenging aspect of leading moving schools is to maintain the momentum. It is easy to become complacent. Leaders must continue to invite pupils, teachers and the community with the ultimate view of developing shared leadership and interesting professional opportunities and challenges. The principal's role is more facilitative of others' leadership and concentrates on maintaining constancy of purpose and coherence of direction. Through staff development activities, staff mobility, evolutionary planning and constant monitoring of the school's context, the invitational leader helps the school to reinvent itself continually.

Cruising schools, ostensibly effective but declining, require a 'wake-up call'. Such schools often do not recognize the signs because the pupils usually perform well on tests and examinations. Cruising schools are in danger of becoming 'boiled frogs'. Most people think everything is 'just fine'. Leaders need to demonstrate through the analysis of value-added data that the school is not performing well for all pupils. Other data of the type mentioned in Chapter 11 will prove useful in checking current reality and getting people's attention. The initiation of staff development combined with the creation of a meaningful school development plan are important ways to stop the slide and recapture the culture of continuous improvement. Principals must be prepared to provide courageous leadership, and occasionally risk overt action to support the learning of all pupils. Such actions might include confronting unprofessional behaviour or poor teaching practices, changing teaching assignments, modifying timetables or arranging for outside support. The school cannot be allowed to slip into the ranks of the ineffective.

Strolling schools are neither particularly effective nor ineffective. They are improving but too slowly to keep up with the pace of change in their context. The leader must expect, express and model a vision of 'greatness' for the school. Average is not good enough. Pupils and their parents deserve better. Through staff development, rigorous school self-analysis, school development planning and other school improvement strategies, the leader accelerates the pace and the focus of change. If structures impede, change them. If individuals undermine the school, it is necessary to deal with them. Simply stated, the leader takes whatever principled actions are necessary to get the school moving.

Struggling schools have the will to change but not the skill. They are ineffective but trying to improve. By definition, they lack direction and planning. It is important, therefore, to start with small solvable problems. Usually schools will begin with management issues. Staff need to be involved in their resolution. Accomplishments should be celebrated before moving on to bigger issues. In the process, the leader works to shape directions through the discussion of vision and uses problem-solving teams to begin to build a more collaborative culture.

Sinking schools are ineffective and getting worse. A principal must be personally and professionally prepared for the challenge. Even the most dynamic principal will need help from governors or school councils, school districts or whatever other partners can contribute. The principal's ability to function politically will be crucial. A sinking school requires strong and rigorous intervention. The principal might ask such questions as: is the building an inviting place? Do the structures of the school, such as discipline, contribute to orderly functioning? Does the school have effective ways to communicate, resolve conflicts, make decisions? These are issues which can be resolved expeditiously. By listening to the concerns of pupils, teachers and parents, and by acting quickly on issues which are fully within the principal's control, the leader builds credibility and sends the message that 'things are changing for the better around here'. Once these basics are in place, then the strategies outlined for struggling and strolling schools may apply. In the last resort, however, truly desperate schools may require dramatic interventions such as an outside takeover or school closure as has been proposed in Britain.

In this chapter, we have tried to develop two themes. The first is that changing and unstable social forces which shape education require a style of leadership which is quite different from that which has been promoted in most educational jurisdictions. Second, we have proposed a leadership style more inclusive than the type currently described in the literature and which is more suited to the moral purposes that we have suggested will be required to assist teachers to teach and pupils to learn. It is to this teaching learning dynamic that we now turn.

eight

CHANGING CONCEPTS OF
TEACHING AND LEARNING

In Chapter 1, we attempted to frame several paradoxes that described the shifting contexts in which schools must operate. Our purpose was to suggest that for schools to do more of what they have always done is to prepare pupils for a world that is rapidly disappearing. There is a saying which describes this mind-set: 'if you always do what you have always done, you will always get what you have always got'. It is unacceptable, therefore, in democratic societies to limit the purposes of education to those learnings which meet the corporate agenda of political and economic élites. As educators we must try to ensure that reform efforts are consistent with our best knowledge about teaching and learning and our best insights into our pupils' needs in a postmodern age.

With so much activity worldwide in the name of educational reform, the very centrality of teaching and learning sometimes gets lost. In this chapter we address the *why* of educational reform, developments in teaching and learning for *all* pupils. To this end, we need to embrace a new, or at least emerging, paradigm of learning. To understand this paradigm it should be viewed in contrast to the traditional and generally accepted model of learning.

The traditional learning paradigm

The most significant ongoing challenge for teachers is the necessity to move from a teaching–learning paradigm or model which has served many teachers and pupils to a different conception which is compatible with the emerging issues of the new millennium.

As we suggested in Chapter 1, the evolution of comprehensive public schooling developed in concert with changing social and economic forces produced by the rapid industrialism of the nineteenth and early twentieth centuries. Just as society had its social order and the economy divided into managers and workers, schools too became social agencies to sort people into their appropriate places in the social and economic worlds according to their intelligence. This led to school systems, which, in the words of Purkey and Novak (1984), 'labeled, libeled, sorted and grouped' children (p. 11).

Intelligence was considered an unchanging trait normatively distributed in the general population. Some people were smart, some of average intelligence and others less intelligent. Intelligence became that which was measured by IQ tests. This led to a very narrow definition of human intelligence and potential. Tests to a greater or lesser degree focused on what Gardner (1983) would call 'logical mathematical' intelligence.

This paradigm of intelligence led to the belief that learning is sequential, that it is an individual activity, and that it occurs best without the assistance of tools like calculators. A certain hierarchy of knowledge evolved which is reflected in contemporary education. Thinkers use their intelligence; artisans use tools. Perhaps more insidious for many pupils is the decontextualized nature of much of what pupils are expected to learn. Getting the correct answer is more important than understanding the concepts behind the problem. Gardner suggests that students who learn at a surface level rarely gain the real understanding which comes through contextualized learning (Brandt 1993). The traditional school paradigm, therefore, came to mean the imparting of 'approved' knowledge through government guidelines, state authorized textbooks and standardized tests.

Pupils were sorted according to ability, thus creating more homogeneous groups. Special education legislation in many countries further exacerbated this sorting by creating new categories. Supported by detailed legislation, schools spent as much time ensuring compliance as they did attending to pupils. Evidence indicates that this sorting process – which has its roots in the early part of the century – still divides pupils; not by intelligence, but by socio-economic class, race and ethnic background (Oakes 1985; Hargreaves and Earl 1990).

It is within this paradigm that teachers are considered quasi-professionals or skilled tradespeople. Since pupils are the inputs in the educative process then the teachers' job is to mould them in accordance with the specifications (courses, hours, texts, tests) designed by educational experts to achieve the proper outputs measured by test scores. The proof of teacher and school effectiveness to many is computed in reading and mathematics scores on decontextualized tests.

This competitive model worked well for many years for the children of middle- and upper-class parents (Bracey 1992). Our societies, for the most part, have been able to absorb young people with basic mathematics and reading abilities who could perform routine jobs in which punctuality and compliance were required qualities. The unsuccessful in the traditional school paradigm found places in society; many have enjoyed the benefits of developed economies. This paradigm may have worked in 1965 but is not working in 1995 and will not work in 2005. The postmodern world requires a different model of schooling which is more in concert with the changing nature of economies and social structures.

The emerging learning paradigm

Among researchers and educators a new paradigm of learning is emerging:

> the capacity for thoughtfulness is widespread, rather than the exclusive property of those who rank high, and our views of students are susceptible to change. Not only may students' capacities leapfrog our predictions but our cultural conceptions of skill and learning inevitably develop (or at least change) . . . learning at all levels involves sustained performances of thought and collaborative interactions of multiple minds and tools as much as individual possession of information.
>
> (Wolf *et al.* 1991: 49)

Everyone has a mind; these minds work in different ways. According to Gardner (1983), there are multiple intelligences. People are more proficient in some areas than others. In addition to a logical-mathematical intelligence, he describes linguistic, musical, spatial, bodily-kinesthetic, and two kinds of personal intelligences, inter-personal and intra-personal. This is a much more democratic and inclusive concept of learning and intelligence. The challenge is not one of sorting the fit and the less fit but rather developing all of these minds.

Research on school effectiveness indicates that ability is not fixed (Mortimore *et al.* 1988). Pupils' ability can be modified by effective instruction. Learning is far more effective within a context. The popularity of cooperative education and work experience is reflective of this notion. In addition to conventional basics there are new basics appropriate to a changing world. Reich (1992) contends that people who will succeed in a postmodern world possess the following four sets of basic skills:

- abstraction, the capacity for discovering patterns and meaning
- systems thinking, to see relationships among phenomena
- experimentation, the ability to find one's own way through continuous learning
- the social skills to collaborate with others.

The compatibility between this new learning model, with its expanded definition of the basics, and the predicted demands of postmodern economies provides a compelling argument for change in schools. Berryman and Bailey (1992), in their study of what they call the 'double helix' – that is, the needs of the new workplace and the imperatives of new approaches to learning – found that:

> our new understanding of both work and learning suggest very similar directions for reform. Strengthening the educational system so that it conforms more to the way people learn will also directly enhance the system to prepare students for the types of workplaces that are emerging in factories and offices throughout the country.

(p. 44)

The Conference Board of Canada (Corporate Council on Education 1992), in its outline of employability skills, corroborates Berryman and Bailey's finding in its list of required academic skills and training targets. The Conference Board expands the conventional basics to include critical thinking, problem solving and technological literacy. The list also outlines personal management skills like positive attitudes, responsibility and adaptability. The skills list adds a set of teamwork skills which include the ability to contribute to organizational goals and to work within a significantly expanded span of control. Similar lists can be found in most developed countries. A cursory analysis of present educational practices suggests that schools are out of step with the needs of the larger society of the 1990s.

While congruent with changing employability needs, what is particularly appealing about this new paradigm is its compatibility with the needs of individuals to develop as fully functioning human beings. This model of learning will flourish in schools which reflect the conviction that:

> a democratic society is ethically committed to seeing all people as able, valuable and responsible; to valuing cooperation and collaboration; to viewing process as product in the making; and to developing the untapped possibilities in all worthwhile areas of human endeavor.

(Purkey and Collins 1992: 8)

What is emerging, therefore, is a much clearer sense of purpose, which not only addresses the cognitive imperatives necessary for all pupils to function in the postmodern environment, but also focuses sharply on the vital sources of pupils' humanity.

Implications of the emerging learning paradigm

While it is not totally clear what this future will look like in practice, there are sufficient successful examples of practices based on the emerging paradigm

Figure 8.1   Learning outcomes

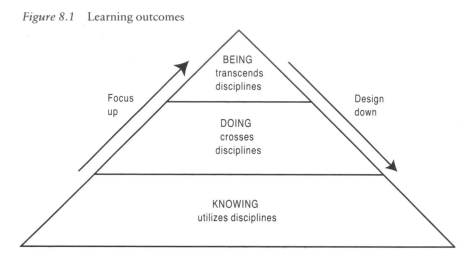

that we can make some fairly educated guesses as to the shape of things to come in the classroom. To this end, we will turn to some basic teaching questions: what do the pupils need to learn, and why?; how do we know when they have learned?; how do we help all the children to learn?

What do the pupils need to learn, and why?

There is no shortage of answers to this question. If teachers taught everything experts and special interest groups recommended, school systems would have to have a retirement plan for pupils! Fortunately, most jurisdictions are defining learning in terms of outcomes for all pupils to ensure curriculum consistency. This is a significant shift from tradition, which defined curriculum in terms of what teachers were required to cover, not what pupils were expected to learn. Accountability has moved squarely to teachers to address the learning of each pupil. Identification of outcomes provides ammunition for critics who have their own list or believe schools are interfering with families and religions. While these issues are being fought out in various governments and district offices, their fallout affects the lives of pupils and teachers.

Drake (1995) provides a useful way for teachers to interpret the types of outcomes teachers use in lessons (see Figure 8.1). Based on Spady's (1994) 'demonstration mountain', she identifies three types of outcomes. At the top of the mountain are the 'being' outcomes: being tolerant, being caring and being responsible. In the middle, the 'doing' level, are the crossdisciplinary or interdisciplinary outcomes like critical thinking, problem solving, using technology, and, among others, communicating effectively; and at the base are 'knowing' aspects of learning found in subject disciplines. It is easier to assess the base, more difficult to measure the 'doing' level, and exceedingly difficult to determine the 'being' level. It is tempting, therefore, to ignore the middle and top and focus solely on the 'knowing' level. Drake's advice is for teachers to 'focus up' but 'design down'.

She advises teachers: 'In developing our daily lessons we need to keep our focus on the kind of person we want the student to be. Then we are in a better position to decide what students should be able to know and do as we design down from the exit outcomes to develop curriculum' (p. 30). By focusing up, teachers can address the key curriculum question: 'Why am I teaching this?' Asking this question – how do these activities contribute to the 'being' level of pupils – on a daily basis obliges teachers to determine principles on which their work is to be based.

The 'doing' level of her model raises another important issue, curriculum coherence. While all curriculum reforms emphasize consistency, few focus on the need for coherence. Each day, in almost every secondary school and many primary schools around the world, pupils are expected to integrate the learning presented by five, six or even eight different teachers teaching their specialities. It is ironic that we expect pupils to do what experts have great difficulty doing. As Beane (1995) points out, pupils are expected to construct a jigsaw puzzle without a picture to guide them. He defines a coherent curriculum as: 'one that holds together, that makes sense as a whole; and its parts, whatever they are, are unified and connected by that sense of the whole' (p. 3).

The emerging learning paradigm requires teachers to function collabora-tively to bring coherence to the curriculum to ensure that pupils succeed at the 'doing' part of national, state or provincial curricula which are the new basics for the twenty-first century. If teachers are to collaborate to bring coherence to the curriculum through integrated curricula, then existing structures which divide pupils by class, stream, subjects and time periods need to be challenged. To change culture, structures require altering. In one Ontario secondary school, teams of teachers were given large heterogeneous groups of 14-year-old pupils and essentially told to achieve the learning outcomes. This left issues of time, place, content, organization and discipline to the teachers to work out collaboratively with the pupils. What started as a small pilot proved so successful that other teachers and pupils have been added to the project. We return to this theme in more detail later.

How do we know when they have learned?

'Assessment is an important part of education, and . . . whenever possible it must be of a type suitable to/and used for the enhancement of good quality learning' (Gipps 1994: 158). The definition of a set of common learning outcomes or goals has and will result in fundamental change in curriculum design and delivery, and necessitate greater assessment literacy among educational professionals: 'As the assessment/evaluation demands become more complex, teachers are left with the sinking feeling that they don't know enough to implement new models of assessment and evaluation' (Earl and Cousins 1995: 13). It is the role of the teacher, in consultation with parents and the pupil, to assess and evaluate the performance of each pupil. If assessment is the gathering of data about a pupil's performance, then evaluation is the application of judgement to that data to place a 'value' on the performance (Cooper and Ward 1988).

To this end we as educators must become assessment literate (Stiggins 1991). Assessment literates can answer such questions as:

- Are these the best assessment practices to assess this learning outcome?
- How well does this assessment sample pupils' achievement?
- Do the pupils understand the achievement targets and assessment methods?
- Does this assessment assess outcomes that matter?
- Are assessment strategies fair for all pupils?
- How are the resulting data to be presented?
- Who will have access to the data?
- How will they be reported and to whom?

While most discussions, and certainly most resources, are directed towards large-scale assessments, this constitutes a very small part of the assessment of pupil achievement which occurs every day in virtually every classroom. Assessment must, therefore, be seen in concert with shifts in curriculum design and teaching strategies.

Traditionally teachers decided on content based on guidelines or district curriculum documents. Once they decided on the 'what' of teaching, they proceeded to design the lesson plans that directed the 'how' of teaching. At some point in the process, usually when examinations or a reporting period loomed on the horizon, the 'how do we know?' pupil evaluation was considered. It was usually an afterthought and not well integrated into the planning process. One can hardly expect teachers to be assessment literate, however, when in many places, initial teacher education skims over the topic, leaving teachers to assess in ways in which they were assessed as pupils. What has changed is that assessment and evaluation strategies now must be developed in conjunction with the choice and delineation of the learning outcomes pupils are expected to achieve, rather than as the final chapter of the planning process. Only after the evaluation is planned can teachers develop teaching and learning strategies to meet the needs of pupils.

This paradigm shift, from planning based on teacher intention to planning directed towards pupil outcomes, requires teachers to determine standards of performance at the beginning of the teaching–learning process rather than at the end. If pupils know what is to be learned – the performance standards which define the outcome – then they have a much better opportunity to learn. There are three types of standards. Pupils can be compared to other pupils. This is certainly what most people think of when they talk about standards. They assume that education is a race and the fittest survive. Unfortunately, many pupils are left at the starting-blocks because they are unable to compete.

Pupils' performance can also be compared to predetermined criteria for the pupils' age or grade. This is a far more democratic approach and assumes that all pupils can learn if given sufficient time and support. A third approach is to assess a pupil's progress. This approach requires an assessment at the pupil's entry into the learning and an assessment of the growth or progress in the pupil's learning over time. This is possible (see Chapter 11) but far more difficult to do. Each of these definitions is appropriate under certain circumstances; the challenge is to decide what standard is acceptable politically and ethically. Equally important as the determination of reference points is the judgement of how standards should be established. Should standards be based on expert opinion, or what pupils actually do, or based on real-world demands? The process to select and define standards is a necessary prerequisite to a quality assessment process.

A teacher must also decide what is the purpose of each assessment. Is it for diagnostic purposes? How can it accommodate pupils' differences? Is it for grading? How is it to be used by others? Who will have input into the assessment? Will the pupil, the pupil's peers, or other professionals be involved? Which assessment strategy is best suited to a demonstration of pupil expertise? Such traditional approaches as multiple choice, true-false, and fill-in-the-blanks assessments have their place if the purpose of the assessment is to sample knowledge in a relatively quick and reliable way. Similarly, essay questions require pupils to use higher-order thinking skills and express themselves cogently and coherently, and oral questions and interviews with pupils are useful to assess understanding of their learning. Performance assessment, however, is gaining considerable support as a valuable technique because it is consistent with the emerging learning paradigm and because of its potential to assess a pupil's ability to apply knowledge and understanding.

Performance or authentic assessment is not new. Music, art, vocational and physical education teachers have always used performance assessment as the basis of their assessment processes. It is interesting that these are the subjects which have been marginalized within schools. In recent years, teachers of other subjects have begun to develop interesting ways to determine their pupils' ability to demonstrate understanding throughout the application of their learning. Such techniques as pupil journals, independent study projects, in-basket simulations, public exhibitions of performance, portfolios and records of achievements provide broad samples of pupil performance over time, upon which a range of pupil achievements can be assessed. The emerging paradigm for learning should result in an approach to learning and assessment which is beneficial to *all* pupils. Performance assessments have the potential to be fairer for all pupils. The jury, however, is still out.

It is clear from years of traditional testing experience that 'the one size fits all' approach to assessment has been inherently inequitable to special education pupils and pupils from cultural and linguistic minorities. Equity for these tests has traditionally been defined as ensuring that all pupils performed the same tasks under the same conditions. A more inclusive approach to equity gives all pupils the opportunity to present themselves in the most positive manner possible. This may mean providing choices of materials, questions or activities, use of tape recorders or computers, or adult assistance during the assessment activities. The type and manner of performance assessment can provide scope for ensuring that assessments are more flexible and equitable. In the hands of trained professionals who understand the multicultural nature of our societies and the support required by special education pupils, performance assessments can promote that difficult balance between quality and equity.

Once assessment strategies have been determined, then teachers can decide on teaching strategies, materials and activities best suited to achieving the desired learning outcomes.

How do we help all the children to learn?

Volumes have been written to address this question. Our discussion of teaching skills and strategies is necessarily short although the areas are rich with recent knowledge. For detailed summaries, see Good and Brophy (1991), Joyce *et al.* (1992), Creemers (1994), Moon and Mayes (1994), Pollard and Bourne (1994) and Harris (1995). We limit our analysis to a three-part organizer and brief survey of each component.

Attend to pupils' self concepts
Researchers have postulated for years that there is a direct connection between how pupils feel about themselves and their achievement in school. The study of self concept and its relationship to learning has been a persistent and controversial theme in educational literature (Kohn 1994). In more recent years, as more behaviouristic reforms have been mandated and fallen short of improving learning, scholars have returned to the study of self concept as a key to improving pupils' learning (Purkey and Novak 1990; Beane 1991). School effectiveness research has also reported that 'school

membership can have an important impact upon the development of children's self concept in relation to school' (Mortimore *et al.* 1988: 196). In general, however, school improvement and school effectiveness research at best understates pupils' affective outcomes (Stoll and Fink 1994).

Simply stated, self concept is a person's personal belief or 'concept' about her- or himself. It is the product of a multiplicity of interactions with significant others. Purkey and Asby (1988) identify five axioms which define how school context impacts a pupil's self concept:

- schools that facilitate affective development also facilitate cognitive development
- 'inviting' practices are related to positive outcomes
- pupils learn more when they see themselves as able, responsible and worthwhile
- pupils learn more when they choose to learn
- people are the most important component of a school.

Unfortunately, ill-conceived self-esteem programmes – in the United States in particular – have been the subject of considerable derision and have provided critics with plenty of ammunition. This has influenced politically motivated reform strategies to ignore or downplay its importance. Practitioners, however, attest to the significance of self concept to learning; we would submit that it is a rich area for further school effectiveness and school improvement research.

Address the basics of classroom management and teaching skills

The importance of teacher behaviour to pupil learning has resulted in considerable research over the past 20 years focusing on teacher practices which are predictably successful. Since this research is based on more traditional teaching–learning models, we would consider that the findings outline fundamental or basic skills necessary to create a climate for learning but are limited in their utility to describe a truly stimulating learning environment. Research confirms the necessity for effective lesson planning; the need to group students according to academic and affective needs; the importance of the efficient use of time; smooth, efficient classroom routines; the importance of higher-order questioning to encourage thinking and reasoning; the significance of explicit, consistent and equitable standards for classroom behaviour; focused lessons; high expectations for student learning as well as maximum interaction between the students and the teacher; and a work-centred environment.

Employ a variety of teaching and learning strategies to engage multiple minds

The new paradigm suggests that since every one has a mind and these minds work in different ways, then a variety of strategies are required to meet these differences. If the focus of instruction is to provide meaningful, contextualized learning so that pupils understand and can transfer learning, then traditional approaches are inadequate for all pupils.

The informed application of technology to the classroom is one obvious strategy to employ but it is not a panacea. There is little question of the need to prepare children for life in the new knowledge-based technologically driven economy, but as Postman (1993) argues, technology has the potential to be both a friend and enemy to humankind. He sees technology as a friend because 'it makes life cleaner, easier and longer' (p. xii) but warns of the dark side:

> Its gifts are not without a heavy cost. Stated in the most dramatic terms, the accusation can be made that the uncontrolled growth of technology destroys the vital sources of our humanity. It creates a culture without a moral foundation. It undermines certain mental processes and social relations that make human life worth living.
>
> (p. xii)

If one accepts that technology is morally neutral, then as educators we must use it in ways which capitalize on the friendly aspects of technology while preserving those aspects of humanity which technology tends to diminish: creativity, memory, common sense, morality and ethics.

Research on cooperative learning suggests that this strategy can prove to be a powerful alternative to traditional competitive instructional models because it has the potential to help all pupils to experience success. It also contributes to affective goals such as cooperation, teamwork, tolerance of others and positive self-esteem. Other research-supported strategies include creative problem solving, use of advanced organizers, graphic representations and metacognition, to mention only a few strategies which – used appropriately – can enhance learning for all pupils.

Restructuring for learning

Many years ago one of our mentors would challenge people who wanted to innovate by saying 'What are you getting rid of?' 'Innovation', he would say, 'was something that you did instead of, not added on.' Drucker (1969), the management expert, captured this idea in what he called organizational abandonment:

> An organization whatever its objectives, must . . . be able to get rid of yesterday's tasks and thus to free energies and resources for new more productive tasks. If it wants to be able to work on opportunities, it must be able to abandon the unproductive and to slough off the obsolete.
>
> (p. 193).

The emerging learning paradigm has profound implications for the way we structure our schools. In fact, it has the potential to challenge our very concept of school as we know it. If the new paradigm – with its requirement for learning for all pupils through contextualized learning experiences, cohesive curricula, authentic assessments and instructional flexibility – is to affect our pupils, then we need to re-examine rigorously the organizational structures of our schools. Restructuring means a total, critical re-examination of our use of time and space, roles and relationships, with a view to adopting new structures which enhance the learning of all pupils and abandoning those structures which are unproductive and obsolete.

As educators, we are in the business of pupil learning. While it may not seem like it on some days, stripped of all the rhetoric it is what we are about. If we accept the essence of the argument about the emerging paradigm, the question becomes how can we restructure to enhance the potential of this model of learning? To start with a conception of learning and develop structures is the reverse of traditional approaches. Furthermore, we must look at any new structures in an ecological way. It will not be enough just to fiddle with the timetable, or to provide more offices for teachers: we must recognize that every aspect of the organization will be affected to a greater or lesser degree. Consider, then, some possible implications of the emerging learning paradigm on the structure of school.

Time as a structure

A usual first reaction to the suggestion that we should consider a different approach to teaching and learning is: 'That's all very well, but where do we get the time?' There is no question that a major implication of the emerging paradigm will be the need to find time for teachers to collaborate to develop cohesive learning programmes for pupils. Authentic assessments are time-consuming. Teachers will need time to meet with pupils as individuals and in groups. Participative leadership requires time. Building partnerships will need time. As long as we think about time in conventional ways it becomes an excuse to do nothing. We don't want to give the impression, however, that there are easy answers out there just waiting to be discovered, but there are answers. Not all will be totally palatable.

As Schlechty (1990) states, perhaps more than any other organization, schools are 'time bound and time-conscious' (p. 72). Schools have a definite time cycle which is comforting, predictable and largely unquestioned. Why, for instance, do many schools close down for two months in the summer? Since less than five per cent of the populations of developed countries work in agriculture, the traditional answer is no longer applicable. While this is being written on a hot summer's day, pupils are enrolling in school in Calgary. Year-round schools have been a fact of life in Los Angeles. While we suspect this movement has more to do with finances than pupils' learning, it does provide one example of how a traditional conception of time is being challenged. Why does school begin at 8.30 or 9.00 a.m. and end around 3.30 or 4.00 p.m? Why is the school day usually five to five and a half hours? There are secondary schools that operate from 8.00 a.m. to 8.00 p.m.

Why should the school year for teachers be almost the same as that for pupils? Teachers need time to work together, design and develop materials, enhance their professional knowledge and skills. Perhaps the trade-off is to trade time for salary. In Japan, the reported length of the school year is 220 days, compared to less than 200 in most western jurisdictions. Critics of western education point to this to prove the superiority of the Japanese school system; more must be better. They fail to appreciate that Japanese teachers are in front of classes considerably less than teachers in most western countries. Japanese teachers have time during the course of the normal working day to collaborate, meet pupils or prepare for classes. Perhaps we need to think of different configurations of the school year and the school day. Why must period lengths be 40 or 55 or even 70 minutes, when the time bears no relationship to what is being taught? The structure dictates the teaching and learning not the other way around. Are inflexible master timetables still relevant?

Restructuring school years and school days are fairly obvious answers, but an approach more consistent with our stated educational purposes is to take Schlechty's (1990) advice: 'Perhaps the most powerful way to create time, especially time for teachers and time for students, is to organize the rhythm of school life around the work of students rather than around the instructional performances of teachers' (p. 75).

This implies more use of technology, flexible schedules, teams of teachers and pupils working together, and the abandonment of departmental and subject organizations; it may even mean totally different organizational metaphors. We have already mentioned the shamrock organization (Handy 1991). How might this look in a school? It could mean a small cadre of highly skilled, intellectually eclectic and dedicated professional teachers. The teachers would enjoy salaries comparable to other professions and would be accountable for the pupils in their charge. To augment the teaching core in this scenario would be part-time instructors, not necessarily teachers, who have a particular expertise which they might share with a number of schools as it is required. Finally, this 'shamrock' school might, for example, contract out such non-teaching duties as playground and cafeteria supervision, and the organization of school events and secretarial tasks (Hargreaves and Goodson 1996). By removing functions which do not need to be done by qualified professional teachers, they would have the time to collaborate to improve the school. If this seems somewhat bizarre, it might be instructive for educators to look at how other public services are restructuring to meet changing needs.

Spaces as structure

Schools are places where both adults and pupils work and learn. It has been said that schools are places where pupils go to watch the adults work. Traditional egg-carton school designs certainly can give this impression. They reinforce the culture of isolation, individualism, compartmentalization and the factory metaphor. There are many examples around the world, however, of flexible inviting architecture which supports rather than inhibits collaborative cultures. The challenge comes from what to do with older buildings designed for another age. Money for renovations is usually in short supply, so serious modifications are out of the question. One answer is to use the community – the parks, museums, shopping centres, historical sites, streams and woods. Here is where we need to tie time and space. Field trips are usually one-day excursions which are seen by pupils as a diversion and by teachers as a disruption to the daily timetable. If teams of teachers taught the entire curriculum to groups of pupils and used time in ways which supported learning, then out-of-school experiences could contribute significantly to understanding through contextualized learning. For example, if the teacher responsible for science wanted a two-day stream study and used volunteers from the community to help supervise, then the remaining teachers would have two days to plan collaboratively.

Roles and relationships

In Chapters 6, 7 and 9 we outline in some detail how roles and relationships will need to change within and outside the school. In this chapter, we have already suggested an entirely different relationship between teachers and pupils. We would, however, go even further and suggest that the organizational structures which define the various roles will need to be re-examined. Do schools need principals? Could schools be operated effectively through staff collaboration? While we are sceptical, it is worth considering.

Is the role of the assistant principal still relevant? There have been many successful experiments in which the organizational, administrative and disciplinary roles of assistant principals have been reallocated with some success. Do schools need specialized guidance counsellors or could other professionals assume the role? Is this a task which could be contracted out? Do we need department heads who look after narrow subject interests? In most schools, this structure works against collaboration and cohesion and promotes balkanization (Hargreaves 1994a). In our view, this entire structure could be dramatically reshaped. A more sensible approach might be to assign individuals to provide leadership on various school goals or system initiatives within the school. These appointments would last as long as the project and have a termination date. Responsibility allowances, which now go directly to people as part of salary, might go directly to the school to decide how it needs to support leadership in the school.

Answers to the questions we have raised can only be found in individual school contexts. Our purpose has been to ask a few 'what if' kinds of questions. A cursory reading of research and other educational journals indicates that the changing conception of teaching and learning which we have described as an emerging learning paradigm is not a passing fad. The 'kidney stone' approach won't work. Now is the time to start examining our school structure, policies and procedures and asking 'what if'?

Conclusion

'Changing our schools' raises the initiating question, 'for what purpose?' In this chapter we have tried to answer that question by demonstrating the centrality of teaching and learning. In doing so we have sought to answer some of our own 'what if' questions by suggesting some possible implications of the emerging learning paradigm for schools. Schools, however, are not isolates; they are part of a larger ecological system made up of many stakeholders. These stakeholders have the potential to be powerful partners or time-consuming adversaries. In the next chapter we develop the 'need for partnerships'.

nine

THE NEED FOR
PARTNERSHIPS

Despite an increased belief that the school is the centre of change and that its relationship with the school system and the world outside is important, no definition of school improvement has specifically articulated this, although Fullan (1991) highlights the need for improvement capacity to permeate all aspects of the system. Schools exist within a context of parents, community, school districts, other educational organizations and institutions, and levels of government. Each of these groups or institutions has an agenda, each has 'turf' or self-interest to protect, and each wants to have an impact on schools and through schools, pupils. Schools can, as many do, isolate themselves to maintain control and avoid criticism. In so doing, they not only build barriers against potential partners; they contribute to the incoherence of pupils' lives.

We have already described the need for coherence in curriculum. We would submit that the first reason to reach out to others beyond the school walls is to bring some cohesion to the fragmentation and mixed messages in the lives of many pupils, particularly those in lower socio-economic areas. The goal should be to have these outside forces act in ways which are complementary and mutually supportive. Fullan (1990) captures this idea:

> Our attention in policy, practice and research has shifted in recent years, away from preoccupation with single innovations toward more basic integrative, and systematic reform. Changes in the culture of schools, in the roles and relationships of schools, districts, universities and states, and in integrating teacher development, school improvement, leadership and curriculum toward more engaging learning

experiences for students and teachers, dominate the current scene and will continue to do so for the rest of the decade.

(p. 137)

To express it more metaphorically, we see schools in their contexts as being somewhat like spiders' webs. Each web and each school community is unique in size, setting and configuration. The purpose of all spiders' webs is fundamentally the same: to catch unwary insects. The purpose of all schools is fundamentally the same: the learning of pupils. Because the school in most communities is the central social agency, it is in a unique position to create a partnership 'web' with all the individuals, groups, organizations and institutions which share responsibility for the growth and development of pupils.

A second reason for partnerships is to enable schools to maintain a firm notion of current reality. To this end they need 'critical friends'. Costa and Kallick (1993) describe a critical friend as

> a trusted person who asks provocative questions, provides data to be examined through another lens, and offers critique of a person's work as a friend. A critical friend takes the time to fully understand the context of the work presented and the outcomes that the person or group is working toward. The friend is an advocate for the success of that work.

(p. 50)

Schools need critical friends, individuals and groups who, at appropriate times, listen and help them sort out their thinking and make sound decisions, who are not afraid to tell them when expectations for themselves and others are too low and when their actions do not match their intentions. They also help schools raise their expectations because critical friends are concerned about schools and want the best for them. In this chapter, we look at the immediate potential partners and critical friends for schools, parents, community, governing bodies or school councils, and the pupils themselves. We then examine some partners who, although physically more distant, have equally important roles to play in the network that links schools and their external environment.

Parents as partners

Virtually every reform effort has placed a heavy emphasis on parental involvement in schools. Some reforms have given parents governance roles, whereas others such as Ontario, Nova Scotia and Ireland have legislated an advisory function for parents. These initiatives are based on the premise that involved and interested parents contribute significantly to a pupil's success in school. Whether these mandated changes will facilitate the necessary school-home partnerships is questionable. The fact remains that parents and teachers need to be 'reading from the same page' to promote pupil learning and development.

The long history of schools reaching out to parents and parents trying to understand and influence schools has often been fraught with misunderstanding and wariness. As a result of surveying parents in Halton, we concluded:

> There is a high degree of uncertainty and in some cases misinformation about contemporary education and what is going on in schools ... Perhaps the major message of this study is the need to communicate meaningfully with parents, not only on the progress of their child but also in terms of educational issues. Parents want an opportunity to provide input into the educative process. A number of schools were praised by parents for their inclusionary approach. It would appear that elementary schools, because of their size and the age of their students, have an advantage.
>
> Parents feel somewhat uneasy about changing curriculum and unsure of what is going on in the classrooms of Halton. This uneasiness is no doubt the product of general societal unrest with its social institutions, but there is no question that the parents of Halton students have many questions to which the system must respond in meaningful ways. Parents need to be involved in schools in major decisions such as staffing, budget and curriculum. The traditional approach to parents is no longer satisfactory.
>
> (Halton Board of Education 1993c: 20–1)

Hargreaves (1994b) makes this point succinctly:

> While many schools are trying to build cultures of collegiality among teachers in their staffrooms, they are, at the same time, often retaining and perpetuating autistic cultures of miscommunication and misunderstanding in their classrooms and communities.
>
> (p. 7)

Schools continue to put forth great effort to involve parents. The best schools have built true partnerships with parents but in many schools, particularly ineffective schools, the gulf is wide and increasing. Parents have often become the scapegoats for unsatisfactory school performance. There are some teachers who seem to believe that the parents are 'sending the wrong children'. As a friend has said, 'parents send the best children they have'! Conversely parents have often seen schools as places to be feared, especially by those who were unsuccessful in their own school experiences. Certainly the size, structure and complexity of secondary schools is daunting for the most confident of parents, let alone a secondary school drop-out or a semi-literate parent. It is not a case of doing the old thing better or harder; rather, our changing social context requires a total rethinking of parental involvement in schools:

> It is necessary to sort out the group called 'parents', noting the range in their experiences, in their relationships with their children, and in their feelings about school. Some have high regard for education; for others, their children's schooling is a relived struggle amid more pressing concerns. The goals and values of individual families will vary and may differ from those of the teacher and the school. It is this individuality that parents bring to parent involvement efforts.
>
> (Edwards and Jones Young 1992: 74)

If, as we indicated in our Halton report, parents need to understand the changing nature of schools, it is equally important that schools 'acknowledge the range of dispositions, experiences and strengths among families' (Edwards and Jones Young 1992: 76). To this purpose, Epstein (1995) provides a useful framework to understand types of parental involvement in schools. She lists:

1 Parenting – helping each home to create an environment which supports learning, such as the school providing advice on supportive learning practices which can be carried out at home.
2 Communicating – developing two-way, jargon-free, meaningful communications about school programmes, practices and pupil progress.
3 Volunteering – recruiting and supporting parental and community help in the school.
4 Learning at home – helping parents to support their children's homework, and other curriculum and school-related activities.
5 Decision making – including parents in meaningful school decisions as well as encouraging parental leadership on important school issues.
6 Collaboration with the community – identifying and integrating appropriate resources and services from the community to support the family and the pupils.

In the leadership chapter we outline an approach to stimulating school improvement. It was based upon four principles: trust, optimism, respect and intentionality. Developing strategies to address Epstein's six involvement patterns – when looked at through the lens of this invitational framework – provides a basis for partnerships with parents to enhance not only pupils' academic achievement but also their social well-being.

Community and school council partnerships

Pupils are not only a part of schools and families; they are part of community groups, neighbourhoods, clubs, gangs, teams and other social, economic and political units. Partnerships mean recognizing all these influences and attempting to bring some coherence to the multiple messages pupils receive. This may mean initiating adult learning programmes to enable adults to help their children. It may mean involving the community in developing school development plans, as is done in Denmark (Kruchov and Hoyrup 1994). It may mean 'wrapping' various health and social agencies around the school to ensure coordinated services. It may mean building bridges to local businesses to introduce young people to the world of work. It may also mean, as Hallinger and Murphy (1986) discovered in effective low SES schools, working hard to separate the school from the negative features of the surrounding community. There is no shortage of engaging ideas but there is a limit to the time, energy and resources people can expend to build these linkages. Morgan and Morgan (1992) suggest that the following seven issues must be considered if partnerships are to be helpful:

- Partnership programmes or activities require a focus if they are to sustain interest and conserve time, energy and resources.
- Collaboration has to have a human face – many partnership programmes run aground on the shoals of bureaucratic intransigence and structures. People involved want to be informed of all the relevant information, listened to, and feel they have some influence.
- Parameters have to be clear – there are limitations and restrictions within which partners must operate. These should be out in the open. If people are to be called together to disseminate information it should be clear that this is not a decision-making forum. There is nothing more frustrating than what one of our colleagues called 'planned discovery'. The decision had been made but the person in charge created a pretence of decision making by inviting discussion until someone discovered the 'right' answer. Then the discussion concluded!
- School personnel must take the lead – it is important that the school itself has a collaborative culture if others are to feel invited and accepted as partners in a larger collaborative experience.
- Conflicts of interest must be aired – one problem with parent councils and other representative bodies is that people may be there to promote a personal agenda to the detriment of the organization as a whole.
- Adequate resources have to be provided – time, energy and financial and material resources need to be determined to make programmes work. If, for instance, there is an effort to reach out to immigrant parents, then translators will be required. Too many promising programmes have

disappeared because of inadequate funding. It is wonderful to advocate parental involvement and community outreach but new or reallocated resources are necessary.

• Equity issues need to be confronted – schools have different community resource bases. Some communities can quickly raise money to buy computers, sports equipment, library books or other perceived school needs. How do school jurisdictions ensure some degree of equity? If the focus of education is moving from inputs to results then funding agencies must ensure equal opportunity for all children to learn. It makes little sense to spend millions on new curricula and tests when many children lack basic learning resources. Similarly, ways must be found to ensure that parents from all socio-economic groups are involved in school activities, school councils and governance. There is a very real danger that these emerging structures will be just another way for the contented middle class to entrench the *status quo*.

Some of these guidelines are particularly important in partnerships between schools and their school councils or governing bodies. Earley (1994a) cautions: 'The term partnership is . . . a much overused word and subject to a great deal of rhetoric; so there is a need for governing bodies to decide what is the precise nature of that partnership or how it might be achieved' (p. 106). In a changing world with new roles and responsibilities, there is a lot of uncertainty about the part school councils play. Many members are in full-time employment and do not have considerable amounts of time to visit schools, and yet good partnerships between governors and teachers depend on trust and respect that only develops if they meet frequently (Creese 1995). Whether or not school councils have a governance role, this does not mean that they are responsible for the daily management of the school: that is the duty of the principal and staff. Working as critical friends, however, and by asking the right questions they can ensure that the work of the school is carried out effectively and efficiently. These 'right questions' must relate to the purpose, outcomes and processes of the particular school, the *why*, *what* and *how*: in other words, they must assure themselves that the school is a good school for today and tomorrow, not for 1965; that it evaluates outcomes related to this purpose; and works on the processes, conditions and cultural norms that will best support its improvement to this end. School council members should also be advocates for the school and actively support improvement efforts.

Pupils must be partners too

Innovation and change in schools affect pupils but they are usually considered the ultimate purpose of the school improvement process rather than as partners in that process. We tend to focus on teachers' working conditions, cultures and contexts but often forget that school is also the workplace for pupils: 'it seems evident that students are much more than raw materials, since their ideas and behaviour have an enormous influence on how the process of education unfolds' (Levin 1994: 759). Phelan and colleagues (1992) note that pupils have their own list of factors which make for a supportive work environment:

- visibility and accessibility of the principal
- the collective message and level of support students receive from the professional staff
- the perceived degree of safety or violence
- types of interaction between student groups
- availability of extra-curricular activities
- student involvement in decision making
- condition of the school facilities
- opportunities for non-English speaking students to speak their native languages in informal settings.

Our own work suggests that many teachers are resistant to the notion of partnership which includes pupils. Our questionnaires to teachers and students at both the primary and secondary levels not only revealed little student involvement in school decision making but also reflected teachers' belief that students should not be involved. Results of the effective schools questionnaire administered to secondary pupils throughout Halton in 1992 demonstrated that while many (71 per cent) felt they were encouraged to think for themselves, only half believed that teachers listened when they had an opinion about school-related issues such as school rules. Furthermore, approximately one-quarter did not feel that their teachers were interested in them as people or that they were treated with understanding or concern, and one-third were either not sure or did not believe they were given opportunities to take on extra jobs and/or responsibilities (Halton Board of Education 1992b). The Halton profile is not unusual. The engagement of pupils and their involvement in school life is important but some teachers, it appears, teach subjects not pupils (Sarason 1990). Yet pupils are the reason for teachers' existence. Fullan (1991) points out that adults 'rarely think of children as participants in the process of change and organizational life' (p. 17). It is not surprising that pupils would rather be elsewhere if their opinions are not sought and they have no opportunity to contribute to decisions that affect them.

When pupils do speak up, Phelan and colleagues (1992) report,

we find that their perspectives on school and learning rather than being at odds with those of teachers are remarkably similar. Teachers want to be respected and want to work with students who care; who exhibit humour, openness, and consideration; and who are actively involved in subject-area content. Furthermore teachers want to be in safe and tension-free environments. Students say they want the same things from their teachers and schools.

(p. 704)

Pupils can and should be partners too.

The school district as partner

Most schools operate within some kind of a school system, whether the system is a tightly knit district, an LEA, or a loosely structured network of schools. School systems throughout the world, however, are in the process of reorganization, redefinition or in some cases dissolution. From our work we concur with Fullan (1991) when he states:

> The role of the school district is crucial. Individual schools can become highly motivated for short periods of time without the district, but they cannot *stay* innovative without the district action to establish the conditions for continuous and long term improvement.

(p. 209)

It is difficult though for an effective school to be constrained within an ineffective system. At their best, school systems can be powerful partners for schools (Coleman and LaRocque 1990; Stoll and Fink 1994). Where decision making is decentralized, however – for example in Britain – severe reductions in LEA powers have forced them to carve new roles for themselves that emphasize not only leadership but also their willingness and ability to work with schools and other partners; 'losing an empire, finding a role' (Audit Commission 1989). Some have been more successful than others in developing this 'co-managed' partnership.

How districts can aid change

Based on Halton and subsequent experience, we suggest ways in which this partnership can help schools.

Teacher and leadership development – while professional development is every teacher's, principal's and support person's business, school systems have a great responsibility to support the professional growth of all their people, as we outline in the next chapter.

Assistance to schools – school districts have been found to play a major role in supporting school improvement (Huberman and Miles 1984; Corbett and Wilson 1992). While the focus of policy directions in many countries has shifted towards outputs, the school system plays an important role in most countries in ensuring the equitable and purposeful distribution of resources – not only monetary resources but human, material and psychological support. It is our view, based on observations of American, British and Canadian schools that inputs such as staff development, psychological services, data collection and analysis, transportation of pupils, school maintenance and budget support can be delivered more efficiently, effectively and equitably within a larger network.

Some school systems, in the name of site-based management, have devolved all budgets and responsibilities to the schools. Principals and staffs are not only responsible for academic programmes, but also buses, custodians or school keepers, ordering light bulbs and arranging for building maintenance. This clearly thrusts educators into roles for which they were not trained and detracts from their focus on pupil learning. Effective systems are not necessarily centralized or decentralized. Responsibilities must be assigned on grounds of efficiency and efficacy and linked to the school's pre-eminent goals of teaching and learning for all pupils. Like so many other things in education, a good idea like site-based management has become so politicized it has become an article of faith. Louis (1990) suggests that 'Essentially, the picture is one of co-management, with co-ordination and joint planning enhanced through the development of consensus between staff members at all levels about desired goals for education' (p. 161).

Support for development planning – schools need training, support and resources in school development planning. This is a major system role. Hargreaves and Hopkins (1991) suggest seven district-related issues are likely to affect the success of schools' development planning attempts:

- how the district determines its development planning policy
- its conception of development planning
- the fit between its own plan and those of schools
- integration of district and school plans
- if and how it uses schools' development plans
- its support system for development planning
- how it interprets the relationship between monitoring and evaluation and development planning.

Creation of interconnections between innovations – our work in Halton indicated that school development and system development went hand in hand. One could not be maintained without the other. Personnel at both central office and schools needed to learn about change, school culture and school-based planning, and where their particular role fitted into the jigsaw. In its search for new ideas to support schools, the system had to engage in simultaneous development as schools progressed with growth planning and began to make diverse demands that required a response. Essentially, the strategic plan at system level mirrored the growth plan at school level. The coordination of system and school plans gave schools considerable flexibility to pursue their own areas of interest within a framework and to adapt ideas to their own context and needs.

Provision of an overarching vision, focusing on teaching and learning – this provides a framework for each school to develop a *version* of the system's vision (Schlechty 1990), which provides cohesion because schools are interrelated, often serving the same families and communities. Halton's system focus on improved instructional strategies was mirrored in different ways in each school's growth plan.

Monitoring of school effectiveness and school improvement – through supporting and encouraging schools' own quality assurance efforts, districts can ensure that the gap between more and less effective schools does not widen when decision making is decentralized to schools. In Lewisham LEA in south London, Quality Assurance and Development (QAD) advisers work in partnership with schools, through improvement strategies, professional, management and curriculum development and assisted school self-review (Stoll and Thomson 1996). QAD aims to support the development of self-regulation. Schools are helped to make judgements on their own practice and performance, and to measure their effectiveness. Provision of useful and user-friendly data to schools on the progress and development of all of their pupils is also an essential part of this supportive partnership.

Building networks – this is an area of real importance for schools. Districts can support teacher subject groups, principals' associations and school development team networks, to mention just a few. Isolated schools miss out on the rich interaction with peers in other schools. Districts, themselves, can also build networks with other districts, higher education, the business community and other partners so that they keep looking outwards and ensure they are learning organizations.

Partnerships with higher education

The scope for university involvement in school improvement has mushroomed with decentralization of decision making from districts to schools. In some countries the role of universities in initial teacher education has shifted and many institutions have developed partnership programmes with schools. Rudduck (1992) expresses caution about such 'liaisons dangereuses', and warns potential partners of the need for mutual respect of each other's strengths and needs, clarification of principles and purposes, shared commitment to exploration of alternatives, maintenance of momentum of slow-paced change and a shared perception of the complexities of teaching.

Three-way partnerships between schools, school systems and universities are also being forged for specific projects. Increasingly, schools and districts have started to work with partners in higher education institutions on improvement initiatives in the action research mode. As a consequence of interest in school effectiveness research findings, as well as those from school improvement studies, others are beginning to mesh the two. No two approaches are identical, nor are the schools and districts that are involved, and therefore no blueprint for improvement can be offered. None the less, the partners involved from schools, districts and higher education continue to try to identify the strategies that lead to improvement and promote pupil progress, development and achievement. The relationship has to be one of equals, as one professor argues:

> we cannot hope to influence the restructuring movement unless some of us work more closely with the schools. This means climbing down from our proverbial ivory towers and working with schoolpeople . . . If we see ourselves working with schoolpeople – not on them – we can indeed exert an influence.
>
> (Lieberman 1990: 533)

The two examples we cite here are partnerships in which one or both of us have been involved. In both cases, the partnership is extended by collaboration between several external partners, as well as collaboration between external partners and schools.

The Learning Consortium

The Learning Consortium was established in 1988 as a collaborative teacher education partnership between four Canadian school districts, one of them Halton, and two higher education institutions, in and near Toronto. Fullan (1993) describes its intent:

> The aim of the Consortium is to improve the quality of education for schools and universities by focusing on teacher development, school development, and the restructuring of districts and the faculty of education to support improvement on a continuous basis.
>
> (p. 121)

The rationale behind the consortium is ongoing development of educators that, in turn, works towards improvement of students' learning and development. Initiatives have included investigation and implementation of a variety of models of learning, in particular cooperative group learning; beginning teacher support programmes; leadership training programmes; new teacher preparation pilot partnership programmes; international conferences; structural changes in the higher education institutions; and coordination of school and district level developments. Initiatives are documented, researched and disseminated. Now entering its eighth year, the partnership is still largely funded by an annual base budget of $20,000 from each partner. Watson and Fullan (1992), commenting on the Learning Consortium, conclude that strong partnerships are not accidental and do not arise purely through good will or *ad hoc* projects. They require new structures, activities and rethinking of the way each institution operates as well as how they might work as part of a network.

From Halton's perspective, the consortium brought a workable but research-based model of components of classroom improvement (Fullan *et al.* 1990). Linked with the district's commitment to school growth planning and staff development, this model provided a clear instructional focus. It also opened up a continuum of interlinked professional development from pre-service through to leadership.

International School Effectiveness and Improvement Centre

In Britain in the last few years, school effectiveness and school improvement researchers have started to move together in their thinking and have realized that they have a considerable amount to offer each other (Reynolds *et al.* 1993; Stoll 1996). This is none too soon for practitioners in search of support for improvement efforts. To bridge the two fields and the worlds of theory and practice, an International School Effectiveness and Improvement Centre (ISEIC) was established at the Institute of Education at the University of London in 1994. Its aim is to draw on, extend and link the two bodies of knowledge in order to support schools in systematic programmes that:

- improve the quality of teaching and learning
- improve pupils' academic performance, attendance, self-image and attitudes towards continuing education and training
- ensure progress for pupils of all backgrounds
- develop improved educational indicators
- promote the concept of lifelong learning within schools for adults as well as children
- develop the internal capacity of schools for managing change and evaluating its impact
- encourage effective working relationships within schools
- enhance relationships between schools and their partners: pupils, parents, governing bodies, LEAs, the business community and higher education.

Various models of partnership and networking have been developed. These are under constant refinement as higher education and other partners endeavour to find the most effective ways to support schools in the provision of the best possible learning opportunities for pupils and adults alike. Work to achieve these is focused on developmental work, research, teaching and dissemination.

Developmental work

ISEIC works with schools engaged in effectiveness and improvement projects in three ways. It undertakes *action research* with individual schools, groups of schools and LEAs to develop the appropriate culture to support and evaluate their school improvement activities. Schools are aided and studied as they investigate and implement the most effective teaching and learning strategies in order to raise pupil attainment, achievement and morale. Different programmes are developed for and with schools and various partners, including LEAs and governing bodies. Successful work from other countries, particularly Canada and the United States, has been adapted for English schools.

It has developed *a team of associates* around the country who provide consultancy support to schools engaged in improvement efforts. These people act in the role of external change agents and critical friends. They are not inspectors or line managers

> but people with a 'license to help'. Their role seems crucial, because such school improvement programs, taken seriously, require much time and care, are an effort to change the school as an organization, and usually have to compete with the ordinary demands of keeping schools running.
>
> (Miles *et al.* 1988: 158)

External change agents have an important role to play in school improvement because they do not have a particular 'axe to grind'. To be successful, however, they require specific skills. As a result of their study of skills needed by educational change agents, Saxl and colleagues (1990) have developed six training modules related to trust and rapport building, organizational diagnosis, dealing with the change process, resource utilization, managing implementation, and building skill and confidence in people to continue.

ISEIC has also established the *School Improvement Network* (SIN) which brings together people engaged in school improvement to share and discuss experiences, debate issues of mutual concern, solve common problems and further refine improvement strategies. Network members also receive listings of people involved in school improvement, newsletters and summaries of research findings. By summer 1995, 18 months after the first meeting, nearly 500 schools or individuals, 20 LEAs, several clusters of schools, and several government agencies and professional associations had joined the network. From feedback, it appears that such a network enables educators to combat isolation and realize that others share their concerns, and promotes deeper thinking about teaching, learning and organizational issues.

SIN participants have also been asked in what ways they think higher education can support school improvement. Responses indicate that educators look to higher education to feed in research findings in an accessible form; to help them make the links between theory and practice; to offer staff development, act as facilitators, and provide an impartial outside view as critical friends; and to offer expertise in the areas of data collection and analysis, monitoring and evaluation of school improvement and school effectiveness.

Research

A vital function of ISEIC is to continue to expand the knowledge base about school effectiveness and the challenge of school improvement. In this work ISEIC also collaborates with a variety of partners, including other higher education institutions, LEA personnel, educational consultants and government agencies. Of their research projects, one is an exploration of the differential school effectiveness of secondary school departments, to establish whether it is possible to talk in terms of whole-school effectiveness or whether and why some secondary school departments are more effective than others (Sammons *et al.* 1994). It is interesting that when an initial letter was sent to schools to ask them if they would be prepared to be involved as case-study schools, the almost universal response was favourable, even from less effective schools, because they wanted to participate in a study that would help them better understand department differences.

Another subject under investigation is the Improving School Effectiveness Project, a collaborative study with the University of Strathclyde of Scottish schools engaged in improvement activities in the areas of school development planning, developing a 'moving school' culture, and teaching and learning, and the impact of outside interventions on such efforts (MacBeath and Mortimore 1994) (see Chapter 4).

Teaching

Lifelong learning through continuous professional development is a key message of this book. Much of this learning takes place in schools. For this reason, accredited courses are available for teachers involved in school improvement projects. Other pre-service and in-service, masters and doctoral level courses have been specifically developed related to school effectiveness and school improvement. School practitioners and other partners are invited to present at these courses as well as to attend them.

Dissemination

Another important function of ISEIC is dissemination. One example of partnership has been involvement in production of a videotape and supporting materials (Resource Base 1995). Several schools throughout England were featured. A second example is an international conference, entitled 'Learning

From Each Other'. Its specific purpose was for practitioners, local and national policy makers, researchers and other partners in the improvement process to share and debate perspectives.

Governments as partners

In recent times the rush by governments to make structural changes in education has left many educators feeling like conscripts rather than partners. Gradually, however, some governments and their departments of education are realizing that substantive changes require the involvement and support of educators. As important partners in the educational web, governments need to be part of the partnership network if substantive school change is to occur. There are some excellent examples of governments playing meaningful roles in the development of schools. For example, government-sponsored teachers' centres in Ireland, principals' courses in Ontario and the Headlamp programme for heads in England (TTA 1995) perform important professional development functions.

An 'improving schools' initiative by the Department for Education in England and Wales (DFE 1995) plans to redistribute its Grants for Education Support and Training (GEST) in 1996–7 in three directions. First, schools may claim a grant when they submit their post-inspection action plan. Second, an annual school effectiveness grant will be paid to all maintained schools. Third, LEAs will keep part of the grant to support improvement of schools with serious weaknesses. While resources for schools are always welcome, new money is needed in excess of redirected budgets. More positive in this initiative are a focus on promotion of effective teaching and teacher training, identification of schools with good systems of target setting, and post-inspection action-planning seminars, linking action-planning with school improvement.

If governments are to be true partners we suggest the following activities are part of their legitimate role in democratic societies:

1 Articulate society's expectations for schools.
2 Develop and administer equitable ways to ensure that schools and districts provide quality education.
3 Ensure equity of treatment for all the children of all people, not just those who can afford it.
4 Consult educators widely before the initiation of change, hear and respond to concerns and inform them after changes have been undertaken.
5 Provide the resources to support educational change.
6 Support the professional development that changes require.
7 Provide direct professional support to isolated and remote schools.
8 Recognize and act on the premiss that 'change is a process not an event'.

Partnership is a two-way street. Real change occurs in schools and classrooms, not legislatures, government or district offices. Teachers and principals who are treated like partners work more willingly and more effectively than they do if coerced like conscripts.

Other partners

There are many other important potential partners of schools: business and industry, teaching unions (see Chapter 8) and social services, to name a few. For example, one of the key ingredients of the Comer School Development Program (Comer 1988) in the United States is a mental health support team. Many non-teaching staff also offer specialized skills that enhance the school's capacity for effective management, but there is a tendency for some to feel that they are perceived as outsiders rather than members of a multidisciplinary team (Mortimore *et al.* 1994).

In an overview of school improvement in Canada, Kilcher (1994) reported a variety of approaches, including provincial programmes, funding mechanisms, administrator and facilitator training, networking structures, university-school district collaborations, a range of related professional development activities, and business-education partnerships. In Manitoba, the Walter and Duncan Gordon Charitable Foundation grants approximately $400,000 annually to individual secondary schools who submit proposals for improvement projects with 'at risk' pupils. Grants awards are based on principles of school effectiveness and school improvement. There are many similar foundations in the United States that support school improvement initiatives. In Britain, support of this kind is considerably harder to procure, although several businesses and foundations have funded specific initiatives, a notable recent example being the Paul Hamlyn Foundation, which funded the National Commission on Education (1993) and 11 case-studies of school improvement 'against the odds' (National Commission on Education 1996).

The International Congress on School Effectiveness and School Improvement provides opportunities for international partnerships among researchers and school practitioners. The organization produces a journal, *School Effectiveness and School Improvement*, a newsletter and organizes an annual conference. It is presently sponsoring a ten-nation research project which looks at school effectiveness in different contexts (Reynolds *et al.* 1994).

Conclusion

We can now add one more paradox to our growing list. As policy decisions force schools to use market approaches, divisiveness and isolation tend to follow. Individual schools cannot begin to meet the needs of pupils in this complex and diverse world without help from other sources. Rather than separateness, schools require togetherness with their various stakeholders to ensure coherence in the lives of children and to continue to develop as organizations. To achieve these goals, schools, districts and other partnership institutions and agencies must become learning organizations and function within a larger learning community. It is to the topic of 'learning for all' that we now turn.

ten

LEARNING FOR ALL: BUILDING THE LEARNING COMMUNITY

An essential theme of this book is that the rapidly changing context of our world requires organizations to continue to improve. As we have stated previously, schools are either improving or declining. There will be periods of consolidation and the pace of change might speed up or slow down but standing still is an illusion. A most difficult aspect of change is the problem of sustaining momentum. Garratt (1987) states that for an organization to survive and develop, the rate of learning within the organization must be equal to, or greater than, the rate of change in the external environment. To be effective, therefore, a school must become a learning organization. Handy (1991) provides two definitions of a learning organization: an organization that learns; an organization that encourages learning in its people.

To this point, our focus has been on organizations that learn: organizations that have a sense of direction and a firm fix on current reality through scanning their contexts; who plan effectively, efficiently and flexibly; organizations in which continuous development and improvement are integral parts of their culture. In this chapter, therefore, we briefly review the qualities of learning organizations before we focus in more depth on the second definition, 'learning for all'.

Learning organizations

Learning organizations which invite others professionally have the following qualities. They all:

- Treat teachers as professionals – learning organizations assume that pupils are not standardized and that teaching is not routine. Within this model, teachers need knowledge of child development, multiple teaching strategies and a variety of assessment strategies. Learning organizations trust teachers to make decisions which benefit children.

- Promote high quality staff development – Fullan (1991) states: 'As long as there is the need for improvement, namely, forever, there will be need for professional development' (p. 344). If we expect to change pupil learning, learning organizations must attend to and invest in teacher learning.
- Encourage teacher leadership and participation – successful principals are 'leaders of leaders' (Barth 1990). There is evidence that there is a strong relationship between participative decision making and systemic curricular and instructional change (Bryk *et al.* 1994).
- Promote collaboration for improvement – the key to collaboration within a learning organization is to promote norms of both collaboration and continuous improvement while respecting the individuality of pupils and teachers.
- Develop ways to induct, include and develop new organizational members perpetuation of a learning culture is dependent upon the organization's ability to develop practices, procedures and customs which draw new people into the culture and compensate for the loss of key participants.
- Function successfully within their context learning organizations exist within the context of a nation, a community and, often, a district. They constantly read their various contexts and develop the political skills to function successfully within these contexts.
- Work to change things that matter – learning organizations move beyond first-order change, which is to do more or less of the same thing, to second-order change which requires the reframing of issues in a larger context (Garratt 1987).
- 'Sweat the small stuff' – learning organizations have processes and procedures in place which staff, pupils and parents trust. They address such issues as discipline, routines, decision making, conflict resolution, communications and public relations in ways which prevent issues of structure from interfering with curricular, teaching and learning changes. Effective administration of day-to-day activities, what some may consider the 'small stuff', is fundamental to the development of a learning organization.

Learning for all

The evidence to support this concept of schools as learning organizations is fairly clear. A study of effective large-scale change in the United States reported that teachers who made effective adaptations to students of today shared one quality: 'each belonged to an active professional community which encouraged and enabled them to transform their teaching' (McLaughlin and Talbert 1993: 7). In our thinking this concept needs to be extended to all the school partners. In short, 'everyone must want to learn and have ample opportunity and encouragement to do so' (National Commission on Education 1993: xv).

In the rest of this chapter we argue that teachers, like their pupils, must be learners. We consider how teachers learn and explore implications for professional development. Traditionally, staff development has implied external workshops. Increasingly, however, teacher development needs to take place within schools. We examine the role of the school in teacher development. We also focus our lens on the teacher and ask the question, 'what should the teacher's role be in her or his own development?' Finally, extrapolating from our discussion of teacher as learner, we look at leaders as learners and initiate a discussion of parents, community members, school councillors or governors as partners and thus part of the learning organization.

Teachers as learners

While the ultimate outcomes of the educational process must be pupil progress, development and achievement, a crucial contributor to pupil learning is teacher learning. When teachers are professionally fulfilled, demonstrate job satisfaction, skills and knowledge, and have a strong feeling of efficacy around their practice, they are more likely to motivate pupils to want to learn. Barth (1990) argues, 'Probably nothing in a school has more impact on students in terms of skills development, self-confidence, or classroom behaviour than the personal and professional growth of their teachers' (p. 49). Teacher learning has to be a goal and intermediate outcome of school improvement. In effective schools, lifelong learning incorporating adults as well as children is a norm, and emphasis is placed on developing the school as a learning organization.

We have already asserted that improvement is change. Change is experienced by teachers both personally and developmentally. Indeed, change is dependent on the thoughts and actions of teachers, which means that the role of teacher development as a process of school improvement is fundamental. Thus teacher development is both a process and intended outcome of school improvement. Where, however, does teacher development fit within the school improvement process? Essentially, school improvement depends on the involvement of teachers, which has major implications for their own development. If classrooms are going to be effective, schools must be effective as well, and teachers are a major part of the school. As Fullan and Hargreaves (1991) say:

As individuals, they must therefore take responsibility for improving the whole school, or it will not improve. If they don't, their individual classrooms will not improve either, because forces outside the classroom heavily influence the quality of classroom life: forces like access to ideas and resources, timetabling arrangements, and sense of purpose and direction.

(p. 11)

For teacher development to occur, we need greater understanding and appreciation of the ways in which teachers learn.

How teachers learn

Earlier we examined ways that young people learn. While there is some overlap between this and the means by which adults learn, there are also differences. These are influenced by many factors, including age, career and development stage. Fundamentally important to teacher development, but all too often neglected, is a consideration of the teacher as a person. Just as no two children are the same, neither are two teachers. Adults are influenced by what goes on in their lives, both on a daily basis and over time, and yet many approaches to staff development treat teachers as if they are all the same. In considering teacher development, it is imperative to pay attention to their priorities and lives (Goodson 1992). Age and gender influence teacher development (Krupp 1989; Oja 1991; Sikes 1992). A 20-year-old teacher has different needs and interests than one who is 30, 40 or 50. In their early twenties people explore new options in the world, whereas at 40 many go through a midlife transition or crisis, where they question whether they are doing what they had anticipated for themselves or if they have achieved their goals. During their forties, men also often show a greater desire to nurture. If their own children have grown up by this time, school may provide opportunities for nurturing, for example through mentoring relationships.

Teachers also go through different stages in their career. Huberman's (1988, 1992b) examination of the career cycles of Swiss teachers in the early to mid-1980s emphasizes connections between their careers and school improvement, as their interest in change and learning fluctuates during particular phases. In some ways, career cycles mirror life cycles, but they are also influenced by educational experiences. For example, 'positive focusers' are teachers once very involved in innovations but now, later in their careers, happy to focus on the classroom, taking on less outside responsibilities. In contrast, others at the same stage of their careers experience disenchantment due to bitterness of the failure of reforms and perceived lack of follow-through by administrators. Treating these two groups' needs and desires as identical in terms of professional development would be a travesty. Our speculation, however, is that increased external demands on teachers have changed the ages at which teachers go through particular career cycles.

Based on the premiss that 'stage theorists focus on underlying patterns of thought and problem solving that play a central role in determining an individual's approach to the world' (p. 41), Oja (1991) examines different stages of ego, moral, intellectual and interpersonal development and discusses implications for staff development. She points out that what may appear to be a challenge to new learning at one stage could easily feel like a support at a subsequent stage, and further argues that knowledge of adult development is helpful to facilitate interactions between teachers in staff and committee meetings.

There are implications for adult learning. Adult learners (Knowles 1980; Dalellew and Martinez 1988):

- are more self-directed – are not dependent on others and can develop their own learning environments
- bring their own experiences – that shape their readiness to learn and influence assumptions about learning
- go through transitional phases – that influence their perspective towards learning
- learn for specific purposes – forcing them into learning situations will not ensure that they 'absorb' knowledge
- are problem-centred – and want to apply what they learn immediately to solve specific problems.

Using adult learning principles, Moore (1988) offers guidelines we consider useful for anyone involved in developing a school's staff development policy or facilitating teacher development. She proposes teacher learning opportunities should:

- be collaborative, involving participants in diagnosing needs, decision making, designing, implementing and evaluating staff development
- help learners achieve self-direction and be able to define their own objectives, using professional content to meet their needs
- capitalize on learners' experiences, using them as a starting point
- foster participation, with learners helping to decide learning methods and structure the learning environment
- cultivate critical, reflective thinking, helping learners examine cultural and organizational assumptions as well as their own practice
- foster learning for action, with opportunities for decision making and strategy planning
- encourage problem posing and problem solving, as closely connected as possible to learners' real problems

- have a climate of respect, with interchangeable facilitators and participants, opportunities for small-group interaction, comfortable furniture
and, we would add, food!

The changing face of professional development

The implications of adult learning for professional development are significant. In the same way that we see an emerging paradigm of pupil learning,
there is considerable international evidence of an emerging professional
model or paradigm of teacher learning. The one-off in-service sessions
designed to impart the 'right way' of doing something are being replaced by
more sustained, coherent, inquiry-based programmes. Attempts are been
made to bring teachers' and schools' development needs together so that
individuals feel personally and professionally fulfilled while whole-school
improvement occurs. There is an increased orientation towards viewing
professional development as a continuum. Bolam (1993) defines continuing
professional development (CPD) as 'an on-going process which builds upon
initial teacher education and training, begins with induction into teaching,
includes in-service training, staff development and management development
and concludes with preparation for retirement' (p. 18). Within this framework, education, training and support activities are offered for the purpose of
helping teachers and principals to add to their professional knowledge,
improve their professional skills, and help them clarify their professional
values. The ultimate purpose, Bolam argues, is that they will be able to
educate pupils more effectively. Here we outline a few forms of professional
development that, we believe, offer variation and choice to individuals while
at the same time ensuring a focus on whole-school improvement.

Reflective research and study

Teachers are action-orientated, practical people. Faced with pressures of new
curricula, demands of principals, school systems and governments, and
pupils who bring a diversity of backgrounds, needs, learning styles and
attitudes to learning, simple solutions are often attractive. It is often easier to
do what you have always done or to try something that worked for the
teacher in the next class than develop new strategies or evaluate current ones
to assess whether they address teaching goals. Classroom research, however,
is a meaningful activity that engages teachers in a process of refinement, helps
create autonomy in professional judgement and enhances practice. Elliott
(1991) describes two different ways in which teachers reflectively develop
their practice through research. In one, reflection initiates action: research on
a practical problem leads to new understanding that requires a change in

some aspect of teaching. In the other, action initiates reflection: some aspect of teaching is changed in response to a practical problem and the teacher self-monitors the change's effectiveness, which leads to new understanding. A third stimulus we encountered in Halton was some teachers' response to research findings. Many teachers may not actively seek out or be aware of significant research findings on more effective practices. During the course of the project, teachers' access to and consciousness of such findings increased. Several reflected on it as it related to their own current practice, which prompted them to ask themselves questions and to use research in their classrooms to diagnose areas of need. There is a need for researchers from higher education and school districts to devote more time to collaborative work with teachers to help them design suitable research techniques that will enable them to reflect on their planned curriculum and strategies in the light of what actually occurs in the classroom.

Classroom research provides not only an opportunity for individual teacher development but also potential for the development of collaborative partnerships. Research support networks could be set up within schools and districts where teachers could share ideas, formulate strategies, provide feedback and also formulate joint classroom research projects. Study groups can also be set up where staff meet on a regular basis to discuss topics they have selected. To help stimulate and focus discussion an article can be circulated in advance. Teachers can set their own agenda and time to meet. As well as being a forum for increasing professional knowledge, study groups can also become places for solving professional problems, sharing classroom ideas and techniques and gaining social support from colleagues. Sometimes the reading and discussion raise issues that require more detailed investigation and reflection through classroom research. Coaching relationships can also be used to extend the exploratory work of study groups.

Mentoring and coaching relationships

It is never too early for new teachers to learn about school development, their role as a member of staff and its implications for their career development. At the end of their first year, the major need expressed by new teachers is personal support and encouragement from experienced colleagues (Earley 1994b). A colleague of ours describes his early months in teaching: 'I looked into my bag of tricks and pulled out anger.' Mentoring of newly qualified teachers offers experienced teachers the opportunity to take on leadership roles as they help induct an inexperienced colleague into the working and social life of the school. It is not, however, merely a one-way process: the agenda for the relationship needs to originate from both teachers (Watkins and Whalley 1993). In Halton several experienced teachers viewed mentoring as a chance to reflect on their own practice through observing their partner in the classroom or being observed by them. If a trusting relationship is built, the new teacher can act as a fresh pair of eyes on the mentor's classroom practice. In Halton a district-level programme was also developed for first-year teachers paired with experienced mentor teachers from the same school. Partners attended sessions together and worked together throughout the year. This meant that mentor teachers also received input, which they reported benefited their personal professional development as well as their ability to assist their less experienced partner.

Peer coaching relationships are in some ways similar, but involve a more equal partnership in terms of length of experience or interest. Joyce and Showers (1982) define coaching relationships as those that follow up, continue and extend in-service training in school as teachers attempt to master and implement new knowledge, skills and strategies. Essentially, during training, a new idea or strategy (theory) is presented and demonstrated, after which time participants practise the new skill and receive feedback. Joyce and Showers have found that incorporation of the new skill into the teacher's regular repertoire is most likely to occur when teachers engage in coaching activities that include observation of each other in the classroom and provision of feedback that is accurate, specific and non-evaluative. Coaching may also include joint problem solving, planning of lessons and analysis of materials.

Appraisal

In their reflections as a result of their evaluation of the School Teacher Appraisal Pilot Study, Bollington and colleagues (1990) highlighted the connection between appraisal and school development. They suggested that linking appraisal and school review can result in a more powerful school improvement strategy because teachers can set their own appraisal within the context of the school's 'appraisal', and appraisal can, therefore, be viewed more as a developmental than accountability experience.

We provided an example in Chapter 2 of Halton's teacher appraisal (CS&E) and its links to school growth planning. This approach has much in common with descriptions of personal development planning (Day 1994). In Halton, through discussion with their principal, vice-principal or department head, each teacher expressed their commitment to focus on particular areas of the school's growth plan and to develop themselves in this area. This is not to say that their own professional interests were ignored, but that they also assumed a responsibility to participate in the development of the whole school, committing themselves to a range of professional development activities that both served their own and the school's needs.

Developing change process understanding and skills

We have already noted that all school improvement involves change. Initial stages of the change process are frequently associated with turbulence and anxiety (Fullan 1991; Huberman 1992a). Understanding the change process and its implications, both personally and developmentally, can help teachers, particularly through the early stages. In Halton, as the emphasis shifted towards collaborative decision making, group skills became increasingly important. For teachers to work and plan together, and to become increasingly involved in decisions at school level, staff development is necessary in the area of shared decision making, group processing and conflict resolution. Working with school staffs to help them reflect on and analyse their school's culture and its implications for school improvement was a key element of staff development in Halton.

A voluntary five-day workshop was developed for school teams. Practitioner knowledge gained through early attempts at growth planning was incorporated into the training, codeveloped by school and system-based personnel. Workshops emphasized strategies to help teams work with colleagues back at school to conduct needs assessments, set goals, and implement and evaluate them. Particular emphasis was paid to necessary process skills for organizational development: team building, problem solving, decision making, conflict resolution, understanding change and people's reactions to it and stages of adult development. Time was also devoted to the development of shared values and beliefs, a collaborative culture, and vision building, as well as an understanding of school effectiveness, school improvement and the change process.

Another programme was process consultation (Schein 1969). This prepared people to participate in or lead group situations and to facilitate work group issues, including needs assessments, communication, problem solving, decision making, group norms and growth, leadership and authority, team building, contracting, improving motivation, interpersonal effectiveness and evaluation. Thus it focused on both political and cultural facets of the change process.

While Halton's school growth plan team training was offered centrally to help develop change agentry capacity, teachers within a school might choose to study, discuss and apply the literature on organizational development (Schmuck and Runkel 1985), school improvement, change and school culture through setting up study groups.

The role of the school in teacher development

If teachers' professional development is essential to school improvement, then it is the role of the school to ensure that the climate is one in which ongoing adult learning can flourish and where adult learning needs can be met. The school as a workplace with its unique culture has an enormous capacity to support and enhance teachers' learning, as we have emphasized in Chapter 6.

Conditions under which teachers attempt to learn in schools vary, however. Some are more conducive, for example provision for teachers' physical needs and an appropriate context for learning, such as adequate time, sufficient space and necessary materials; emotional support and a sense of belonging; facilitative leadership; and the presence of colleagues committed to learning (Nias *et al.* 1992). Schools also vary in the structures and processes that support teacher learning. Leithwood (1995) describes structures and processes that influence organizational learning. The former include school-based professional development, informal meetings, mentor programmes, school accreditation and opportunities to attend external workshops. The latter comprise consultation with colleagues, personal reflection, experimentation and reading.

Professional staff development requirements are clearly spelled out and addressed in schools with more effective development planning processes. A staff development policy should attend to adult learning principles and provide opportunities for teachers to pursue their own learning needs as well as school development needs. Such a policy will ensure that time is provided for discussion, reflection, mutual observation, curriculum development and coaching and mentoring activities, as well as the more traditional workshop-style events. Development of non-teaching staff also needs to be incorporated.

In schools that are learning organizations the ten cultural norms we outlined previously thrive. While schools are fundamentally important to teacher development through the activities and supportive conditions offered, the kind of role we have tried to demonstrate provides a culture that promotes and supports teacher as learners and self-developing professionals (Bolam 1993). Within such a culture, the onus gradually shifts to each person to play the major role in their own development.

The role of teachers in their own development

Barth (1990) reminds us that on airlines, flight attendants tell adults to place their own oxygen masks on before placing masks on children, yet 'In schools we spend a great deal of time placing oxygen masks on other people's faces while we ourselves are suffocating' (p. 42). If, Barth says, teachers want children to breathe in new ideas, they must reveal themselves to children as learners. The work of Nias and her colleagues emphasized that teachers had the most fundamental role in their own learning, and that those who wished to improve were characterized by four attitudes:

they accepted that it was possible to improve, were ready to be self critical, and to recognize better practice than their own within the school and elsewhere, and they were willing to learn what had to be learned in order to be able to do what needed or had to be done.

(Nias *et al.* 1992: 73)

If teachers are involved in improving their whole schools, and not just their own classrooms, teacher development in its broadest sense can be seen to take place because teachers become part of a learning community where they see themselves as responsible, on a daily basis, for their own and colleagues' development. Fullan and Hargreaves (1991) offer teachers 12 guidelines for 'interactive professionalism' to help create, sustain and motivate them throughout their careers. These guidelines are intertwined and are ineffective in isolation from each other. Rather, they build on each other. We feel they both aptly summarize the professional development of teachers that takes place in schools that are learning communities, and also demonstrate respect for teachers as whole people, people who have important lives outside of teaching:

1 Locate, listen to and articulate your inner voice – each teacher is an important individual and needs personal time and solitude to develop their values and ideas.
2 Practise reflection in action, on action and about action – deep reflection on the activities one is engaged in, getting feedback from pupils or asking colleagues to provide other pairs of eyes and perspectives on one's work.
3 Develop a risk-taking mentality – change and improvement are accompanied by anxiety, uncertainty and stress, particularly in early stages of doing something new. The risk can be reduced by trying out a new practice on a small scale and, gradually, attempting to be the first person to act on the other guidelines.
4 Trust processes as well as people – teachers also need to take risks in terms of involvement in organizational processes, such as shared decision making, problem solving, and commitment to continuous enquiry.
5 Appreciate the total person in working with others – it is important to consider both professional and non-professional realms of colleagues' lives, and understand the many routes to professional development, some more appropriate for certain people or at particular times than others.
6 Commit to working with colleagues – the many possibilities include: mentoring; peer coaching; participating in a school improvement team, group trying out new teaching strategies or collaborating to develop a topic-based activity; or joining a school-wide committee.

7 Seek variety and avoid balkanization – teachers need to seek diversity to avoid cliques, and to understand the culture of their school.

8 Redefine your role to extend beyond the classroom – 'classroom conditions will never improve until teachers take action to improve the conditions surrounding classrooms' (Fullan and Hargreaves 1991: 104).

9 Balance work and life – the importance of developing lives, interests and selves outside school, as well as in, is an important protection against burn-out. It also leads to more interesting teachers and teaching.

10 Push and support principals and other administrators to develop interactive professionalism – teachers need to have strong expectations that principals and other administrators will model interactive professionalism. Principals, however, face many responsibilities, are also subject to overload and stress, and also must balance their professional and private lives.

11 Commit to continuous improvement and perpetual learning – to repeat two cultural norms, the best teachers never stop learning and they are always looking to improve their practice.

12 Monitor and strengthen the connections between your development and students' development – 'The value of teacher development and teacher collaboration must ultimately be judged by whether these changes make teachers better for their students in ways that teachers themselves can see' (p. 110). In effective schools, teachers monitor and measure what is important as it relates to pupil learning.

The link between teacher development and pupil development

Fullan and Hargreaves's final guideline brings us back to the ultimate purpose of teacher learning: pupil learning. Louis and colleagues (1994) find a link between the strength of teacher professional community in schools and teachers taking greater responsibility for student learning: teacher efficacy and high teacher expectations for students. Both of these have been found to influence student outcomes positively. While there is still limited evidence of the impact of staff development on pupil learning outcomes, Joyce (1993) points out that many studies of effects of teaching strategies and curriculum implementation supported by staff development demonstrate evidence of significant effects on students, not seen in large-scale field tests of generic staff development programmes. His own work with Showers on coaching demonstrates the power of the technique in helping teachers incorporate new strategies into their everyday repertoire and subsequent impact on students' learning (Joyce and Showers 1982, 1988). Further links between teacher and pupil learning need to be explored.

Leaders as learners

Barth continues his oxygen analogy by suggesting that if the principal wants teachers to learn, she or he too must learn. The role of the principal as a driving force in inviting a culture of collegiality and development is vital. Indeed, Barth views the principal as 'head learner', with the potential to act as 'a catalyst assisting teacher growth' (Barth 1990: 50). This can be achieved through principals inviting themselves professionally (see Chapter 7) but leaders need help and support with this. School systems and governments must play a role. Much of what we have said to this point concerning principles of adult learning and 'interactive professionalism' also applies to leadership preparation. Strength of leadership, particularly at the school level, sustained Halton through good times and bad. We attribute this strength to the following factors which contribute to the learning of leaders:

- A system-led and sponsored leadership course – virtually all people who aspire to any leadership post in the Halton system complete 'the leadership course'. From its origins in 1969, it has provided opportunities for people, regardless of role, to deal with important theories and concepts about leadership and education, build career-long networks and test their own potential.
- Rigorous selection processes for appointments – role expectations are defined and continually updated. Applicants for principal jobs must be supported by their principal, be observed in action by a member of the selection committee and complete a thorough interview process. For many years Ontario has required teachers to complete two summer courses conducted by both ministry and school board personnel before they receive certification to be a principal in the province.
- Induction programmes – as part of the overall staff development programmes, newly appointed leaders are provided with opportunities by the system to interact with more experienced leaders on an ongoing basis. The Halton principals' associations provide a powerful network of mentors for new appointees. The new government-sponsored Headlamp scheme in Britain (TTA 1995) for headteachers in their first two years fills a gap for these recently appointed leaders, for whom no leadership preparation courses prior to appointment exist.
- Ongoing leadership development – Leaders in Education Assisted by Peers (LEAP) has been described in detail elsewhere (Zywine *et al.* 1995). This is a model of collaborative staff development in which leaders work in partners to assist each other's learning. Principal centres in the United States, Australia, Singapore and Ontario also provide significant support networks and coaching opportunities for experienced principals. Such support is essential for all principals.

- The 'Manager's Letter' process – in this process, described in Chapter 2, leaders and the person to whom they report include the leader's professional growth as an integral part of the supervisory system. This system is a form of psychological contracting; the onus is on both partners to attend with integrity to the leader's development. Supervisors are required as part of their own appraisal to be accountable for the growth and development of the people who report to them.

Parents, governors and school councils as learners

One of the compelling messages from our effective schools work with parents in Halton is their desire to know what is going on in schools. They know schools have changed. Most thinking parents recognize that change is natural and predictable, but they ask, why 'these' changes? It is ironic that in an age of information and communication this is such a pervasive problem. Part of it results from the 'psychological moat' which many parents feel exists around schools. They are invited in on festive occasions for a 'show and tell', but kept quite separate from the ongoing life of the school. Parents who feel cut off from schools are prepared to believe the worst and accept aberrations as the norm.

We have emphasized the need to invite parents as school partners. This is a fundamental role for all school leaders, especially principals. Parents who feel like partners will listen to school people and act as critical friends. Uninvited parents will just be critical. In many ways the educational learning of parents and significant community members should be approached in much the same way as the learning of teachers. Similar principles of learning should guide a partners programme for parents and community. Contexts will determine precise strategies. There are enough examples in some of the most challenging situations of building drawbridges to invite parents to refute the charge that this desire to involve them is all rhetoric and no substance.

Entirely new areas of need for learning are opened up by the move to school councils with quasi-governance roles, and governing bodies – such as in England and Wales – who govern the school. There are two compelling reasons that education of school councillors or governors is crucial; one is for the sake of the pupils, and the other is for the sanity and security of the principal and staff. Since these are new areas of legislation, there are many grey areas; roles and responsibilities are often not well defined. There are sufficient number of horror stories to motivate people in schools, school systems and departments of education to consider the learning of councillors and governors.

A publication in England, jointly commissioned by the Department for Education, OFSTED and Banking Information Services, advises governors that

To help their schools most effectively, governing bodies need to take their own development seriously. They should consider their training and support needs carefully, and be prepared to allocate funds for external courses, visits to schools, or training for the whole governing body.

(Barber *et al.* 1995b: 6)

The document lists the following features of effective governing bodies:

- working as a team
- good relationships with the headteacher
- effective time management and delegation
- effective meetings
- knowing the school
- training and development.

Clearly each of these items has implications for governors' learning. In the same way that schools have different cultures, governing bodies seem to have different cultural identities that include norms and expectations about training and development (Earley 1994a). While much of this might take place in-house, in addition, Earley maintains, governors need ongoing access to high quality external training. This has financial ramifications and training budgets are always limited. Schools are unable to provide for all the needs of governors. Governments, who have in most cases mandated school councils and other governing bodies, bear a responsibility to provide at least some of the support to these new structures. Training for all school board members in Scotland has been organized by the Scottish Office Education Department, to give them greater understanding of their role in school development (MacBeath *et al.* 1992). If the situation in England is any barometer, however, the possibilities of such support are only wishful thinking.

Conclusion

Many teachers and others say they do not want to 'be developed'. In other words, they are not looking for other people to be responsible for their learning. Within the right school which provides opportunities and motivation for self-development teachers', principals', parents' and others' learning can thrive. Little (1990) points out it is possible to become a better teacher just by being a member of staff at a particular school. We would add that it is possible to be a better parent, governor, community member by being a partner of a particular school. In such a school ultimately everyone, supported by colleagues, is responsible for their own learning. There is a saying: 'Some people make things happen; some people watch things happen: some people ask "what happened?"'

If practitioners and their partners want to ensure that they are continuing to learn, they should be asking themselves three questions:

- To what extent is my school a learning organization for adults as well as children?
- Am I part of that learning organization?
- How can I play my part in developing my school as a learning organization for myself, my colleagues and partners?

eleven

EVALUATE WHAT
YOU VALUE

Performance and accountability are watchwords of the 1990s. A common thread to the reform plans of virtually every nation, state or province is that improvement will happen if we just test pupils, and make schools and teachers accountable for the products of schooling. The metaphor of 'product' to describe pupils reflects the market-place and choice consider-ations which motivate much of this political activity. In Britain, for example, this rationale underpins development of league tables of raw examination results, attendance and truancy figures, and the external inspection system operated by the government's Office for Standards in Education (OFSTED). A cruel irony is that there is very little evidence that external assessments actually improve the quality of education. In fact, there is substantially more evidence of their negative effects on teaching (Haladyna *et al.* 1991; Smith 1991) and many examples of 'teaching to the test', where test content drives what is taught. None the less, governments have spent millions on such strategies, while cutting proven approaches like staff development.

Why have non-educators determined a narrow range of outcomes on which schools are to be judged? It is too easy to point outside education and say 'they' are misguided or perverse. If there is a problem for educators and researchers, we did it to ourselves. We have never demonstrated to ourselves, let alone anyone else, that schools make a difference to pupils' learning, knowledge, skills and attitudes which will enable them to be successful citizens in the twenty-first century. If most educators are not assessment literate how can we expect our publics to understand the issues that relate to assessment?

Assessment and testing are a high stakes business. We all know from our own school days, what gets measured, or assessed, gets valued. If schools do not measure what they value, what others choose to measure will be valued. The onus to find a way out of this dilemma is not just on people in schools. For too long, researchers have agonized over difficulties of comparing more authentic forms of assessment despite their accepted validity within the teaching profession. Even those practitioners who understand the importance of assessment reliability are frustrated. The following example, admittedly oversimplified, helps to describe the challenge of developing meaningful ways to assess learning and, therefore, schools.

One of us has a mother who is over 80 years of age and must take an Ontario driver's test each year to retain her licence. She must successfully complete two tests. First she completes a multiple choice test on rules of the road and road signs. She rarely misses an answer. This test has many advantages. It assesses the basic knowledge necessary to be a driver and it determines whether a person can recognize shapes and colours and read instructions in context. The test is very reliable: that is, different markers arrive at the same score for the applicant. Such tests are also relatively inexpensive to administer, and produce a numerical total easily understood and communicated. Would you accept these results as satisfactory demonstration that a person should be driving on the same roads as you? We think the answer is obvious – no! Every day, around the world, similar types of tests are accepted as proof of pupil literacy, mathematical abilities and scientific skills. Such tests are used to sort pupils; compare pupils, schools, districts, states, provinces and even countries; and to make significant policy decisions.

Fortunately for those of us who drive, in many countries elderly people, as well as new drivers, must take a road test to maintain or receive their driving licence. A certified examiner puts the driver through a series of practical tests to see if the applicant has the necessary skills to operate a car, can apply knowledge of the rules of the road, and can demonstrate appropriate attitudes such as courtesy. The result of the in-car test is combined with the written test to determine success. It is, in effect, an assessment of the whole driver, not just the driver's ability to remember facts and details. The in-car examination is a valid test because it actually assesses skills, knowledge and attitudes necessary to drive a car safely. This is an example of performance assessment. While it is valid, it is not as reliable as paper-and-pencil tests because different examiners have different standards. This can be overcome, however, through thorough training of examiners. This type of assessment is labour intensive and, therefore, potentially more expensive. It is also not as easy to reduce results to numbers or draw generalizable conclusions about the quality of what has been assessed. It is a matter of great urgency, therefore, that ways be found to ensure greater reliability of authentic forms of assessment so that the full range of achievement can be measured.

A related but no less vital issue is to balance the drive for accountability and outcomes with attention to the process of change. Given what we know about difficulties of implementing new ideas, both monitoring and evaluating the change process are essential to school improvement. In fact, we would argue that when school improvement activities fail, it is often because insufficient time was taken to determine how the initiative was progressing and whether it made any difference. Assessment should not only tell you which rung of the change ladder you are on but also whether the ladder is leaning against the right wall.

In this chapter we consider some issues that impinge on the judgement of school effectiveness and improvement and propose a framework for the evaluation of key aspects of effectiveness and improvement.

What should be the purposes of evaluating schools?

Different educational stakeholders vary in their perceptions of the purposes for evaluating schools. While external accountability appears to be a perennial favourite of politicians, many people view empowerment, teacher development and school improvement as more important. The question is, are the two incompatible? From our experience, the twin pillars of accountability and empowerment (Glickman 1990) are compatible. Before a system or government gets heavily involved in accountability activities, however, educators must be empowered through effective processes and support to control the nature and extent of change in their school. This approach builds confidence, risk taking and openness to accountability practices (Stoll and Fink 1992).

We believe that the key purposes for any judgements of school quality should be to:

- Promote school self-accountability, translatable into wider accountability – teachers and principals need to know they make a difference to their pupils' progress, development and achievement. Assessment-literate educators have nothing to fear about open access to data if they have taken the time to educate interested stakeholders in interpretation and use of data. School governors and parent councils, for example, need to understand the impact of context on pupil progress.
- Provide useful indications of what works well and what needs to be improved – it is important to know what works well so it can be celebrated and analysed to understand its success. Knowing what does not work well does not explain how to change it, but offers a starting point for reflection on why something is not as effective as it might be, the barriers that prevent improvement and what needs to occur to ensure improvement. Even summative data, collected at the end of an initiative, project or schooling phase should be used for formative, ongoing monitoring purposes.

- Guarantee equal opportunities for all pupils – equity is a fundamental tenet of school effectiveness. Some schools are differentially effective: they offer better opportunities to one pupil group than another, for example girls rather than boys, younger rather than older pupils, pupils of one particular ethnic or social class background, pupils taking particular subjects or courses, or pupils in different levels or streams. During evaluation, data should be disaggregated to examine differences between such groups.
- Determine trends in schools' effectiveness and improvement over time – teachers need to know if their school is improving or declining over a period of years. Evaluation information for one year alone only provides a limited picture of the school's effectiveness and cannot ascertain the extent to which it has attempted to act on previous evaluations.
- Lead to further development – information on schools' effectiveness and improvement is only helpful if it is used. All too often people who provide data to schools assume that teachers know what to do with it, and some school staffs believe they have achieved their purpose once they have collected data. Cousins and Leithwood (1993) argue the importance of 'knowledge utilization': that is, the use of evaluative data or judgements for improvement purposes. Data cannot just be collected or provided. Clear explanation and staff development may be necessary, as well as an understanding of the history, context and culture of the school from which data have been collected and into which they will be fed back. Guidance and directions on what needs to be done to improve are also important.

Who should evaluate schools?

Real improvement comes from within and is not externally imposed or mandated. Many school self-evaluation models of the 1970s and 1980s were underpinned by this assumption. Appropriate self-evaluation provides the ultimate demonstration of self-accountability. Is only the school in a position to judge its effectiveness and improvement? An inherent danger in self-evaluation is that a school might not always identify its weaknesses. Insiders may be too close to problems to be able to diagnose them adequately, or may have limited expectations about what is possible with particular pupils. The vast majority of teachers also have no training in inspecting and auditing skills (D. Hargreaves 1995b). People within the school, none the less, do know it best. In contrast, an outside eye may spot important issues unintentionally overlooked in everyday school activity, and bring a broader frame of reference. The rationale that school practitioners are not the best people to judge their own schools and may be subject to bias underpins many inspection models, notably the OFSTED system in Britain. A problem with such external models is pressure on schools to conform to the inspection model and criteria, in the same way as standardized tests promote teaching to the test. More seriously, they inhibit creative and critical teacher reflection on the judgement and evaluation of school effectiveness and school improvement, and cost a lot to identify the aberrant. This is one area where experience of business organizations appears to have been ignored. Quality control inspection systems have been rejected by business and industry in favour of quality assurance that puts responsibility for quality at the door of the workplace (D. Hargreaves 1995b).

It is not a case of choosing one or the other. Systems that blend internal and external evaluation can combine the best features of both. One example is the Quality Assurance school review approach developed in several Australian states (Cuttance 1995) where inspections are 'done by' rather than 'done to' school communities. The school is primarily responsible for developing review focus areas through carrying out a self-audit, including analyses of its own student learning outcomes. Computerized software is provided to the school to assist in this task. The principal and a teacher attend all review team sessions where evidence is discussed. The review team comprises principals, teachers and administrative staff from other schools, school system quality assurance staff and a local community member from the reviewed school. Team members are seconded for up to a year and receive training in quality assurance review practices and procedures. The benefits of this are that a large number of teaching staff participate in the experience and then return to their schools with enhanced evaluation skills. Practitioners also help to develop statements of outcomes that can be obtained from best practice.

The use of critical friends in self-evaluation efforts provides another opportunity for internal and external eyes to examine jointly a school's effectiveness and improvement. Such outsiders might help schools collect, analyse and interpret data on pupil achievement, progress and development, teacher practices and general school functioning. They might also be invited to observe specific aspects of the school agreed in a pre-specified agenda and, from this, provide feedback, pose questions and engage in discussion about possible improvement routes. This is a particular benefit of critical friendship, not shared by most inspection models that fall short of guidance on specific improvement strategies. Such an approach has occurred in Lewisham in south London where, for example, a primary headteacher commissioned LEA advisers to assist her in a joint audit to evaluate the quality of learning and teaching and standards of achievement in the school. In this school, where the ethos reflected a collegial feeling of mutual support and pride, but standards of pupil achievement were unsatisfactory because of low staff and parent expectations of themselves and the pupils, the findings provided necessary data to galvanize action to move the school forward (Stoll and Thomson 1996). Governors or parent council members might be invited to fulfil such a role.

Figure 11.1 Evaluating school effectiveness and school improvement

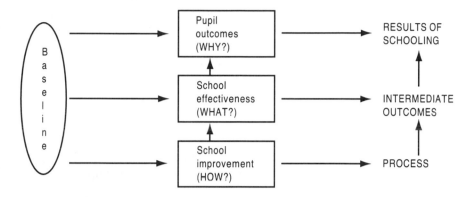

Whether or not the school chooses to invite outsiders to assist self-evaluation, a variety of perspectives on the school's workings and relationships needs to inform audit and evaluation. Parents and non-teaching staff have important opinions; and, all too often, pupils' perspectives on the educational process are neglected. In appraisal, for example, perspectives other than those of line managers are important. Pupils' views should be incorporated in teacher appraisal systems and teachers should provide input into headteachers' appraisals. Pupil attitudes to school can be tapped through surveys or informal interviews. For example, Scottish teachers have found creative ways of administering ethos indicators (SOED 1992) to elicit young children's attitudes (MacBeath 1994).

What aspects of school improvement and school effectiveness should be evaluated?

An improving school is a self-evaluating school. To fulfil the purposes outlined at the beginning of this chapter, the process of improvement as well as intermediate and final outcomes of improvement and effectiveness must be monitored and evaluated. We have developed a model to guide such self-evaluation (see Figure 11.1) and outline its components.

Collecting baseline information

In order to know where you are at any point, it is essential to know where you were when you started: this is baseline information. It may be an initial audit or needs assessment to be repeated at some later point. It may be specific data gathered once a development plan or improvement project target has been set to determine the starting point. Baseline data are vital and are an often neglected part of improvement initiatives. When schools have embarked on improvement efforts they appear to understand better the need for and importance of collecting baseline data against which they can measure increased effectiveness. There is, however, a tension between encouraging school ownership of improvement while persuading schools of the import- ance of processes they may not fully understand as being essential to self-evaluation and accountability (Stoll *et al.* 1995).

Evaluating the process of improvement

Measuring change is a challenge. A key feature of school effectiveness research is the demonstration of effectiveness in terms of pupil outcomes. Until recently school improvement, in contrast, has emphasized process over outcomes. School improvement is often described as a journey. If it is viewed as a particular type of journey, a climb up a staircase, the top stair represents effectiveness as demonstrated in positive pupil outcomes, but each stair has to be climbed to reach the top. Near the top are other intermediate outcomes of teacher and organizational effectiveness. They are also part of the process: the means to the end. Without arriving at these, however, the top cannot be reached; the journey up the stairs is not complete until the last stair, positive pupil outcomes, has been climbed. This becomes more complicated because once the top is reached, the journey must begin again. Given there is no such thing as complete effectiveness, if you do not continue climbing upwards, the chances are that you will start to move downwards.

In their study of urban high schools, Louis and Miles (1990) found that coping with problems was 'the single most important influence on outcomes' (p. 280). Readers might ask what this has to do with evaluation. Earlier we discussed the inevitability of problems in all school improvement efforts. Part of coping with problems involves actively searching out and finding them. A key function of formative evaluation is concerned with locating problems: seeing where the process of change is not running as smoothly as it might and where individual pupils, groups, or whole classes do not appear to be benefiting from a new initiative. Monitoring and analysing the process of change is as important as evaluating its intended outcomes.

Hopkins (1995) argues the case for 'more user-friendly yet penetrating techniques' to investigate and measure the complexity of the school change and improvement process. Let us turn to some examples of such techniques, developed to help schools and districts monitor and critically examine different facets of the improvement process. The first three examples focus specifically on the change process and the reactions to it of individuals and whole staffs. The fourth enables a school to analyse its culture over time.

Implementation profile

Change is both personal and developmental. Individual teachers differ in readiness towards new initiatives (Loucks and Hall 1979), as do whole schools faced with external mandates and even internally derived change. In the early years of growth planning in Halton, schools were at varied stages of understanding of and comfort with the process. It was important, politically, for administrators and school board trustees to know and accept the fact that all schools cannot and do not march together. Contexts vary. This might appear a problem, and yet we accept that there are children of different abilities in classrooms and that teaching strategies need to be differentiated.

To help school staffs see what stage their school had reached in various growth planning activities and supportive conditions, an implementation profile was developed. The key use of such self-evaluation profiles is to indicate process and to open up issues for debate and improvement. It can also be used by districts to monitor process and progress throughout the system and identify support needs. The implementation profile is based on the Levels of Use scale of the Concerns-Based Adoption Model (C-BAM) (Loucks and Hall 1979). Information can be gathered over a period of years and examined for changes. Implementation profiles identify critical components or key elements which must be present for an innovation to succeed. Educators may be at different stages of development in the critical components. These are described as four levels of use:

- awareness   'beginning stages', acquiring information and early use
- mechanical   'getting a good start', experimenting and trying to master strategies
- routine   'well on the way', having achieved a degree of mastery
- refined   'best practices working', introducing new developments and re-evaluating quality to achieve increased impact on pupils.

The four stages of the school growth planning process and four conditions associated with more successful planning efforts formed eight critical components of a school growth planning implementation profile. Each was elaborated into levels of use (see Figure 11.2 for examples of the stages).

In examining results on a growth planning profile, school staff might ask themselves the following questions:

- With which aspects of growth planning are people in this school most and least comfortable?
- Is pupil information systematically collected and used to select goals?
- Do each of the goals have success criteria that state what successful goal achievement will look like?
- How can we address aspects of growth planning that are a challenge?

Figure 11.2 Halton's implementation profile – the planning cycle

	Awareness	Mechanical	Routine	Refined
Assessment	The staff makes no or only occasional reference to data.	The staff refers to data but doesn't use them in a systematic way.	The staff uses data in an ongoing and systematic way in preparation of the school growth plan.	The staff uses the existing data and initiates its own ways to gather information.
Planning	The principal is aware of the effective schools movement and that a body of research exists. The principal knows the attributes of effective schools can be identified. The principal attempts to bring the effective schools movement to the awareness level of the staff. The principal attempts to implement one or two attributes of effective schools.	The principal can identify the critical attributes of effective schools. The principal is becoming familiar with the effective schools research. The principal conducts one or two staff meetings to familiarize staff with the concept of effective schools. The principal selects one or two attributes on the basis of perceived needs and incorporates the attributes into the school plan.	The principal and staff understand the concept of effective schools and can identify the attributes. The principal appoints a school growth plan team. The principal and planning team review data, regional trends, and set priorities for new goals and directions. The principal and staff determine the goals, and develop an implementation plan for the school growth plan.	The principal and staff know and use the characteristics of school effectiveness as a basis for the school growth plan. The principal and staff develop a school growth plan based on a thorough assessment, an understanding of regional trends and the involvement of students and parents in the process.
Implementation	The staff is aware of the school growth plan but does not implement it.	The staff implements parts of the school growth plan. Of the parts implemented, some are done better than others. Implementation is not always consistent.	The staff understands the school growth plan and supports it. All parts of the plan are implemented on a consistent basis. The plan has been integrated with the board's strategic plan, and makes an impact on personal growth plans.	The staff understands the plan, and has assumed ownership for it. Each member of staff supports the others, and all parts of the plan are fully implemented, according to the agreed criteria.
Evaluation	The staff is aware that evaluation is an important part of school growth planning, but does not have an effective process.	The staff has a partial process for the summative evaluations of the school growth plan, usually in areas such as student achievement and self concept.	The staff makes a formative and summative evaluation of key components of the plan such as: • student achievement • self concept • teacher attitudes • community attitudes.	Staff continually evaluates all aspects of the growth plan as part of an ongoing process of formative and summative evaluation.

- How can implementation of goals be enhanced?
- What methods do we use to measure successful goal accomplishment?
- What help is needed for evaluation?
- How will people inside and outside the school know that all our effort implementing goals has been worthwhile?
- What difference does growth planning make to pupil outcomes?

Stages of concern
C-BAM also addresses stages of concern teachers go through when faced with a change (Loucks and Hall 1979). Personal concerns – reflected in comments such as 'this means more work' – precede management concerns, where teachers want to know 'how do I do this?' These, in turn, precede pupil-orientated concerns: 'will this make a difference to the pupils?' Gradually, teachers consider how they could work with colleagues to refine the initiative and improve its impact. Teachers' concerns need to be elicited. Using surveys, interviews or asking teachers to write down their worries can help analyse particular problems. From these, a profile can be drawn for the whole staff to see where support needs to be targeted, individually or school-wide.

Agreement trial response types
A similar rationale underlies a response scale developed in Britain to examine how staff feel about agreement trialling of the National Curriculum key stage assessments (Clarke 1995). Agreement trialling is the discussion of pupils' work as it relates to statements of attainment in the original ten-level scale; its purpose is to come up with a consistent view of performance. Teachers have been asked, at different points in time of involvement, to indicate on a five-point response scale which response type most reflects its view.

- Reactive   'This change is of no use to me'
- Engaging   'This might be of some use to me'
- Active   'This is useful to me and I'll get involved'
- Reflective 'How has this been of use to me?'
- Creative   'Now we know what we can do, how can we develop it?'

An advantage of this approach is use of the friendly outside adviser or researcher, the critical friend, who works with teachers to help them reflect on and understand reactions to change, while at the same time developing a clearer understanding of strategies that enhance improvement. The response scale could, however, be used by a staff on its own.

Assessing the school's cultural norms
We have described ways to examine responses to change and stages of development over time. Another vital part of formative evaluation is ongoing

monitoring of the school's cultural norms. Using the norms described in Chapter 6, each staff member could assess the extent to which they are evident in their school, using the following scale:

1 = not at all
2 = to a limited extent
3 = to some extent
4 = fairly widespread
5 = school-wide.

Once results were collated, follow-up discussion could focus first on evidence for and celebration of areas rated positively, celebration being a vital norm of successful school improvement. Subsequently attention would turn to areas to which teachers gave poor ratings and those where there was disagreement between staff, for example where one-third felt problems were school-wide and another third felt they were limited.

Another simple but important way to monitor the improvement process is through observation and asking questions to locate implementation difficulties. The purposes of such ongoing monitoring are to:

- ascertain the types of problems being faced and their reasons
- determine how these might be resolved
- see whether teachers feel they have ample and relevant support
- find out whether too much has been taken on
- understand what works well and badly
- establish to what extent strategies might need adaptation
- ensure that morale remains good.

Intermediate outcomes

It is often difficult to distinguish between processes and outcomes, which is why teachers and schools often view successful implementation as an outcome. It may be helpful to think of intermediate outcomes, for example teacher attitudes and institutional change, as process indicators because this suggests that outcomes exist that are more final: namely, pupil outcomes. None the less, process indicators are valuable and need to be included in the evaluation of any change effort. Process indicators are vital as part of any formative evaluation because they are part of ongoing monitoring efforts to refine improvement goals.

Effective schools questionnaire
In addition to their use as part of a school development planning needs assessment (see Chapter 5), questionnaires can enable schools and districts to examine indicators related to the characteristics of effectiveness, school organization and development planning as an intermediate outcome to

evaluate the progress and attainment of various process strategies. In Halton, we collected data from a sample of teachers, students and parents throughout the system. Surveys were also made available and analysed if schools wished to use them with all staff or larger samples of students or parents. Schools could thus compare their own results with those of the system. Such surveys might be used at the start of an improvement initiative and repeated annually or every two years, to determine change in attitudes. Figure 11.3 shows examples of teacher survey items (Stoll 1992).

Intermediate outcome data may need contextualizing in the same way that pupil outcome data must be adjusted to take account of pupils' background and initial attainment. Contextual factors that might influence teacher attitudes, for example, include phase, location and size of school, pupil population characteristics, years experience as a teacher, length of time at present school, sex and role. Further work is needed to explore this issue.

Teacher as learner

Our cultural norms express the importance of continuous improvement and lifelong learning. If schools are to be filled with teachers who are lifelong learners, and if most of the difference in schools' effects on pupils can be seen at the classroom level, an appropriate intermediate outcome we would want to see is some evidence of 'the teacher as learner'. This might be demonstrated through attitude surveys, informal interviews, appraisal, evaluations of staff development and through classroom observation of, for example, strategies for grouping pupils, classroom management, promoting positive pupil self concept and engagement of multiple minds.

Pupil outcomes

Having monitored and evaluated *how* the improvement process progresses and *what* effects there are on intermediate teacher and school organizational outcomes, the final measure to be made relates to the *why* of schooling. The ultimate question that needs to be asked about the processes that occur at different levels, whether school, classroom or outside the school, is 'Does the educational experience encountered by pupils make a positive difference to them?' In this section we address the evaluation of effectiveness and improvement, as demonstrated in enhanced outcomes for all pupils.

Evaluating effectiveness

In our age of accountability, the outcomes of effective schools have, for the most part, become externally driven, and defined exclusively by good results on standardized tests or public examinations. Even Ontario, with its 20-year history of no provincial testing, is moving the way of many jurisdictions by introducing language and mathematics assessments at the end of grades 3, 6,

Figure 11.3   The Halton Board of Education effective schools teacher questionnaire

---

Instructions

The statements in the questionnaire have been developed and are grouped according to the characteristics of effective schools. For each statement, please circle two responses on the following scales:

A. First, *the extent to which you agree with the statement as it reflects what is happening in our school at this time.*

      1 = strongly agree
      2 = agree
      3 = uncertain
      4 = disagree
      5 = strongly disagree

B. Second, *how important do you feel that this characteristic is in creation of a more effective school?*

      1 = crucial
      2 = important
      3 = fairly important
      4 = not very important
      5 = not at all important

Frequent monitoring of student progress

Reflects this school
A

Importance
B

1 2 3 4 5   34. Student progress is monitored through a variety of methods of assessment and evaluation.   1 2 3 4 5

1 2 3 4 5   35. Teachers use assessment results to plan appropriate instruction and curriculum priorities.   1 2 3 4 5

1 2 3 4 5   36. Teachers communicate to students how and why evaluation methods are used.   1 2 3 4 5

---

9 and 11. Most of these tests and examinations do not measure the full range of learning experiences offered by schools; nor do they tell us about the development of pupils as future members of society. In fact they tend to promote a narrow curriculum. In 1984, a committee of the Inner London Education Authority described four aspects of achievement appropriate to

the aims of secondary pupils, only the first of which was adequately addressed by the public examination system of the time:

1　Written expression, retention and selection of knowledge at speed, and memorization.
2　Knowledge application, practical and oral problem solving and investigation.
3　Personal and social skills of communication, co-operation, initiative, self-reliance and leadership.
4　Motivation, commitment, perseverance and self-confidence.

(ILEA 1984).

While the last ten years in Britain have seen some changes, notably in attempts to incorporate the second aspect in the General Certificate of Secondary Education (GCSE), the third and fourth aspects are still relatively untapped. Elsewhere in this book we have offered views of learning emanating from cognitive psychology. Gardner (1993) argues that an assessment initiative being planned today

> should be sensitive to developmental stages and trajectories. Such an initiative should investigate human symbolic capacities in an appropriate fashion in the years following infancy and investigate the relationship between practical knowledge and first- and second-level symbolic skills. It should recognize the existence of different intelligences and of diverse cognitive and stylistic profiles, and it should incorporate an awareness of these variations into assessments; it should possess an understanding of those features that characterize creative individuals in different domains. Finally, a new assessment initiative should acknowledge the effects of context on performance and provide the most appropriate contexts in which to assess competences.
>
> (p. 173)

Gardner agrees that this is a 'tall order' but maintains that, unlike many current assessment systems, this would be 'both true to the individual and reflective of our best understanding of the nature of human cognition' (p. 173). This, as we have noted, proves a major challenge in terms of reliability, particularly when assessments are heavily dependent on teachers' delivery. None the less, it is time to put higher-order academic outcomes, and social outcomes, at the top of the agenda alongside ongoing favourites. An effective school cannot only be judged by its pupils' ability to read, write and be numerate. Schools have a larger role to play in pupils' lives.

Demonstrating value added

Even if assessments are appropriate, valid and reliable, other problems exist. Raw results, while they may demonstrate actual levels of attainment, do not tell those inside or outside schools how effective they are because results partly reflect what pupils had already achieved when they entered school and the influence of their home background. Proper assessment of progress, the 'value added' by the school, requires statistical adjustment for various background factors at the level of the individual child, and for prior attainment that has an even greater influence (McPherson 1993; Thomas *et al.* 1995).

This is compounded by the use of results, whether raw or adjusted, to compare schools. This can be seen in Britain's 'league tables' of schools' raw results where schools are rank-ordered, and in various American states where the national flag is still raised on school buildings when test scores rise and lowered when they decline. Given the importance of prior attainment and background factors to pupils' later attainment, to assess the effectiveness of schools without taking such differences into account is highly problematical, as a government-sponsored reviewer of the British National Curriculum and assessment system reported:

> Without a value-added dimension, the obvious basis for judgement is that 'higher' scores represent better practice and 'lower' scores worse. This could lead to unwarranted complacency on the part of some schools . . . and, conversely, to despair on the part of others.
>
> (Dearing 1993: 77)

Unless schools are compared on a like-with-like basis, judgements will not be fair or valid. Increasingly in Britain, schools, LEAs, the media and, most recently, the government have been looking for ways to establish adequate contextual control measures in the analysis of educational outcomes. These range from simple manual disaggregation of academic results and attendance information by, for example, sex, year and ethnic background, to the use of sophisticated multilevel modelling techniques (Goldstein 1995). Having established the impact of a range of different intake factors, such analyses can provide estimates of value-added scores.

Proponents of value-added analyses are, none the less, cautious about their use and interpretation. In particular, even when value-added analyses are used, confidence intervals for school 'effects' are wide. This means that many schools cannot be separated reliably; therefore it is inappropriate to produce fine rank orderings of schools. Goldstein (1992) cautions: 'even with "adjusted" league tables, the results need to be interpreted carefully, and are most useful for identifying extreme schools or departments which may be performing much better or worse than predicted' (p. 313).

While Thomas and Goldstein (1995) argue that problems occur when assessments are set within an accountability framework which leads to institutional comparisons, they see use for a range of value-added measures for different outcomes 'if provided confidentially and with caveats about accuracy, for stimulating and informing school self-evaluation and initiatives for improving educational standards'(p. 17).

The real use of any evaluation data should not be for invidious school comparisons. It should enable an individual school to assess where it is, determine areas for improvement and, having addressed these areas, evaluate whether it has made the intended progress.

Differential effectiveness

It is often assumed that an effective school is effective for all its pupils. If some pupils do better than others within a school, the school is displaying differential effectiveness. To determine whether this is the case, the school's outcome data, whether academic or social, needs to be disaggregated to look at the progress, achievement and development of different groups. Depending on the intake and phase of the school, results might be disaggregated by:

- sex
- social class background
- ethnic background
- age within classes – older compared with younger pupils
- year group, for example year 2 compared with year 3 or grade 9 with grade 10
- ability level, determined by prior attainment or level of class
- language of instruction, for example French immersion
- subject in secondary school departments.

In the name of equity, it is vital to know that all children are given the opportunity to achieve and to have a strong sense of self-worth.

Evaluating improvement

There are several ways for schools to evaluate improvement in pupil outcomes. An increase in raw examination or assessment results over a period of time does not necessarily indicate school improvement because influential background factors related to the pupil intake may change over time. Using contextualized results that have been collected over a period of years, however, a school can determine whether it continues to boost pupils' progress and 'add more value' each year (Gray *et al.* 1995). This can be examined for the pupils as a whole group as well as for pupils differentiated according to factors outlined in the previous section. To do this properly requires the use of multilevel modelling techniques and background information for individual pupils. Some districts and several higher education institutes provide such a statistical service for schools. This needs to become more widely available, as does support for interpretation of data to make it user-friendly.

Success criteria

When schools engage in development planning or particular improvement initiatives they need to identify particular pupil learning goals or targets. Success criteria are then required, specifically matched to particular targets, to determine their achievement. For example, if a goal is orientated towards incorporating information technology across the curriculum, success criteria might include examining the impact of target implementation on pupils' attitudes towards, usage of and performance on computers in different subjects. Some schools find this difficult, and evaluation is limited to an end-of-year round-up of strategies implemented to meet objectives. The underlying assumption of this 'check off the ones we have done' approach is that implementation is equated with improvement. Ongoing monitoring and final evaluation of success criteria related to intended outcomes are essential to all school improvement efforts.

A core question to be considered in selecting success criteria is 'What will be different in this school if this target is achieved?' Answers to this question enable choices of appropriate success criteria to be monitored to determine progress in meeting the target. Means to measure achievement of the success criteria can then be developed. The key message, however, is that pupil outcome measures need to be clearly defined at the beginning of any improvement initiative. This provides the potential for subsequent measurement of pupil outcomes and examination of change.

A particular challenge is that when schools go through the 'implementation dip' common to all change efforts, they are often afraid to measure what might look like failure. Thus, while some schools seek to evaluate their goal achievement from the start of their improvement effort, many need encouragement and support in selecting success criteria and related monitoring and evaluation devices.

District or group improvement projects

Evaluation of improvement projects containing more than one school is a different but equally important challenge. Barber and colleagues (1995a) found a significant minority of English urban improvement initiatives were set in motion with little clarity about desired outcomes, and several others where 'the implementation of noticeable change' or reports of participants were the sole evaluation criteria. Whether internal or external evaluation is selected, a formal evaluation plan is essential, including collection of baseline pupil data related to the specified goals of the project against which progress can be measured. Background information and prior attainment measures at the level of individual pupils are also necessary to provide a basis for progress to be examined. For a system-level project, two key questions emerge related to measuring pupil outcomes: 'can it be assumed that any change in broadly stated outcomes, such as academic progress, attendance, drop-out rate or pupil attitudes, is related specifically to the improvement project? Is it appropriate for a system to identify broadly stated pupil outcomes as a demonstration of such a project's impact?

Causality is extremely difficult to infer. School performance may result from more than school improvement activities within a school. Other concurrent projects may account for achievement gains. Similarly, at district level any one of many innovations might affect pupil outcomes. Equally, they might have more effect on teachers who, as a result, change their classroom behaviour (intermediate outcomes), which affects pupil outcomes. This is more likely. While evidence of improvement in pupil outcomes is essential, three points must be borne in mind. First, as we have already argued, these outcomes should be of a more comprehensive kind than those used to measure the success of many previous improvement efforts. Second, 'quick fixes' will not work. It is inappropriate to measure change in pupil outcomes throughout the system until the change effort has had time to take effect. This may take several years. It may be that some outcomes can be enhanced more quickly. As a result – particularly for schools experiencing difficulties – interim level outcomes such as pupil attitudes and attendance may be the most appropriate early targets (Reynolds 1996). Third, it may still be difficult to prove that any increases in pupil performance were due to such a project.

For district or other external partnership initiatives involving several schools, appropriate improvement process measures must be identified as well as indicators of intermediate and pupil outcomes. Because each school that participates is unique, it is also likely to have its own specific targets. Schools need support in identifying and setting appropriate success criteria; collecting, analysing and using baseline data; and monitoring and evaluating what they value.

Indicators

The concept of indicators has woven its way throughout this chapter. Internationally, increasing interest in indicators has broadened the scope of information that might be used to judge school effectiveness and improvement. An indicator is a single or composite statistic which reflects the health of an educational system and can be reliably and repeatedly obtained. For example, the drop-out rate in Ontario is 18 per cent. This is an indicator. By itself it tells us very little until we put some kind of interpretation around it. Indicators 'do not provide the diagnosis or prescribe the remedy; they are simply suggestive of the need for action' (Nuttall 1994: 17). An indicator system is a network of indicators. Developing an indicator system, however, does signal that a school, district, province or nation measures what it values.

To use a medical analogy, if you have an annual check-up, you go through a battery of tests. Each is an indicator of physical health. A series or system of tests together provide a comprehensive picture. One measure may identify a concern, whereas a number of measures in combination help to confirm good health, or pinpoint problems and allow for purposeful remediation. Further information is required for accurate interpretation of any indicator. To take another medical example, without supporting information, it would be impossible to tell whether the indicator of empty hospital beds meant that a hospital has cured patients and sent them home or whether beds are empty because patients have died! (Riley 1994).

Indicators are complex. Politicians who seek clear output measures like dials on a car's dashboard (Carter 1989), do not wish to accept that 'Measures of performance are, instead, more contestable notions, influenced by a complex range of factors and are perhaps more aptly described as "tin openers" which open up a "can of worms" and lead to further examination and enquiry' (Riley 1994: 87).

Indicators are not easily developed. While they are most often quantitative measures, those related to processes of schooling may require qualitative judgements to be made, which involve value judgements and subjective assessments (Gipps and Stobart 1993), and some aspects of schooling are not easily measured.

Drawing on ideas from participants in the OECD/CERI International Educational Indicators (INES) project (Bottani and Tuijnman 1994; Riley and Nuttall 1994), we have summarized key considerations for those wishing to set up indicators at school, district, provincial or national level:

- The purpose and audience for collecting information need to be clear.
- It is important to measure and acknowledge outcomes.
- Performance indicators are only part of the whole-school story.
- There is a danger of overvaluing easily measured outcomes at the expense of ones less quantifiable.
- Indicators should measure enduring features of schools so trends can be analysed over time.
- Indicators should be readily understood by broad audiences.
- Information should not be collected merely because it is available.
- Indicators should address quality, equity and efficiency issues.
- Collecting too few indicators may lead to interpretation difficulties because of insufficient information. Too many can be overwhelming.

At all levels of the education system, from school to national, there needs to be a public and open debate on what indicators are the most appropriate to demonstrate schools' effectiveness and improvement in the broadest sense. Perhaps most important is the need for teachers to be involved in designing and implementing any national monitoring system for, as Willms (1992) argues, their involvement 'increases the likelihood that performance indicators will inform school policy and practice' (p. 26). Teacher involvement and commitment, however, is insufficient, as has been demonstrated so starkly in the abrupt termination of the barely five-year-old Californian Learning Assessment System (CLAS) due to political lobbying of external pressure groups (Chrispeels 1995).

At school level, making choices between many possible indicators is difficult. Each school needs to consider its own purpose and evaluate the pupil outcomes it values, as well as selecting or developing appropriate ways to monitor and evaluate intermediate outcomes and the improvement process. We have offered ideas based on our work, but the final choice must be up to each school.

Making evaluation data manageable and useful

We have mentioned manageability. So often, data collected are not used because they are presented in non-user-friendly ways. Many districts produce compact school profiles or data organizers of key information for their schools. The better ones include graphical representations of data and are presented to schools with linked training on their interpretation and use. What is required, however, is a way to present data conceptually, visually and emotionally to capture peoples' attention and aid understanding. Changing our schools means changing the way data are communicated. School improvement is a process and not a product; what we need are new means of displaying evaluations that we value. These might include visual displays of data, videotapes, computer discs and other modes of representations more in line with postmodern society.

Conclusion

Once teachers, school communities and school systems have articulated their shared values on desired outcomes of schools for pupils, and have developed and implemented plans and strategies to reach these targets, it cannot be assumed that such strategies have had the desired impact. It is vital for schools to evaluate what they value. This, as we have argued, can be complicated, particularly when what you value is not easily assessed. Not everything that is important, however, can be counted; assessing complex skills, attributes and 'intelligences' by simple tests fails to capture the educational process. On the never-ending improvement staircase, moving schools monitor process as well as progress and final outcomes.

twelve

CHANGING OUR SCHOOLS: LINKING SCHOOL EFFECTIVENESS AND SCHOOL IMPROVEMENT

What started out as an attempt by a Canadian school district to improve school quality through the implementation of school effectiveness research findings evolved into the blending of the content of the school effectiveness knowledge base and other facets of this research with the processes of school improvement and planned change. From this and subsequent experience, and drawing on school effectiveness and improvement theories, we propose a theoretical but practical model to link school effectiveness and school improvement, through the school development planning process (see Figure 12.1). It provides a synthesis and summary of this book. The theoretical concepts that underpin the model are now described.

Context

Context is viewed as important to school improvement. In this model, it has two facets. The *internal* context includes some features sometimes considered as inputs or, in research studies, intake measures: for example, the nature of the school, its pupil population and current programme. It also incorporates teachers' professional, personal, political and learning experiences and a key contextual influence, the current culture.

The *external* existing context comprises government, ministry and local district initiatives and expectations, and societal trends. These must be considered before planning and development start. They may, however, continue to influence the improvement process once implementation is underway.

Figure 12.1 A model linking school effectiveness and school improvement

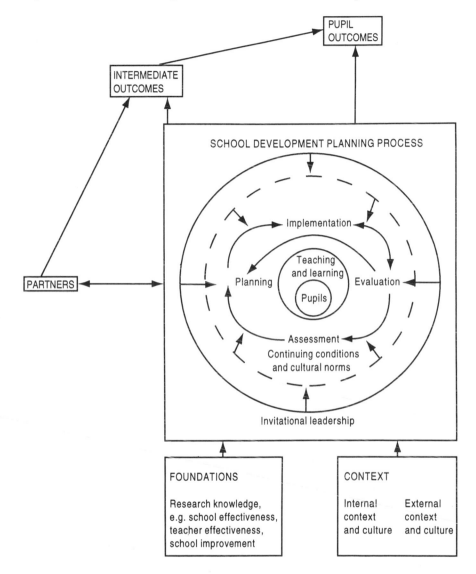

Context is one initial influence on the school development process. It acknowledges key differences, for example between primary and secondary schools, and it is what makes the process unique to each school. The second part, however, is its foundations.

Foundations

While contextual understanding might provide some information on which to base school development planning, research knowledge complements it and adds a further dimension. There are three bodies of research knowledge combined within foundations:

1 Research findings on school effectiveness.
2 Research findings on teacher effectiveness and cognitive psychology, to provide greater detail on successful teaching and learning strategies.
3 Research findings on school improvement.

Foundations and context together form the basis for school development planning. Both are scanned during the audit stage to help a school get a clear picture of its current state. Neither provides sufficient information on its own. Schools need to know what has proved successful in other places. Equally, they must be aware of their own particular situation and culture of external educational initiatives, and also keep an eye on society and the world of the future so that they do not prepare pupils for the past.

While school and teacher effectiveness characteristics are foundations for development planning, they also provide a constant reference point throughout the entire process.

School development planning process

The school development planning process is the vehicle that blends the school effectiveness research findings with the school improvement process. It incorporates two outer layers, an inner cycle and a two-layered central core:

1 Invitational leadership, the outermost layer, is supported by an understanding and feel for the change process. While leadership is a characteristic associated with school effectiveness, it merits separation as it fuels the engine of school improvement, and filters its influence through the next layer.
2 Continuing conditions and cultural norms, the next layer, include climate setting, vision, the development of collegiality and a collaborative culture, involvement and empowerment, a lifelong learning and improvement orientation, monitoring and problem solving, staff development and amending management structures. These conditions and development of norms may or may not precede development planning but they pervade the process and require constant attention.
3 The four-stage development planning cycle of assessment, planning, implementation and evaluation.

4 The outer layer of the central core is the essential focus on the teaching–learning process and curriculum.
5 The pupil, who is not only the product of improvement but is a participant in the process is, and should be, at the heart of school development planning.

Given that the school is perceived as the centre of change, this model addresses not only its external context, scanned during the audit phase, but also the ongoing active contributing components of the various external partners.

Partners

The school is both influenced by and reaches out and influences its partners (denoted by a two-way arrow). The external influences may include:

- support, through staff development, assistance, critical friendship, materials, research support and money
- information and data
- politics, both at the macro- and micro-level
- a strategic framework
- access to outside agencies
- educational networks.

School development planning and involvement of partners emphasize processes associated with school improvement. The ultimate purpose of schools, however, is to produce positive results. There are two key sets of outcomes in our model: intermediate outcomes and pupil outcomes.

Intermediate outcomes

In line with our argument that school development and teacher development are inextricably linked, earlier success as the result of the link between school effectiveness and school improvement should be demonstrated through intermediate teacher and organizational outcomes. Two key outcomes are outlined: first, identification of the characteristics of the *teacher as learner* that include a broad and varied technical repertoire, collaboration, mutual observation and feedback, reflection, and research or inquiry; second, positive attitudes towards the existence of the effectiveness characteristics, belief in their importance, and willingness to work towards them.

These outcomes may be influenced by the development planning process within the school, but also by involvement of various partners.

Pupil outcomes

The ultimate outcomes of the link between the two paradigms at school level should be those related to pupils. Returning to our definition, from knowledge gained from school effectiveness research, both in terms of its strengths and its omissions, five components are necessary:

1 A range of outcomes, both academic and social, that measure the goals of the school.
2 An emphasis on progress, to demonstrate the 'value' added by the school.
3 The highest standards possible.
4 A focus on equity, so that success is experienced by *all* pupils.
5 Standards that improve over time.

These pupil outcomes may be influenced both by the school-wide development planning process as well as more directly by the teacher as learner.

Thus, in this model, school effectiveness and school improvement are blended closely and complement each other's functioning. This model also links the internal doors to school improvement described in Chapter 4. It is the task of further research to investigate the practicality and validity of this model in other settings.

Two further issues remain. Governments in many countries are currently mandating significant external educational changes. Whole systems are being 'restructured'. What, therefore, are the implications of the link between school effectiveness and school improvement for restructuring?

School effectiveness, school improvement and restructuring

Certainly, in North America, restructuring has become a commonly used word with a variety of sets of definitions that include:

- school choice, mandated curriculum, standardized tests and open competition among schools and districts
- site-based management and the involvement of teachers in decision making
- contemporary notions of child development and cognitive psychology.

In Britain, the first two sets of definitions are combined within the 1988 Education Reform Act.

McLaughlin (1990) has suggested that processes which try to coerce restructuring through policy and mandate are unlikely to succeed: 'We have learned that we cannot mandate what happens to effective practice; the challenge lies in understanding how policy can enable and facilitate it' (p. 15).

This message is depressing for educators in schools, systems and countries where change has, indeed, been mandated, as it implies that reforms of such kind are doomed to failure. It would seem, however, that schools with a solid understanding and base of first- and second-wave change, as described in Chapter 2 and illustrated throughout this book, will be better able to cope with the demands required by such reform efforts. The school development planning process gives schools an organizational framework in which to examine reform demands, select priorities and consider their own preferred direction.

Throughout restructuring efforts or third-wave activity, therefore, if the foundations, continuing conditions and cultural norms within the school that support its growth are lost, the school could lose all the energy and creativity it has developed and teachers could remain in isolated classrooms. Thus, while the third wave may carry the school along, the first and particularly second waves must continue as undercurrents. School effectiveness and school improvement are therefore fundamental to each other and to educational reform efforts.

The final ingredient

Our model has dealt with a variety of concepts that link school effectiveness and school improvement: context, planning, culture, leadership, teaching and learning, partnerships, learning organizations, and evaluation – among many others. As we draw to a close we return to the one ingredient that underlies all the concepts we have described, one which will make or break the change process: caring. It not only provides the moral purpose for change, outlined in Chapter 1, it also adds the ethic which invites pupils, teachers, principals, parents and all those interested in educational change to join, contribute and persevere on the change journey. Martin Buber, the philosopher, in a 1939 address to teachers stated that 'education worthy of the name is essentially education of character' (Kohn 1991: 497). Not only are schools in the business of developing good learners, they are in the business of developing good people. This is what Drake (1995) meant when she talked about 'designing up' towards the 'being' level. It is what Purkey and Novak (1984) intend when they indicate that people, places, policies, practices and programmes in schools must communicate to pupils that they are able, responsible and worthwhile. It is what Noddings (1995) has in mind when she writes about the American *Goals 2000*:

> Our society . . . needs to care for its children – to reduce violence, to respect honest work of every kind, to reward excellence at every level, to ensure a place for every child and emerging adult in the economic and

social world, to produce people who can care competently for their own families and contribute effectively to their communities.

(p. 366)

We hasten to add, before anyone concludes that here is another 'soppy' plea to love the children but allow academic failure, as in D. Hargreaves's (1995a) welfarist culture, caring requires expectations of quality work from *all* children. To do less is uncaring. To decide that pupils cannot learn important things, like reading, because they are deprived, handicapped in some way or not academically bright, is to be uncaring and inhumane. Caring teachers expect *all* pupils to do well; they do what it takes to the best of their abilities to help each pupil achieve. The same principles of caring that engage pupils in their learning apply equally to caring for teachers, for parents, for important ideas, or for organizations like schools.

In Chapter 1 we suggested that schools reflected the factory metaphor of standardization, control, compliance, and focus on deficits as opposed to quality. We submit that a better metaphor is the school as a caring family. In contrast to dysfunctional families and ineffective schools described earlier, consider how truly functional and caring families and improving schools work. They have high expectations for all their members; they build on and recognize individual strengths while providing mutual support; they compensate and help individual weaknesses; and they behave in ways based on mutual trust, respect, optimism and intentionality. Learning communities are caring families. We submit that our societies need more moving schools that are based on the cultural norms of caring families and fewer 'good schools if this were 1965'. This should be the direction for the change journey. *Bon voyage.*

REFERENCES

Adam, E. (1987) *Steps to Success: the Principal's Role*. Burlington, Ontario: Halton Board of Education, unpublished manuscript.

Angus, L. (1993) The sociology of school effectiveness, *British Journal of Sociology of Education*, 14(3): 333–45.

Aronson, E., Blaney, N., Stephan, C., Sikes, J. and Snapp, M. (1978) *The Jigsaw Classroom*. Beverly Hills, CA: Sage.

Audit Commission (1989) *Losing an Empire, Finding a Role: the LEA of the Future*, occasional paper 10. London: HMSO.

Ball, S. J. (1987) *The Micro-Politics of the School: Towards a Theory of School Organization*. London: Methuen.

Ball, S. (1993) England and Wales: new relationships and new tensions, in S. J. Crump (ed.) *School-Centred Leadership*. Sydney, Australia: Thomas Nelson.

Banathy, B. (1988) Improvement or transformation?, in *Noteworthy*. Denver, CO: McREL.

Banks, J. A. (1993) Multicultural education: development, dimensions, and challenge, *Phi Delta Kappan*, 75(10): 22–8.

Barber, M. (1994) *Young People and Their Attitudes to School: an Interim Report of a Research Project in the Centre for Successful Schools*. Keele: Keele University.

Barber, M. (1995) *The Dark Side of the Moon: Imagining an End to Failure in Urban Education*. Text of the TES/Greenwich Lecture, University of Keele, May.

Barber, M., Denning, T., Gough, G. and Johnson, M. (1995a) Urban education initiatives: the national pattern, in M. Barber and R. Dann (eds) *Raising Educational Standards in the Inner Cities: Practical Initiatives in Action*. London: Cassell.

Barber, M., Stoll, L., Mortimore, P. and Hillman, J. (1995b) *Governing Bodies and Effective Schools*. London: Department for Education.

Barth, R. (1990) *Improving Schools from Within: Teachers, Parents and Principals Can Make the Difference*. San Francisco, CA: Jossey-Bass.

Bashi, J. (1995) Key national assignments for advancing and improving the Israeli education system during the 1990's, in B. P. M. Creemers and N. Osinga (eds) *ICSEI Country Reports*. Leeuwarden: Gemeenschappelijk Centrum voor Onderwijsbegeleiding in Friesland, January.

Bashi, J. and Sass, Z. (eds) (1992) *School Effectiveness and Improvement: Proceedings of the Third International Congress for School Effectiveness, The Van Leer Jerusalem Institute, Jerusalem 1990*. Jerusalem: Magnes Press.

Beane, J. A. (1991) Sorting out the self esteem controversy, *Educational Leadership*, 49(1): 25–30.

Beane, J. A. (1995) Introduction: what is a coherent curriculum? in J. A. Beane (ed.) *Toward a Coherent Curriculum*. Alexandria, VA: Association for Supervision and Curriculum Development.

Bennis, W. and Nanus, B. (1985) *Leaders*. New York: Harper and Row.

Berryman, S. E. and Bailey, T. R. (1992) *The Double Helix of Education and the Economy*. New York: Teachers College Press.

Block, P. (1987) *The Empowered Manager*. San Francisco, CA: Jossey-Bass.

Bolam, R. (1993) Recent developments and merging issues, in M. Williams and R. Bolam (eds) *The Continuing Professional Development of Teachers*. Swansea and London: University College of Swansea and Department for Education.

Bollington, R., Hopkins, D. and West, M. (1990) *An Introduction to Teacher Appraisal: a Professional Development Approach*. London: Cassell.

Bolman, L. G. and Deal, T. E. (1991) *Reframing Organizations*. San Francisco, CA: Jossey-Bass.

Bottani, N. and Tuijnman, A. (1994) *OECD Education Indicators*. Paper presented at the annual meeting of the American Educational Research Association, New Orleans.

Bowering-Carr, C. and West Burnham, J. (1994) *Managing Quality in Schools*. Harlow: Longman.

Bracey, G. W. (1992) The second Bracey report on the condition of public education, *Phi Delta Kappan*, 74(2): 104–17.

Bradshaw, J. (1988) *Bradshaw on the Family: a Revolutionary Way of Self-discovery*. Deerfield Beach, FL: Health Communications.

Brandt, R. (1993) On teaching for understanding: a conversation with Howard Gardner, *Educational Leadership*, 50(7): 4–7.

Brighouse, T. (1991) *What Makes a Good School?* Stafford: Network Educational Press.

Brookover, W. B., Beady, C., Flood, P. and Schweitzer, J. (1979) *School Systems and Student Achievement: Schools Make a Difference*. New York: Praeger.

Brophy, J. E. and Good, T. L. (1986) Teacher behavior and student achievement, in M. Wittrock (ed.) *Third Handbook of Research on Teaching*. New York: Macmillan.

Brown, S. and McIntyre, D. (1993) *Making Sense of Teaching*. Buckingham: Open University Press.

Brown, S., Riddell, S. and Duffield, J. (1996) Possibilities and problems of small-scale studies to unpack the findings of large-scale school effectiveness, in J. Gray, D. Reynolds, C. Fitz-Gibbon and D. Jesson (eds) *Merging Traditions: the Future of Research on School Effectiveness and School Improvement*. London: Cassell.

Bryk, A. S., Easton, J. Q., Kerbow, D., Rollow, S. G. and Sebring, P. A. (1994) The state of Chicago school reform, *Phi Delta Kappan*, 76(1): 74–81.

Busher, H. and Saran, R. (1994) Towards a model of school leadership, *Educational Management and Administration*, 22(1): 5–13.

Caldwell, B. and Spinks, J. (1988) *The Self-Managing School*. Lewes: Falmer Press.

Capra, F. (1983) *The Turning Point: Science, Society and the Rising Culture*. London: Flamingo.

Carnegie Council on Adolescent Development (1989) *Turning Points: Preparing American Youth for the 21st Century*. Washington, DC: Carnegie Corporation of New York.

Carroll, J. (1963) A model of school learning, *Teachers College Record*, 64. 723–33.

Carter, N. (1989) Performance indicators: backseat driver or hands off control? *Policy and Politics*, 17(2): 131–8.

Chapman, J. and Aspin, D. (1994) *Securing the Future: an Overview of Some Problems, Issues and Trends arising from the OECD Activity on "The Effectiveness of Schooling and of Educational Resource Management'*. Paper prepared for Directorate for Education, Employment, Labour and Social Affairs, Organization for Economic Cooperation and Development, Paris.

Cheung, Y. C. (1995) School effectiveness and improvement in Hong Kong, Taiwan and mainland China, in B. P. M. Creemers and N. Osinga (eds) *ICSEI Country Reports*. Leeuwarden: Gemeenschappelijk Centrum voor Onderwijsbegeleiding in Friesland, January.

Chrispeels, J. H. (1992) *Purposeful Restructuring: Creating a Culture for Learning and Achievement in Elementary Schools*. Washington and London: Falmer Press.

Chrispeels, J. H. (1995) *CLAS Down, but not Out: Continued Learning Assessment Activities in California Result from Earlier Co-construction of Reform Policies between State and Local Level*. Paper presented at the annual meeting of the American Educational Research Association, San Francisco.

Clarke, P. (1995) *Agreement Trialling as a Means to School Improvement*. Paper presented to the Eighth International Congress for School Effectiveness and School Improvement, Leeuwarden, The Netherlands, January.

Coleman, J. S., Campbell, E., Hobson, C., McPartland, J., Mood, A., Weinfeld, F. and York, R. (1966) *Equality of Educational Opportunity*. Washington, DC: National Center for Educational Statistics.

Coleman, P., Collinge, J. and Seifert, T. (1993) Seeking the levers of change: participant attitudes and school improvement, *School Effectiveness and School Improvement*, 4(1): 59–83.

Coleman, P. and LaRocque, L. (1990) *Struggling to be Good Enough: Administrative Practices and School District Ethos*. New York: Falmer Press.

Comer, J. (1988) Educating poor minority children, *Scientific American*, 259(5): 42–8.

Cooper, D. and Ward, F. (1991) *Ontario Assessment Instrument Pool: Basic Level*. Toronto: Ministry of Education.

Corbett, H. D. and Wilson, B. L. (1992) The central office role in instructional improvement, *School Effectiveness and School Improvement*, 3(1): 45–68.

Corporate Council on Education (1992) *Employability Skills Profile*. Ottawa: Conference Board of Canada.

Costa, A. L. and Kallick, B. (1993) Through the lens of a critical friend, *Educational Leadership*, 51(2): 49–51.

Cousins, B. and Leithwood, K. (1993) Enhancing knowledge utilization as a strategy for school improvement, *Knowledge*, 14(3): 305–33.

Covey, S. (1989) *The 7 Habits of Highly Effective People: Powerful Lessons in Personal Change*. New York: Simon and Schuster.

Creemers, B. P. M. (1994) *The Effective Classroom*. London: Cassell.

Creemers, B. P. M. and Osinga, N. (eds) (1995) *ICSEI Country Reports*. Leeuwarden: Gemeenschappelijk Centrum voor Onderwijsbegeleiding in Friesland.

Creemers, B. P. M., Peters, T. and Reynolds, D. (eds) (1989) *School Effectiveness and School Improvement: Proceedings of the Second International Congress, Rotterdam 1989*. Amsterdam: Swets and Zeitlinger.

Creese, M. (1995) *Effective Governors, Effective Schools: Developing the Partnership*. London: David Fulton.

Cuban, L. (1983) Effective schools: a friendly but cautionary note, *Phi Delta Kappan*, 64(10): 695–6.

Cuban, L. (1990) Reforming again and again and again, *Educational Researcher*, 19(1): 2–13.

Cuttance, P. (1994) The contribution of quality assurance reviews to development in school systems, in D. Hargreaves and D. Hopkins (eds) *Development Planning for School Improvement*. London: Cassell.

Cuttance, P. (1995) *Building High Performance School Systems*. Keynote address to the Eighth International Congress for School Effectiveness and Improvement, Leeuwarden: The Netherlands, January.

Dalellew, T. and Martinez, Y. (1988) Andragogy and development: a search for the meaning of staff development, *Journal of Staff Development*, 9(3): 32–6.

Dalin, P. (1993) *Changing the School Culture*. London: Cassell.

Davies, B. and Ellison, L. (1992) *School Development Planning*. Harlow: Longman.

Day, C. (1994) Personal development planning: a different kind of competency, *British Journal of In-service Education*, 20(3): 287–301.

Deal, T. E. and Kennedy, A. (1983) Culture and school performance, *Educational Leadership*, 40(5): 140–1.

Dearing, R. (1993) *The National Curriculum and its Assessment: an Interim Report*. London: NCC and SEAC.

Dempster, N., Logan, L. and Sachs, J. (1994) *The Protean Nature of School Development Planning: an Australian Study* (mimeo). Queensland: Griffith University.

Department for Education (1995) *Improving Schools: Factsheets*. London: HMSO.

Department of Education and Science (1989) *Planning for School Development: Advice for Governors, Headteachers and Teachers*. London: HMSO.

Drake, S. (1995) Connecting learning outcomes and integrated curriculum, *Orbit*, 26(1): 28–32.

Drucker, P. (1969) *The Age of Discontinuity*. New York: Harper and Row.

Drucker, P. (1993) *Post Capitalist Society*. New York: Harper Business.

Earl, L. and Cousins, J. B. (1995) *Classroom Assessment: Changing the Face*. Toronto: Ontario Public School Teachers' Federation.

Earley, P. (1994a) *School Governing Bodies: Making Progress?* Slough: National Foundation for Educational Research.

Earley, P. (1994b) *Initiation Rights: Effective Induction Practice for New Teachers*. Slough: National Foundation for Educational Research.

Edmonds, R. R. (1979) Effective schools for the urban poor, *Educational Leadership*, 37(1): 15–27.

Education Department of South Australia (1991) *A Review of Support for School Development Planning*. Adelaide: Education Department of South Australia.

Edwards, P. A. and Jones Young, L. S. (1992) Beyond parents: family, community, and student involvement, *Phi Delta Kappan*, 72(1): 72–80.

Elliott, J. (1991) *Action Research for Educational Change*. Milton Keynes: Open University Press.

Epstein, J. L. (1995) School/family/partnerships: caring for the children we share, *Phi Delta Kappan*, 76(9): 701–12.

Essen, J. and Wedge, P. (1982) *Continuities in Childhood Disadvantage*. London: Heinemann.

Fraatz, J. M. B. (1988) *Managed Equality*. Paper presented at the annual meeting of the American Educational Research Association, New Orleans.

Frankl, V. (1984) *Man's Search for Meaning*. Toronto: Pocket Books.

Fullan, M. G. (1982) *The Meaning of Educational Change*. Toronto: OISE Press.

Fullan, M. G. (1988) *What's Worth Fighting for in the Principalship*. Toronto: Ontario Public School Teachers' Federation. Published as *What's Worth Fighting for in Headship* (1992), Buckingham: Open University Press.

Fullan, M. G. (1990) Beyond implementation, *Curriculum Implementation*, 20(2): 137–9.

Fullan, M. G. (1991) *The New Meaning of Educational Change*. New York: Teachers College Press and London: Cassell.

Fullan, M. G. (1992) *Successful School Improvement*. Buckingham: Open University Press and Toronto: OISE Press.

Fullan, M. G. (1993) *Change Forces: Probing the Depths of Educational Reform*. London: Falmer Press.

Fullan, M. G. and Hargreaves, A. (1991) *What's Worth Fighting for? Working Together for Your School*. Toronto: Ontario Public School Teachers' Federation. Published as *What's Worth Fighting for in Your School* (1992), Buckingham: Open University Press.

Fullan, M. G. and Miles, M. B. (1992) Getting reform right: what works and what doesn't, *Phi Delta Kappan*, 73(10): 744–52.

Fullan, M., Bennett, B. and Rolheiser Bennett, C. (1990) Linking classroom and school improvement, *Educational Leadership*, 47(8): 13–19.

Gairdner, W. (1993) *The War against the Family*. Toronto: Stoddart.

Galbraith, J. K. (1992) *The Culture of Contentment*. New York: Houghton Mifflin.

Galloway, D. (1983) Disruptive pupils and effective pastoral care, *School Organization*, 3(3): 245–54.

Garcia, J. (1993) The changing image of ethnic groups in textbooks, *Phi Delta Kappan*, 75(10): 29–35.

Gardner, H. (1983) *Frames of Mind: the Theory of Multiple Intelligences*. New York: Basic Books.

Gardner, H. (1993) *Multiple Intelligences: the Theory in Practice*. New York: Basic Books.

Garratt, B. (1987) *The Learning Organization*. Glasgow: William Collins.

General Accounting Office (1989) *Effective Schools Programs: Their Extent and Characteristics*. Washington, DC: United States General Accounting Office.

Gipps, C. (1994) *Beyond Testing: Towards a Theory of Educational Assessment*. London: Falmer Press.

Gipps, C. and Stobart, G. (1993) *Assessment: a Teachers' Guide to the Issues*, 2nd edn. London: Hodder and Stoughton.

Giroux, H. (1989) Rethinking educational reform in the age of George Bush, *Phi Delta Kappan*, 70(9): 728–30.

Giroux, H. (1992) Educational leadership and the crisis of democratic government, *Educational Researcher*, 21(4): 4–11.

Glickman, C. D. (1990) Open accountability for the '90s: between the pillars, *Educational Leadership*, 47(7): 38–42.

Glickman, C. D. (1991) Pretending not to know what we know, *Educational Leadership*, 48(8): 4–10.

Glickman, C. D., Allen, L. and Lunsford, B. F. (1994) Factors affecting school change, *Journal of Staff Development*, 15(3): 38–41.

Goldstein, H. (1992) Editorial: statistical information and the measurement of education outcomes, *Journal of the Royal Statistical Society A*, 155(3): 313–15.

Goldstein, H. (1995) *Multilevel Models in Educational and Social Research* (2nd edition). London: Edward Arnold and Toronto: Halsted Press.

Goldstein, H. and Thomas, S. (1995) School effectiveness and 'value-added' analysis, *Forum*, 37(2): 36–8.

Good, T. L. and Brophy, J. (1991) *Looking in Classrooms* (5th edition). New York: Harper and Row.

Goodson, I. F. (1992) *Studying Teachers' Lives*. Basingstoke: Falmer Press.

Gray, J. and Wilcox, B. (1995) The challenge of ineffective schools, in J. Gray and B. Wilcox (eds) *'Good School, Bad School': Evaluating Performance and Encouraging Improvement*. Buckingham: Open University Press.

Gray, J., Jesson, D., Goldstein, H., Hedger, K. (1995) The statistics of school improvement: establishing the agenda, in J. Gray and B. Wilcox (eds) *'Good School, Bad School': Evaluating Performance and Encouraging Improvement*. Buckingham: Open University Press.

Grosin, L. (1995) School effectiveness research, in B. P. M. Creemers and N. Osinga (eds) *ICSEI Country Reports*. Leeuwarden: Gemeenschappelijk Centrum voor Onderwijsbegeleiding in Friesland, January.

Gustavson, C. G. (1955) *A Preface to History*. Toronto: McGraw-Hill.

Hajnal, V., Sackney, L. and Walker, K. (1994) *Institutionalization of School Improvement Initiatives: an Examination of Government Archive Documents*. Paper presented at the annual meeting of the American Educational Research Association, New Orleans.

Haladyna, T. M., Nolen, S. B., Haas, N. S. (1991) Raising standardized achievement test scores and the origins of test score pollution, *Educational Researcher*, 20(5): 7.

Hallinger, P. and Murphy, J. (1986) The social context of effective schools, *American Journal of Education*, 94(3): 328–55.

Halton Board of Education (1988) *Building a School Growth Plan*. Burlington, Ontario: Halton Board of Education.

Halton Board of Education (1989) *Toward 2000: Learning for the Future: Strategic Directions*. Burlington, Ontario: Halton Board of Education.

Halton Board of Education (1992a) *Perceptions of Implementation of the School Growth Planning Process in Halton Schools*. Burlington, Ontario: Halton Board of Education.

Halton Board of Education (1992b) *Effective Schools: a Summary of Secondary Students in the Halton Board of Education* Burlington, Ontario: Halton Board of Education.

Halton Board of Education (1993a) *The Halton Transition Study: Part Four: Changes in Attitudes and Self Perceptions of Former Grade 8 Students Presently in Grade 9*. Burlington, Ontario: Halton Board of Education.

Halton Board of Education (1993b) *Self Concept Study: a Report of Halton Students in Grades 4 to 8*. Burlington, Ontario: Halton Board of Education.

Halton Board of Education (1993c) *Effective Schools: a Summary of a Survey of Parents of Students in the Halton Board of Education*. Burlington, Ontario: Halton Board of Education.

Handy, C. (1991) *The Age of Unreason*. London: Arrow.

Handy, C. (1994) *The Empty Rain Coat: Making Sense of the Future*. London: Hutchinson.

Hanna, D. P. (1988) *Designing Organizations for High Performance*. New York: Addison Wesley.

Hanushek, E. (1986) The economics of schooling: production and efficiency in public schools, *Journal of Economic Literature*, XXIV: 1141–77.

Hargreaves, A. (1994a) *Changing Teachers, Changing Times: Teachers' Work and Culture in the Postmodern Age*. London: Cassell.

Hargreaves, A. (1994b) *Dissonant Voices: Teacher Voices: Teachers and the Multiple Realities of Restructuring*. Paper presented at the annual meeting of the American Educational Research Association, New Orleans.

Hargreaves, A. (1995) Renewal in the age of paradox, *Educational Leadership*, 52(7): 14–19.

Hargreaves, A., Earl, L. and Ryan, J. (1996) *Schooling for Change: Reinventing Education for Early Adolescents*. London: Falmer Press.

Hargreaves, A. and Goodson, I. (1996) Teachers' professional lives: aspirations and actualities, in I. Goodson and A. Hargreaves (eds) *Teachers' Professional Lives*. New York: Falmer Press.

Hargreaves, D. (1995a) School culture, school effectiveness and school improvement, *School Effectiveness and School Improvement*, 6(1): 23–46.

Hargreaves, D. (1995b) Inspection and school improvement, *Cambridge Journal of Education*, 25(1): 115–23.

Hargreaves, D. and Hopkins, D. (1991) *The Empowered School: the Management and Practice of Development Planning*. London: Cassell.

Hargreaves, D. and Hopkins, D. (1994) *Development Planning for School Improvement*. London: Cassell.

Harris, A. (1995) *Effective Teaching*, Research Matters 3. London: School Improvement Network, Institute of Education.

Helgesen, K. (1991) *The Female Advantage*. New York: Doubleday.

Her Majesty's Inspectorate (1992) *The Implementation of Local Management of Schools*. London: Department for Education.

Hodgkinson, H. (1991) Reform versus reality, *Phi Delta Kappan*, 73(1): 9–16.

Hofkins, D. (1995) Deprivation is the common factor, *Times Educational Supplement*, 12 February, 14.

Holly, P. (1990) Catching the wave of the future: moving beyond school effectiveness by redesigning schools, *School Organisation*, 10(2/3): 195–212.

Holly, P. and Southworth, G. (1989) *The Developing School*. Lewes: Falmer Press.

Hopkins, D. (1995) Towards effective school improvement, *School Effectiveness and Improvement*, 6(3): 265–74.

Hopkins, D., Ainscow, M. and West, M. (1994) *School Improvement in an Era of Change*. London: Cassell.

Houtveen, A. A. M. and Osinga, N. (1995) *A Case of School Effectiveness: Organization, Programme, Procedure and Evaluation Results of the Dutch National School Improvement Project*. Paper presented to the Eighth International Congress for School Effectiveness and Improvement, Leeuwarden, The Netherlands, January.

Huberman, M. (1988) Teachers' careers and school improvement, *Journal of Curriculum Studies*, 20(2): 119–32.

Huberman, M. (1992a) Critical introduction, in M. G. Fullan *Successful School Improvement*. Buckingham: Open University Press and Toronto: OISE Press.

Huberman, M. (1992b) Teacher development and instructional mastery, in A. Hargreaves and M. G. Fullan (eds) *Understanding Teacher Development*. London: Cassell.

Huberman, M. and Miles, M. B. (1984) *Innovation up Close*. New York: Plenum.

Inner London Education Authority (1984) *Improving Secondary Schools: Report of Committee on the Curriculum and Organization of Secondary Schools* [The Hargreaves Report]. London: ILEA.

Jencks, C. S., Smith, M., Ackland, H., Bane, M. J., Cohen, D., Gintis, H., Heyns, B. and Micholson, S. (1972) *Inequality: a Reassessment of the Effect of Family and Schooling in America*. New York: Basic Books.

Joyce, B. R. (1991) The doors to school improvement, *Educational Leadership*, 48(8): 59–62.

Joyce, B. R. (1993) The link is there, but where do we go from here?, *Journal of Staff Development*, 14(3): 10–12.

Joyce, B. R. and Murphy, C. (1990) Epilogue: the curious complexities of cultural change, in B. R. Joyce (ed.) *Changing School Culture Through Staff Development*. Alexandria, VA: Association for Supervision and Curriculum Development.

Joyce, B. R. and Showers, B. (1982) The coaching of teaching, *Educational Leadership*, 40(2): 4–10.

Joyce, B. R. and Showers, B. (1988) *Student Achievement Through Staff Development*. New York: Longman.

Joyce, B. R., Showers, B. and Weil, M. (1992) *Models of Teaching* (4th edition). Englewood Cliffs, NJ: Prentice-Hall.

Kanter, R. M. (1989) *When Giants Learn to Dance*. New York: Simon and Schuster.

Kilcher, A. (1994) *School Improvement in Canada: an Overview.* Paper commissioned by the Walter and Duncan Gordon Foundation, Halifax, Nova Scotia.

King, A. J. C. and Coles, B. (1992) *The Health of Canada's Youth.* Ottawa: Ministry of National Health and Welfare.

King, A. J. C., Warren, W. K. and Peart, M. J. (1988) *The Teaching Experience.* Toronto: Ontario Secondary School Teachers' Federation.

Klein, R. (1995) Where prejudice still flares into violence, *Times Educational Supplement,* 6 January, 9.

Knowles, M. (1980) *The Modern Practice of Adult Education.* Chicago: Follett Publishing.

Kohn, A. (1991) Caring kids: the role of the school, *Phi Delta Kappan,* 72(7): 496–506.

Kohn, A. (1994) The truth about self-esteem, *Phi Delta Kappan,* 76(4): 272–83.

Kouzis, J. M. and Posner, B. Z. (1987) *The Leadership Challenge.* San Francisco, CA: Jossey-Bass.

Kruchov, C. and Hoyrup, S. (1994) *Development of the School System in Gladsaxe Municipality.* Paper presented to the Seventh International Congress for School Effectiveness and Improvement, Melbourne, Australia, January.

Krupp, J. A. (1989) Staff development and the individual, in S. D. Caldwell (ed.) *Staff Development: a Handbook of Effective Practices.* Oxford, OH: National Staff Development Council.

Leithwood, K. A. (1992) The move toward transformational leadership, *Educational Leadership,* 49(5): 8–12.

Leithwood, K. A. (1993) *Contributions of Transformational Leadership Toward School Restructuring.* Address to the University Council for Educational Administration, Houston, TX, October.

Leithwood, K. A. (1995) *An Organizational Learning Perspective on School Responses to Provincial Policy Initiatives.* Paper presented at the annual meeting of the American Educational Research Association, San Francisco, CA.

Leuctenberg, W. E. (ed.) (1963) *Franklin D. Roosevelt and the New Deal.* New York: Harper and Row.

Levin, B. (1994) Improving educational productivity: putting students at the center, *Phi Delta Kappan,* 75(10): 758–60.

Levine, D. U. (1994) Creating effective schools through site-level staff development, planning and improvement of organizational culture, in D. Hargreaves and D. Hopkins (eds) *Development Planning for School Improvement.* London: Cassell.

Levine, D. U. and Lezotte, L. W. (1990) *Unusually Effective Schools: a Review and Analysis of Research and Practice.* Madison, WI: National Center for Effective Schools Research and Development.

Lieberman, A. (1990) Navigating the four C's: building a bridge over troubled waters, *Phi Delta Kappan,* 72(7): 531–3.

Little, J. W. (1982) Norms of collegiality and experimentation: workplace conditions of school success, *American Educational Research Journal,* 19(3): 325–40.

Little, J. W. (1990) The persistence of privacy: autonomy and initiative in teachers' professional relations, *Teachers College Record,* 91(4): 509–36.

Lockheed, M. (1995) *Effective Schools in Developing Countries.* Keynote address presented to the Eighth International Congress for School Effectiveness and School Improvement, Leeuwarden, The Netherlands, January.

Lortie, D. (1975) *School Teacher: a Sociological Study*. Chicago: University of Chicago Press.

Loucks, S. F. and Hall, G. E. (1979) *Implementing Innovations in Schools: a Concerns-based Approach*. Austin, TX: Research and Development Center for Teacher Education, University of Texas.

Loucks-Horsley, S. F. and Hergert, L. F. (1985) *An Action Guide to School Improvement*. Alexandria, VA: Association for Supervision and Curriculum Development and The Network.

Louis, K. S. (1990) The role of the school district in school improvement, in M. Holmes, K. Leithwood and D. Musella (eds) *Educational Policy for Effective Schools*. Toronto: OISE Press.

Louis, K. S. and Miles, M. B. (1990) *Improving the Urban High School: What Works and Why*. New York: Teachers College Press and (1991) London: Cassell.

Louis, K. S., Marks, H. M. and Kruse, S. (1994) *Teachers' Professional Community in Restructuring Schools* (mimeo). Minneapolis, MN: Center on Organization and Restructuring of Schools, University of Minnesota.

Louis, K. S., Kruse, S. D. and Associates (1995) *Professionalism and Community: Perspectives on Reforming Urban Schools*. Thousand Oaks, CA: Corwin Press.

MacBeath, J. (1994) A role for parents, students and teachers in school self-evaluation and development planning, in K. A. Riley and D. L. Nuttall (eds) *Measuring Quality: Education Indicators – United Kingdom and International Perspectives*. London: Falmer Press.

MacBeath, J. and Mortimore, P. (1994) *Improving School Effectiveness: a Scottish Approach*. Paper presented to the Annual Conference of the British Educational Research Association, Oxford University.

MacBeath, J., McCaig, E. and Thomson, W. (1992) *Making School Boards Work*. Glasgow: SOED, Jordanhill College.

MacGilchrist, B. (1994) 'A study of the processes and impact of development planning in nine primary schools', unpublished doctoral dissertation. University of London.

MacGilchrist, B., Mortimore, P., Savage, J. and Beresford, C. (1995) *Planning Matters: the Impact of Development Planning in Primary Schools*. London: Paul Chapman.

McGaw, B., Banks, D. and Piper, K. (1991) *Effective Schools: Schools that Make a Difference*. Hawthorn, Victoria: Australian Council for Educational Research.

McLaughlin, M. W. (1990) The Rand change agent study: macro perspectives and micro realities, *Educational Researcher*, 19(9): 11–15.

McLaughlin, M. W. and Talbert, J. E. (1993) *Contexts that Matter for Teaching and Learning*. Palo Alto, CA: Center for Research on the Context of Secondary School Teaching.

McLaughlin, M. W., Talbert, J. E. and Bascia, N. (1990) *The Contexts of Teaching in Secondary Schools: Teachers' Realities*. New York: Teachers College Press.

McMahon, A., Bolam, R., Abbott, R. and Holly, P. (1984) *Guidelines for Review and Internal Development in Schools* (Primary and Secondary School Handbooks). York: Longman/Schools Council.

McNamara, P. (1995) *Researching Effective Schools: School Development Process – The Application of Research Results into Practical Policy.* Paper presented to the Eighth International Congress for School Effectiveness and Improvement, Leeuwarden, The Netherlands, January.

McNeil, L. (1988) Contradictions of control, part 1: administrators and teachers, *Phi Delta Kappan,* 69(5): 333–9.

McPherson, A. (1993) *Measuring Added Value in Schools,* the Paul Hamlyn Foundation National Commission on Education Briefings. London: Heinemann.

Miles, M. B. (1986) *Research Findings on the Stages of School Improvement.* New York: Center for Policy Research, mimeo.

Miles, M. B. (1987) *Practical Guidelines for Administrators: How to Get There.* Paper presented at the Annual Meeting of the American Educational Research Association, Washington.

Miles, M. B., Saxl, E. R. and Lieberman, A. (1988) What skills do educational 'change agents' need? An empirical view, *Curriculum Inquiry,* 18(2): 157–93.

Mintzberg, H. (1979) *The Structuring of Organizations.* Englewood Cliffs, NJ: Prentice Hall.

Mirel, J. (1994) School reform unplugged: the Bensonville new American school project, 1991–93, *American Educational Research Journal,* 31(3): 481–518.

Mitchell, D. E. and Tucker, S. (1992) Leadership as a way of thinking, *Educational Leadership,* 49(5): 30–5.

Moon, B. and Mayes, A. S. (eds) (1994) *Teaching and Learning in the Secondary School,* Milton Keynes: Open University Press.

Moore, J. R. (1988) Guidelines concerning adult learning, *The Journal of Staff Development,* 9(3): 2–5.

Morgan, G. and Morgan, K. (1992) *Beyond the Glitterspeak.* Toronto: Ontario Teachers' Federation.

Mortimore, P. (1991) The nature and findings of research on school effectiveness in the primary sector, in S. Riddell and S. Brown (eds) *School Effectiveness Research: Its Messages for School Improvement.* Edinburgh: HMSO.

Mortimore, P., Sammons, P., Stoll, L., Lewis, D. and Ecob, R. (1986) *The Junior School Project: Main Report, Part C, Research and Statistics Branch,* London: Inner London Education Authority.

Mortimore, P., Sammons, P., Stoll, L., Lewis, D. and Ecob, R. (1988) *School Matters: the Junior Years.* Wells: Open Books. Reprinted (1994) London: Paul Chapman.

Mortimore, P., Mortimore, J. and Thomas, H. (1994) *Managing Associate Staff: Innovation in Primary and Secondary Schools.* London: Paul Chapman.

Murphy, J. (1992) School effectiveness and school restructuring: contributions to educational improvement, *School Effectiveness and School Improvement,* 3(2): 90–109.

Myers, K. (1995) *School Improvement in Practice: Schools Make a Difference Project.* London: Falmer Press.

Naisbett, J. and Aburdene, P. (1990) *Megatrends 2000: Ten New Directions for the 1990's.* New York: William Morrow.

National Commission on Education (1993) *Learning to Succeed: a Radical Look at Education Today and a Strategy for the Future.* London: Heinemann.

National Commission on Education (1996) *Success against the Odds: Effective Schools in Disadvantaged Areas.* London: Routledge.

Nias, J., Southworth, G. and Yeomans, R. (1989) *Staff Relationships in the Primary School: a Study of Organizational Cultures.* London: Cassell.

Nias, J., Southworth, G. and Campbell, P. (1992) *Whole School Curriculum Development in the Primary School.* London: Falmer Press.

Nikiforuk, A. (1993) *School's Out: the Catastrophe in Public Education and What Can We Do about It.* Toronto: Warner, Walter and Ross.

Noddings, N. (1995) A morally defensible mission for schools in the 21st century, *Phi Delta Kappan,* 76(5): 365–8.

Nuttall, D. L. (1994) Choosing indicators, in K. A. Riley and D. L. Nuttall (eds) *Measuring Quality: Education Indicators – United Kingdom and International Perspectives.* London: Falmer Press.

Oakes, J. (1985) *Keeping Track: How Schools Structure Inequality.* New Haven, CT: Yale University Press.

OFSTED (1995) *The Annual Report of Her Majesty's Chief Inspector of Schools: Part 1 – Standards and Quality in Education 1993/94.* London: HMSO.

Oja, S. (1991) Adult development: insights on staff development, in A. Lieberman and L. Miller (eds) *Staff Development for Education in the '90s: New Demands, New Realities, New Perspectives* (2nd edition). New York: Teachers College Press.

Patterson, J. L., Purkey, S. C. and Parker, J. V. (1986) *Productive School Systems for a Nonrational World.* Alexandria, VA: Association for Supervision and Curriculum Development.

Peters, T. J. and Waterman, R. H. (1982) *In Search of Excellence: Lessons from America's Best Run Companies.* New York: Harper and Row.

Phelan, P., Davidson, L. and Hanh, T. C. (1992) Speaking up: students' perspectives on school, *Phi Delta Kappan,* 73(9): 695–704.

Plowden Committee (1967) *Children and Their Primary Schools.* London: HMSO.

Pollard, A. and Bourne, J. (eds) (1994) *Teaching and Learning in the Primary School.* Milton Keynes: Open University Press.

Postman, N. (1993) *Technopoly: the Surrender of Culture to Technology.* New York: Vintage Books.

Premier's Council on Health, Well-being and Social Justice (1994) *Yours, Mine and Ours: Ontario's Children and Youth, Phase One.* Toronto: Queen's Printer for Ontario.

Purkey, W. W. and Asby, D. N. (1988) The mental health of students, *Person-Centered Review,* 3(1): 41–9.

Purkey, W. W. and Collins, E. L. (1992) The coming revolution in American education, *Quality Outcomes Driven Education,* 1(1): 7–11.

Purkey, W. W. and Novak, J. (1990) *Inviting School Success* (3rd edition). Belmont, CA: Wadsworth.

Purkey, W. W. and Schmidt, J. J. (1987) *The Inviting Relationship: an Expanded Perspective for Professional Counseling.* Englewood Cliffs, NJ: Prentice-Hall.

Pyke, N. (1994) Mangers, but no crib sheets, *Times Educational Supplement,* 23 December, 6.

Reich, R. (1992) *Work of Nations.* New York: Vintage Press.

Resource Base (1995) *Schools Make a Difference: Practical Strategies for School Improvement*. Southampton: Resource Base.

Reynolds, D. (1991) Changing ineffective schools, in M. Ainscow (ed.) *Effective Schools for All*. London: David Fulton.

Reynolds, D. (1996) The problem of the ineffective school: some evidence and some speculations, in J. Gray, D. Reynolds, C. Fitz-Gibbon and D. Jesson (eds) *Merging Traditions: the Future of Research on School Effectiveness and School Improvement*. London: Cassell.

Reynolds, D. and Packer, A. (1992) School effectiveness and school improvement in the 1990s, in D. Reynolds and P. Cuttance (eds) *School Effectiveness: Research, Policy and Practice*. London: Cassell.

Reynolds, D., Creemers, B. P. M. and Peters, T. (eds) (1989) *School Effectiveness and Improvement: Proceedings of the First International Congress, London 1988*. Cardiff: University of Wales College of Cardiff and Groningen: RION.

Reynolds, D., Hopkins, D. and Stoll, L. (1993) Linking school effectiveness knowledge and school improvement practice: towards a synergy, *School Effectiveness and School Improvement*, 4(1): 37–58.

Reynolds, D., Creemers, B. P. M., Nesselrodt, P. S., Schaffer, E. C., Stringfield, S. and Teddlie, C. (1994) *Advances in School Effectiveness Research and Practice*. Oxford: Elsevier Science.

Riddell, A. R. (1989) An alternative approach to the study of school effectiveness in Third World countries, *Comparative Education Review*, 33(40): 481–97.

Riley, K. A. (1994) Following the education indicators trail in the pursuit of quality, in K. A. Riley and D. L. Nuttall (eds) *Measuring Quality: Education Indicators – United Kingdom and International Perspectives*. London: Falmer Press.

Riley, K. A. and Nuttall, D. L. (eds) (1994) *Measuring Quality: Education Indicators – United Kingdom and International Perspectives*. London: Falmer Press.

Rosenau, P. M. (1992) *Post-Modernism and the Social Sciences: Insights, Inroads, and Intrusions*. Princeton, NJ: Princeton University Press.

Rosenholtz, S. J. (1989) *Teachers' Workplace: the Social Organization of Schools*. New York: Longman.

Rossman, G. B., Corbett, H. D. and Firestone, W. A. (1988) *Change and Effectiveness in Schools: a Cultural Perspective*. New York: SUNY Press.

Rudduck, J. (1991) *Innovation and Change*. Milton Keynes: Open University Press.

Rudduck, J. (1992) Universities in partnership with schools: les liaisons dangereuses?, in M. Fullan and A. Hargreaves (eds) *Teacher Development and Educational Change*. London: Falmer Press.

Rutter, M., Maughan, B., Mortimore, P. and Ouston, J. (1979) *Fifteen Thousand Hours: Secondary Schools and Their Effects on Schoolchildren*. Shepton Mallet: Open Books.

Sackney, L. E. (1986) Practical strategies for improving school effectiveness, *The Canadian School Executive*, 6(4): 15–20.

Sackney, L. E. and Dibski, D. (1994) School-based management: a critical perspective, *Educational Management and Administration*, (22)2: 104–12.

Sadker, M. and Sadker, D. (1986) Sexism in the classroom: from the grade school to graduate school, *Phi Delta Kappan*, 64(7): 512–15.

Sammons, P., Cuttance, P., Nuttall, D. and Thomas, S. (in press) Continuity of school effects: a longitudinal analysis of primary and secondary school effects on GCSE performance. *School Effectiveness and School Improvement,* 6(4).

Sammons, P., Hillman, J. and Mortimore, P. (1995) *Key Characteristics of Effective Schools: a Review of School Effectiveness Research.* London: Office for Standards in Education.

Sammons, P., Mortimore, P. and Thomas, S. (1996) 'Do schools perform consistently across outcomes and areas?, in J. Gray, D. Reynolds, C. Fitz-Gibbon and D. Jesson (eds) *Merging Traditions: the Future of Research of School Effectiveness and School Improvement.* London: Cassell.

Sammons, P., Nuttall, D. and Cuttance, P. (1993) Differential school effectiveness: results from a reanalysis of the Inner London Education Authority's Junior School Project data, *British Educational Research Journal,* 19(4): 381–405.

Sammons, P., Thomas, S., Mortimore, P., Cairns, R. and Bausor, J. (1994) *Understanding the Processes of School and Departmental Effectiveness.* Paper presented at the Annual Conference of the British Educational Research Association, Oxford University.

Saphier, J. and King, M. (1985) Good seeds grow in strong cultures, *Educational Leadership,* 42(6): 67–74.

Sarason, S. (1990) *The Predictable Failure of Educational Reform.* San Francisco, CA: Jossey-Bass.

Saul, J. R. (1993) *Voltaire's Bastards: the Dictatorship of Reason in the West.* Toronto: Penguin Books.

Saxl, E. R., Miles, M. B. and Lieberman, A. (1990) *Assisting Change in Education (ACE).* Alexandria, VA: Association for Supervision and Curriculum Development.

Scheerens, J. (1992) *Effective Schooling: Research, Theory and Practice.* London: Cassell.

Schein, E. H. (1969) *Process Consultation.* Reading, MA: Addison-Wesley.

Schein, E. H. (1985) *Organizational Culture and Leadership.* San Francisco, CA: Jossey-Bass.

Schlechty, P. (1990) *Schools for the Twenty First Century: Leadership Imperatives for Educational Reform.* San Francisco, CA: Jossey-Bass.

Schlesinger, A. M. (1991) *The Disuniting of America: Reflections on a Multicultural Society,* Knoxville, TN: Whittle Direct Books.

Schmuck, R. A. and Runkel, P. J. (1985) *The Handbook of Organizational Development in Schools* (3rd edition). Prospect Heights, IL: Waveland Press.

Schon, D. (1983) *The Reflective Practitioner: How Professionals Think in Action.* New York: Basic Books.

Schon, D. (1987) *Educating the Reflective Practitioner.* San Francisco, CA: Jossey-Bass.

Scottish Office Education Department (1992) *Using Ethos Indicators in Primary School Self-evaluation: Taking Account of the Views of Pupils, Parents and Teachers.* Edinburgh: HM Inspector of Schools.

Senge, P. M. (1990) *The Fifth Discipline: the Art and Practice of the Learning Organization.* New York: Doubleday.

Shakeshaft, C. (1993a) Gender equity in schools, in C. A. Capper (ed.) *Educational Administration in a Pluralistic Society.* New York: SUNY Press.

Shakeshaft, C. (1993b) Women in educational management in the United States, in J. Ouston (ed.) *Women in Educational Management*. London: Longman.

Shakeshaft, C. and Cohen, A. (1990) *In Loco-Parentis: Sexual Abuse of Students in Schools*. Paper presented at the annual meeting of the American Educational Research Association, Boston.

Shaw, G. B. (1946) *Man and Superman*. London: Penguin Books.

Sikes, P. (1992) Imposed change and the experienced teacher, in M. Fullan and A. Hargreaves (eds) *Teacher Development and Educational Change*. London: Falmer Press.

Siskin, L. S. (1994) *Realms of Knowledge: Academic Departments in Secondary Schools*. London: Falmer Press.

Sizer, T. R. (1985) Common sense, *Educational Leadership*, 42(6): 21–2.

Sizer, T. R. (1989) Diverse practice, shared ideas: the essential school, in H. Walberg and J. Lane (eds) *Organizing for Learning Towards the Twenty First Century*. Reston, VA: NASSP.

Skelton, M., Reeves, G. and Playfoot, D. (1991) *Development Planning for Primary Schools*. Windsor: NFER Nelson.

Slater, R. O. and Teddlie, C. (1992) Toward a theory of school effectiveness and leadership, *School Effectiveness and School Improvement*, 3(4): 242–58.

Slavin, R. E., Madden, N. A., Dolan, L. J., Wasik, B. A., Ross, S. and Smith, L. (1994) *Success for All: Longitudinal Effects of Systemic School-by school Reform in Seven Districts*. Paper presented at the Annual Meeting of the American Educational Research Association, New Orleans.

Smith, D. and Tomlinson, S. (1989) *The School Effect: a Study of Multi-Racial Comprehensives*. London: Policy Studies Institute.

Smith, G. (1995) Urban education: current position and future possibilities, in M. Barber and R. Dann (eds) *Raising Educational Standards in the Inner Cities: Practical Initiatives in Action*. London: Cassell.

Smith, M. L. (1991) Put to the test: the effects of external testing on teachers, *Educational Researcher*, 20(5): 8–11.

Smith, W. F. and Andrews, R. L. (1989) *Instructional Leadership: How Principals Make a Difference*. Alexandria, VA: Association for Supervision and Curriculum Development.

Southworth, G. (1994) School leadership and school development: reflections from research, in G. Southworth (ed.) *Readings in Primary School Development*. London: Falmer Press.

Spady, W. (1994) Choosing outcomes of significance, *Educational Leadership*, 51(6): 18–22.

Stenhouse, L. (1984) Artistry and teaching: the teacher as focus of research and development, in D. Hopkins and M. Wideen (eds) *Alternative Perspectives on School Improvement*. Lewes: Falmer Press.

Stiggins, R. J. (1991) Assessment literacy, *Phi Delta Kappan*, 72(7): 534–9.

Stoll, L. (1991) School self-evaluation: another boring exercise or an opportunity for growth? in S. Riddell and S. Brown (eds) *School Effectiveness Research: Its Messages for School Improvement*. Edinburgh: HMSO, Scottish Office Education Department.

Stoll, L. (1992) 'Making schools matter: a study of improvement in a Canadian school district', unpublished doctoral dissertation. University of London.

Stoll, L. (1996) Linking school effectiveness and school improvement: issues and possibilities, in J. Gray, D. Reynolds, C. Fitz-Gibbon and D. Jesson (eds) *Merging Traditions: the Future of School Effectiveness and School Improvement*. London: Cassell.

Stoll, L. and Fink, D. (1988) Educational change: an international perspective, *International Journal of Educational Management*, 2(3): 26–31.

Stoll, L. and Fink, D. (1989) *Implementing an Effective Schools Project: the Halton Approach*. Paper presented at the Second International Congress for School Effectiveness, Rotterdam, The Netherlands, January.

Stoll, L. and Fink, D. (1992) Effecting school change: the Halton approach, *School Effectiveness and School Improvement*, 3(1): 19–41.

Stoll, L. and Fink, D. (1994) School effectiveness and school improvement: voices from the field, *School Effectiveness and School Improvement*, 5(2): 149–77.

Stoll, L. and Thomson, M. (1996) Moving together: a partnership approach to improvement, in P. Earley, B. Fidler and J. Ouston (eds) *Improvement through Inspection: Complementary Approaches to School Development*. London: David Fulton.

Stoll, L., Harrington, J. and Myers, K. (1995) *Two British School Effectiveness and School Improvement Action Projects*. Paper presented to the Eighth International Congress for School Effectiveness and Improvement, Leeuwarden, The Netherlands, January.

Stringfield, S. (1995) Attempting to enhance students' learning through innovative programs: the case for schools evolving into high reliability organizations, *School Effectiveness and School Improvement*, 6(1): 67–96.

Teacher Training Agency (1995) *Headteachers' Leadership and Management Programme*. London: TTA.

Teddlie, C. and Stringfield, S. (1985) A differential analysis of effectiveness in middle and lower socioeconomic status schools, *Journal of Classroom Interaction*, 20(2): 38–44.

Teddlie, C. and Stringfield, S. (1993) *Schools Make a Difference: Lessons Learned From a 10 Year Study of School Effects*. New York: Teachers College Press.

Teddlie, C., Stringfield, S., Wimpelberg, R. and Kirby, P. (1989) Contextual differences in models for effective schooling in the USA, in B. P. M. Creemers, T. Peters and D. Reynolds (eds) *School Effectiveness and School Improvement: Proceedings of the Second International Congress, Rotterdam 1989*. Amsterdam: Swets and Zeitlinger.

Thomas, S. and Goldstein, H. (1995) Questionable value, *Education*, 185(11): 17.

Thomas, S., Sammons, P. and Mortimore, P. (1995) Determining what adds value to student achievement, *Educational Leadership International*, 58(6): 19–22.

Thurlow, L. (1992) *Head to Head: the Coming Economic Battle among Japan, Europe and America*. New York: William Morrow.

Tizard, B., Blatchford, P., Burke, J., Farquhar, C. and Plewis, I. (1988) *Young Children at School in the Inner City*. Hove: Erlbaum.

Toffler, A. (1990) *Powershift*. New York: Bantam Books.

Townsend, A. C. (1994) *Effective Schooling for the Community*. London: Routledge.

Tuchman, B. (1984) *The March of Folly*. New York: Alfred A. Knopf.

United States Department of Education (1987) *What Works: Research about Teaching and Learning* (2nd edn.) Washington, DC: United States Department of Education.

van Velzen, W., Miles, M., Eckholm, M., Hameyer, U. and Robin, D. (1985) *Making School Improvement Work*. Leuven, Belgium: ACCO.

Wallace, M. (1991) Flexible planning: a key to the management of multiple innovations, *Educational Management and Administration*, 19(3): 180–92.

Wallace, M. (1994) Towards a contingency approach to development planning in schools, in D. Hargreaves and D. Hopkins (eds) *Development Planning for School Improvement*. London: Cassell.

Wallace, M. and McMahon, A. (1994) *Planning for Change in Turbulent Times: the Case of Multiracial Primary Schools*. London: Cassell.

Waterman, R. (1988) *The Renewal Factor*. New York: Bantam Books.

Watkins, C. and Whalley, C. (1993) Mentoring beginning teachers: issues for schools to anticipate and manage, *School Organisation*, 13(2): 129–38.

Watson, N. and Fullan, M. (1992) Beyond school district-university partnerships, in M. Fullan and A. Hargreaves (eds) *Teacher Development and Educational Change*. London: Falmer Press.

West, M. and Ainscow, M. (1991) *Managing School Development: a Practical Guide*. London: David Fulton.

Wideen, M. (1994) *The Struggle for Change: the Story of One School*. London: Falmer Press.

Willms, J. D. (1992) *Monitoring School Performance: a Guide for Educators*. London: Falmer Press.

Wolf, D., Bixby, J., Glenn, J. and Gardner, H. (1991) To use their minds well: investigating new forms of student assessment, *Review of Research in Education*, 17: 31–74.

Zywine, J., Stoll, L., Adam, E., Fullan, M. G. and Bennett, B. (1995) Leadership effectiveness and school development: putting reform in perspective, *School Effectiveness and School Improvement*, 6(3): 223–46.

INDEX